SCREENWRITER

SCREENWRITER

The Life and Times of Nunnally Johnson

TOM STEMPEL

SAN DIEGO • NEW YORK
A. S. BARNES & COMPANY, INC.
IN LONDON:
THE TANTIVY PRESS

© 1980 by A. S. Barnes and Co., Inc.

A. S. Barnes and Co., Inc.
San Diego, California 92121

The Tantivy Press
136-148 Tooley Street
London SE1 2TT, England

Library of Congress Cataloging in Publication Data

Stempel, Tom, 1941-
  Screenwriter, the life and times of Nunnally Johnson.

  Filmography: p.
  "Produced stage plays of Nunnally Johnson": p.
  "Published short stories of Nunnally Johnson": p.
  Bibliography: p.
  Includes index.
  1. Johnson, Nunnally—Biography. 2. Screen-
writers—United States—Biography. 3. Authors,
American—20th century—Biography. I. Title.
PS3519.02834Z86   812'.5'2 [B]   78-75339
ISBN 0-498-02362-1

1 2 3 4 5 6 7 8 9 84 83 82 81 80

Printed in the United States of America

FOR KERSTIN

Contents

Acknowledgments

A proper acknowledgment of the help provided by the people and organizations listed below would take a volume half again the size of the present one. Nonetheless, a few words of thanks are due at this time to:

The late Nunnally Johnson, who supported my efforts on this project in ways both large and small. In more ways than one, there would have been no book without him.

Professor Howard Suber at UCLA, who got me started interviewing Johnson as part of the Oral History of the Motion Pictures Project, which was funded by grants from the National Endowment for the Humanities and the American Film Institute. Professor Suber then supervised my work on the doctoral dissertation that grew out of the interviews. Also helpful at UCLA were James V. Mink, Rae Lindquist, Lynn Merrick, Alain Silver, Elyseo Taylor, Diana Dreiman, and Professors Robert Hethmon, Alexander Saxton, Theodore Saloutos, and Carl Mueller. The final transcript of the Johnson interviews is available to scholars at UCLA, UC Berkeley, and the American Film Institute's Center for Advanced Studies in Beverly Hills.

At the American Film Institute, where I worked on a Research Associateship from the Louis B. Mayer Foundation: Rick Thompson, Jerryl Taylor, Don Knox, Ursula Bucher, as well as the subjects of the oral history interviews done as part of that Associateship: Barbara McLean, Philip Dunne, Robert D. Webb, Henry King, and Charles G. Clarke. The final transcripts of those interviews are available to scholars at the AFI's Center for Advanced Studies in Beverly Hills.

At Twentieth Century-Fox: John Friedkin, Alex Babcock, Dan Paulson, and especially Jack Yeager at the corporate records center.

Nunnally Johnson's family: Dorris Bowdon Johnson (who in addition to submitting to interviews provided most of the photographs for the book), Marjorie Fowler, Gene Fowler Jr., Nora Johnson, Patrick Johnson, Christie Johnson, Roxie Johnson Lonergan, Scott Johnson, Alice Mason Johnson, and Marion Flynn.

9

Johnson's friends and associates: Mrs. Marian Thompson, the late Robert Emmett Dolan, Joseph L. Mankiewicz, Mrs. Marvin Stahl, Joe Bryan III, Bob Goldstein, Finis Farr, Joel Sayre, Colin Miller, Allen Rivkin, Betty Baldwin Stewart, and Joanne Woodward.

At the Mugar Memorial Library and Boston University: Dr. Howard R. Gotlieb and his staff.

At the Margaret Herrick Library at the Academy of Motion Picture Arts and Sciences: Mildred Simpson and her staff.

The New York Times for "Confessions of a Confederate," © 1947 by The New York Times Company. Reprinted by permission.

Assorted friends, relatives, and co-workers of mine: Stu Miller, John Hochmann, Ernest Callenbach, Barbara Walts, William Harris, Aubrey Solomon and my students at Los Angeles City College.

Lynn Rosbrugh, who typed the various drafts of the manuscript.

Richard Dyer MacCann, whose precise editing of the manuscript both eliminated the trivia (and a few good anecdotes) and helped bring the principal points into clearer focus.

At A. S. Barnes and Company: Thomas Yoseloff, Julien Yoseloff, and their associates.

And finally, my wife Kerstin and my daughter Audrey, whose support over the years has been essential to the completion of this book.

Introduction

In the beginning, unfortunately, was not the Word.* In the beginning,
moving pictures were exactly that: pictures that moved. They were made
not by directors, or producers, or even cameramen, and certainly not by
writers, but by the inventors and developers of the motion picture
equipment—men like the Lumiere Brothers in France, and Edison and
his assistant, William Kennedy Laurie Dickson. They shot anything that
moved: trees blowing in the wind, waves at the seashore. There was no
attempt to tie the elements together into a story, and so there was no need
for anybody to write down what was to be shown. It was just photographed.

As "the flickers" became more popular, they got longer, and it was not
enough just to have pictures that moved. In the early years of this
century, George Méliès and Edwin Porter began to realize the possibilities of putting together different individual shots to tell a story.
Still, there was no great need for a writer; the man making the movie
rearranged the elements of the story himself so they could be filmed.
Since the man photographing the scene had to crank the camera, his job
was separated from that of the man who had to tell the actors what to do.
Thus, the jobs of cameraman and director were established.

Benjamin Hampton, in his *History of the American Film Industry*, says
the first screenwriter came to the movies in 1900. A young newspaperman named Roy McCardell first thought of the possibility of writing
for "living-picture shows." He went to the office of the Biograph

*The reference is not only to the Bible (John 1:1), but to virtually every official and semiofficial
pronouncement from the Writers' Guild of America, West. The "unfortunately" refers to the way the
screenwriter has been treated by critics and historians as well as by the men who ran the business.
The "unfortunately" is one of the reasons for the writing of this book.

Company and asked if they needed somebody to prepare manuscripts. He was offered a job writing ten scenarios a week at ten dollars per story, fifteen if they were good. He borrowed a typewriter, wrote out ten stories in one afternoon, and was hired at the higher rate.

When the movies got longer still, running up to two reels (twenty exciting minutes!), the demand for more coherent story material became greater. Moviemaking was a small-scale, individual-entrepreneur business, and there was still no organized way in which stories were bought. Anybody and everybody could sell stories to the movies. Many small companies put advertisements in the trade papers offering good prices for stories. Mack Sennett, then working as an extra in D. W. Griffith's early films, learned from Mary Pickford that the Biograph Company actually paid money for stories. He went home, sat down with a penny pencil, copied stories from newspapers, and sold them.

The people making films eventually decided to hire well-known writers like Richard Harding Davis, Rex Beach, and Elbert Hubbard, but few of them were very successful. They were used to thinking of stories in terms of words rather than pictures, and they found it difficult to adapt to the demands of the silent film. However, some writers were able to write for silent films, and many of the most successful had started out, as Roy McCardell had, in newspaper work, where the emphasis was not on literary style but on speed, energy, and discipline—values which were equally appreciated by moviemakers.

The writers were not considered as important as the directors since it was the directors on the set who decided what was to be filmed. Because there was no dialogue except in titles, the emphasis had to be on the visual, and the best directors began to develop the basic techniques for cinematic storytelling. Because making movies was relatively inexpensive, directors were fairly free in their choice of what to shoot; the film could be cut in almost any way possible and any gaps in the story could be filled in with explanatory titles. The meaning of the story could be completely changed by adding or revising a few titles.

The standard procedure of the time was similar to the way D. W. Griffith is reported to have made *The Birth of a Nation*.[1] The film was based on Thomas Dixon's novel *The Clansman* and on the play made from it, but Griffith borrowed material from another Dixon story, "The Leopard's Spots," as well as from tales he heard his father tell about the Civil War. There was supposedly no script and Griffith kept it all in his head. But *The Birth of a Nation* runs close to three hours and there may have been more screenwriting going on than we have been told about. The main credits on the picture give a "story arranged by" credit to Griffith and Frank E. Woods. Woods was a former newspaperman and one of the first critics to realize what Griffith was doing in the Biograph films (see the quotes from Woods's reviews in George C. Pratt's *Spellbound in Darkness*). Woods became not only the head of Griffith's story department, but also head of publicity and production supervisor for Griffith. Linda Arvidson Griffith, in *When the Movies Were Young*, says it was Woods who suggested to Griffith the possibility of filming *The Clansman*. Karl Brown, in his *Adventures with D. W. Griffith*, indicates that much of Griffith's legend was created by Woods and the publicity department, and Griffith never called Woods to the set as he did others, but left the set to see him. And the script? Was Frank E. Woods to D. W. Griffith what Herman Mankiewicz was to Orson Welles? Without a doubt, this is a subject for further research.

Because *The Birth of a Nation* made such an enormous profit, men realized the making of motion pictures could be a big business. In the years immediately afterwards, money was poured into the movies. With that money came the organization of motion-picture making as an industry. This meant a decline in the smaller operations of independent producers, since they were unable to keep up with the large-scale production, distribution, and exhibition divisions the big companies developed. Part of that increased organization of production involved standardization which meant less freedom for the directors. One of the methods of standardization was the use of detailed shooting scripts which were prepared by writers under the constant supervision of the studio production managers, a method pioneered and perfected by Thomas Ince (1882-1924), the first important "supervisor" or executive producer.

This trend toward organization was well underway in 1927 when sound pictures were introduced into the industry. Many of the changes in the business were simply continuations of the trends that had already begun. The cost of sound equipment was enormous, and this meant that the men running the studios had to get bank loans to keep in business. The banks insisted on more control over the studios and the organization of methods of production. Since sound films could not be as easily recut and retitled as silent films, there was the necessity of greater pre-production planning, which involved getting a good script before shooting began. This did not mean that the writer had more say in the making of a film. The studio heads did not want to give up the power they had begun to develop in the early twenties. They simply used the necessity of written scripts as a club to control the directors, insisting that the director shoot the script as written.

Because the directors were not, as a rule, writers, the studios sought people who could write sound films. In some cases, they brought in playwrights who had experience in writing dialogue.

Others who became successful in the first twenty years of sound had in common a background in newspaper work (a trait shared with a number of the screenwriters who were successful in the early days of silent films). The stories used were often told in the fast-moving style of the journalism of the period. Former newspaper writers could also write the tough-sentimental dialogue that seemed to suit the realistic settings of the screen as opposed to the more stylized dialogue appropriate for the stage.

Former newspapermen also adapted easily to the conditions of moviemaking. Working in noisy, overcrowded city rooms for arrogant, tyrannical editors would seem to have been the perfect preparation for going to work in noisy, overcrowded story conferences for arrogant, tyrannical producers. These writers were used to working in the middle of the action. The jump from newspapers to films was not a large one, except in terms of money, which made it all the easier. Writing for films meant a pleasanter climate than Chicago or New York, good drinking companions, and a couple of thousand dollars a week. How could anybody refuse? Not many did, if given the opportunity.

The screenwriters who came to prominence in the thirties brought to the movies energy, wit, iconoclasm, and vitality, but, on the whole, the screenwriters were ignored by the critics. Undoubtedly, some of this was envy on the part of critics who were still writing for newspapers at far less salary than the screenwriters were getting, and there was certainly a feeling that the writers who had gone to Hollywood had "sold out." But the major reason writers were ignored was that the critics were still locked in the view that the director was the sole artist who "created" the film. While this was often true to a great degree in silent films, it was not true in the studio productions of later years, or even during the era of the "independent" film-makers from the fifties to the present. Still, this view of the director as demigod persisted among critics. It was a very convenient way of talking and writing about a film, particularly if there were several writers credited with having worked on the adaptation, the screenplay, additional scenes, and additional dialogue. Quite often, more than one director worked on a film, but usually only one was given credit. For critics who had grown up with the romantic view of the solitary artist who creates the work of art in painting or literature, it was easy to shift that principle from the other arts to film.

This convenient way of speaking about the creation of a film soon became a convention and was in turn elevated to the level of theory, the notorious *Politique des auteurs,* promulgated in France by Francois Truffaut and in this country by Andrew Sarris. Both Sarris and his critics soon discovered that, instead of becoming a starting-point, the auteur theory quickly achieved the status of dogma.

There are two basic problems with the auteurist approach to film history. One is that, as indicated above, it is historically inaccurate in its suppositions about how films get made. The second problem is more complex. The auteurist approach puts an emphasis on the director's contributions, which tend to be primarily visual. It also strays into giving directors credit for elements they may have no control over or interest in. The implication is that the most important component of a film is the visual, and that this component is at the center of the art of the film. In fact, a film is made up of two components, the visual and the narrative. The visual consists of the organization of the physical elements within the frame. The narrative consists of the organization of the actions in sequence of time. It is the narrative component that is the responsibility of the screenwriter. He arranges the order of the story and the actions of the characters.

While the visual, or graphic, aspect of a film may be the most important in some kinds of short films, animated films particularly, in the feature film, because of its running time, the narrative values predominate. This is particularly true in films designed for the mass audience, whose interest has always been held more by a strong narrative line than by visual nuances. If we concede that films are either a popular or fine art, or both, and are therefore worth study, it would seem apparent that much can be learned from an examination of the craft of the screenwriter.

Curiously enough, it is only in recent years that any serious critical attention has been paid to the craft and history of screenwriting. Most of this attention has been in the form of articles, such as Pauline Kael's two essays, "Bonnie and Clyde" and "Raising Kane." Occasionally, scholarly magazines will print an article or two on screenwriting: a survey of writers' attitudes toward Hollywood appeared in *Cinema Journal* in the fall of 1971. *Film Comment* (Winter 1970-71) devoted an entire issue, later published as a book, to the Hollywood screenwriter. The editor of that magazine, Richard Corliss, in his book *Talking Pictures*, selected certain writers for the same kind of critical overview Andrew Sarris gave to directors in *The American Cinema*. William Froug collected a dozen interviews in *The Screenwriter Looks at the Screenwriter*.

It is time for a full-length critical biography of a screenwriter as a screenwriter.

Why Nunnally Johnson? First of all, Johnson wrote some of the best, most interesting, and most successful films of his time, from *The House of Rothschild* (1934) to *The Dirty Dozen* (1967), including *Jesse James, The Grapes of Wrath, Woman in the Window, The Desert Fox, How to Marry a Millionaire, The Man in the Gray Flannel Suit, The Three Faces of Eve,* and *The World of Henry Orient*. His work, because it was seldom changed or added to by other writers, shows a continuum of themes, skills, and methods that represent his own contribution to his films. He spent the largest part of his career at Twentieth Century-Fox when the major-studio system was at its height. His career reveals how movies were made within that system and how the screenwriter fitted into it: how he worked with producers, directors, actors, and the other contributors to his films. Johnson also worked outside the studio system, both while the system existed and after its decline. He also worked both as producer and director at various points in his career.

Richard Corliss, looking over Johnson's career as a screenwriter, pronounces it "long and distinguished." If Johnson's craftsmanship is what makes his career distinguished, his longevity, indicating that his films connected with their audiences, is what makes it significant. One of the purposes of this book must be to examine those connections for what they reveal not only about Johnson and his development both as a person and a writer, but also about the society which responded to his films.

SCREENWRITER

1
Georgia

Home for Nunnally Johnson, in the beginning, was Columbus, Georgia. When he was writing short stories for *The Saturday Evening Post* in the twenties, he romantically fictionalized Columbus as "Riverside." In one story, he describes "Riverside":

> The town . . . was just a normal, very slowly growing community, now at that point in civic progress where its old-fashioned, modest Board of Trade was slightly surprised and embarrassed to find itself tonily rechristened the Chamber of Commerce. Wide shaded streets meandered lazily through a half-dozen blocks and then petered out into areas known as suburbs mainly because they weren't yet built up. Distances were short and cool under the trees; business men walked home for their midday dinners, and none but traveling salesmen and other out-of-towners used the two dispirited restaurants. . . .
>
> Entertainment they found in the movies and a country club. Hucksters brought sweet fresh vegetables directly from the earth to their back doors. They gossiped a little, retired early, and were simple in their tastes. They did not know that Edgar Guest was not regarded as the greatest of living poets; they would not have cared had they known; they liked him nevertheless.
>
> Little happened that was exciting. Once or twice a month they drove to Atlanta to raise whatever particular hell they fancied, and occasionally they went to New York and returned exhausted. For the rest, it was all very easy, very leisurely, very amiable, very soothing. The sun shone and there was no harshness.[1]

It was, in other words, one of those many small towns that produce one of three reactions in its citizens: contentment, madness, or a desire to escape.

The contentment possible in such a place Johnson suggests in the quoted passage. It is the contentment found in the joys of family, home, community and the stability of a social order on a human scale. The madness possible in such a place is described by such varied writers about small-town America as Sinclair Lewis, Sherwood Anderson, Grace Metalious, and William Faulkner. It comes from the agonies and pressures of family, home, community, and the stability of a social order that can seem stifling, with no possibility of escape. However, for some people who feel the heavy restrictions of small town ideals, escape becomes not only a possibility but a necessity. So it was with Johnson. What is unusual in his case is that he took with him the values he was escaping from. Throughout his life, there was a tension in Johnson between the desire for the order and stability represented by the idea of home and the excitement and adventure represented by the idea of escape. Because these two sides were both such a strong part of him, he could write successfully for those who felt themselves pulled by either side.

Nunnally Hunter Johnson was born on 5 December 1897, the first of two sons born to James Nunnally Johnson and Johnny Pearl Patrick Johnson. James N. Johnson eventually became superintendent of the pipe and sheet metal department of the Columbus Division of Shops of the Central of Georgia Railroad. He had left school at nine and had become a journeyman mechanic working on the repair of the State Capitol building in Atlanta after the end of the Civil War. He later moved to Macon, Savannah, and finally to Columbus. After he had come to Columbus, a friend of his, Charlie Patrick, invited him to dinner one Sunday after church. James Johnson went to dinner and was pleasantly surprised to discover that the "angel" he had seen singing in the church choir was Charlie's sister, Johnny Pearl Patrick. They were married shortly thereafter.

James Johnson was a tall man with a dry sense of humor he passed on to his eldest son. The late composer Robert Emmett Dolan noticed that James Johnson "had a gleam in his eye that told you that humorous talent did not start with Nunnally, but was a bit bequeathed." The elder Johnson was, in spite of his lack of formal education, a prodigious reader, and each Sunday afternoon would walk down to the library with his two sons. They would read the newspapers and magazines and James Johnson would bring home a stack of five or six books to read during the week. He also wrote occasional articles for the Central of Georgia's company magazine.

Nunnally Johnson's younger brother, Pat, remembers another cultural benefit derived from their father:

As a railroad man he got passes for all of us but not on the Pullmans.

So when he went on overnight trips we strapped pillows on our suitcases and slept in the day coaches. Both of our parents believed in educating us on trips so Nunnally and I visited every important building or site, museum and art gallery in Washington and New York. They would never venture into New England until I lived there because of the New England carpetbaggers during the Reconstruction days—they just didn't like or trust New Englanders. Our first day in New York was an exciting one. Papa went seeking a hotel we could afford, Nunnally found his way to his first big league baseball game, while Mama and I guarded the luggage at the depot.[2]

Mrs. James Johnson guarded the home in Columbus as well as the luggage in New York. She was a small, round, warm woman who resembled actress Maude Adams. Her first granddaughter, Marjorie Fowler, remembers her as "A little tiny lady with a whim of iron. When she couldn't get her own way she had fainting fits." She tried as best she could to housebreak her husband. She insisted that he not come home in his overalls but change in the shop. This he agreed to do, as well as to stop smoking cigarettes in public. She tried unsuccessfully to get him to stop smoking completely, but he would rise early enough in the mornings to sneak a cigarette and blow the smoke up the chimney along with the smoke from the wood fire.

Mrs. Johnson managed the family well on what was probably a middle income of the period. Certainly her values were middle class. The family was well-housed, well-clothed, and well-fed, and they had enough money for trips to Atlanta, Washington, and New York (helped by Mr. Johnson's free passes on the trains). Mrs. Johnson saved enough money to build a second house on the large lot next to their house. From the money she got from renting out the second house, Mrs. Johnson was able to buy other rental properties. These provided enough extra money for the family to move up to more "respectable" neighborhoods. Johnson remembered the series of moves: from the house on Fifth Street to a house between Seventh and Eighth, on up to Thirteenth, a succession he used as the basis for a collection of street signs that show the social climb of the heroine in his film *Black Widow*.

Mrs. Johnson was also something of a social climber, but with a streak of romantic idealism about her. She had come from a poor family and had not finished high school. She had dropped out, according to her son Pat, on a curious show of principle. When she was in high school, the standard procedure when one student misbehaved was for the other students to whip him. Mrs. Johnson had refused to participate in the whipping. After her marriage, she served for nearly twenty years as a member of the Board of Education in Columbus. Her particular goal was proper treatment and proper pay for teachers. In spite of the prejudices of the time and area, which she shared, she worked consistently to see to it that as often as possible black teachers received equal treatment and equal pay. A school is named after her in Columbus.

Mrs. Johnson was also one of the founders of the Mothers' Club in Georgia, a predecessor of the Parent-Teachers Association, and she was state parliamentarian for the PTA for several years. In 1917, she was president of the Columbus Federation of Women's Clubs. The local society ladies were always willing to let Mrs. Johnson do the work, but they did not accept her socially until after Nunnally Johnson had become successful as a short-story writer for *The Saturday Evening Post*. Ironically, Johnson's feeling when he ended up in New York and Hollywood was that his mother should not be ashamed of the way he turned out—that it was not her fault—while in fact it was his success that gave her the kind of social status she wanted in Columbus.[3]

Johnson's later feeling that his mother might be ashamed of him probably came from a sense of guilt over what may have seemed to him a repudiation of the value system he left. On the surface, his way of life seemed very different from his early days in Georgia. He was financially well off, he was living in the big cities, and he was eventually to marry three times; the first two marriages ending in divorce, one of the few things he ever openly expressed guilt over. In fact, his values remained those of his parents. He still believed in marriage, the family, and the home. He retained the qualities of kindness, loyalty, and good manners, and, in his personality, he was very much the child of his parents. Johnson felt he was most strongly influenced by his mother, particularly her warmth and romantic idealism, but in many ways he was more like his father. There was the same dry wit and personal reserve with other people. There was the same orderliness his father showed in the weekly trips to the library, and there was also the same lack of willingness to become completely domesticated.

Nunnally Johnson's own view of his childhood was that it was "strictly Norman Rockwell, which is why Norman Rockwell is my favorite painter." Johnson and his brother Pat both delivered newspapers, starting out with the local *Columbus Enquirer-Sun* and working their way up to the Atlanta papers, the *Georgian*, the *Constitution*, and the *Journal*, which they had to pick up from the 6:10 A.M. train. They also sold *The Saturday Evening Post* at five cents each door-to-door. They used their earnings to see the early movies of the period, to go to the circus when it came to town every year, and to see the stage shows at the Springer Opera House: the "10-20-30" melodramas (so called because the ticket prices were ten cents, twenty cents, and thirty cents) of the Jewel Kelly Stock Company. They put on their own plays in their back yard on Saturdays. Pat was the more stagestruck of the two, and he was the first author of the plays. On one occasion he announced that the new play would begin with "Pat and Nunnally out in a field shooting Yankees."

In 1911, Caruso came to Atlanta in Puccini's *The Girl of the Golden West,* and the Johnsons went up to see it. Pat was so taken with the story that he had his friends performing it every week. Nunnally saw them repeating it over and over again and decided to write a better script for them: his first try at playwriting. Nearly all of the plays the boys concocted involved them as some sort of superheroes escaping from jails, prisons, or dungeons which were made from flimsy fruit crates obtained from the local grocery store.

The theme of escape was not inappropriate. The society was comfortable. It was also closed and confining. Johnson began to develop a vision of himself living what he saw as the exciting life of a newspaperman. It was not so much the work that intrigued him as the pictures he saw of Richard Harding Davis in his war correspondent's outfit: "That looked to me like the kind of life I'd like to lead." Being a newspaperman "seemed to be within the possibilities of my life," especially after he first broke into print at the age of twelve. With his fascination for baseball, Johnson arranged a list of the names of the players on the Columbus team so that if one letter in each name was emphasized the result would be a vertical spelling out of "The Rag is Ours," a slang expression meaning the team had won. The item was printed in the *Enquirer-Sun*. The following year Johnson wrote a review on the activities of the major leagues based on his reading of the accounts in the newspapers as he delivered them.

Johnson's newspaper work led him to the editorship of the school magazine, *The Electron,* during his senior year at Columbus High School. Since there were only twenty-four people in Johnson's class of 1915, he not only was editor of *The Electron,* but also played football, basketball, and baseball for the school, as well as acting the part of the hero's father in the class play.

In Columbus High School at that time, one of the graduation requirements was the successful completion of a course in public speaking. Johnson worked out an arrangement with the English teacher who taught it: he would agree to be class poet two years in a row if he could get out of taking that speech course.

Johnson also fell in love during his junior year in high school, or so he thought. The girl's name was Kitty and she was a year ahead of him. Both she and Johnson were convinced that she looked like the silent film star Anita Stewart, an idea they both spent a great deal of time mooning over. They would sneak out of school and go down to the local movie theatres,

the Elite and the Dreamland, to see such stalwarts as E. K. Lincoln and
Carlisle Blackburn.

When Johnson was graduated from Columbus High School in 1915, he
tried to decide what to do with himself. He wanted to go to Yale because
he had grown up reading Frank Merriwell stories, but his grades,
particularly in math and the sciences, were not good enough. The
Central of Georgia, where his father worked, did not win his enthusiasm
the summer he worked there. As he later wrote for the Central's magazine:

> In time, when I was on vacation during my high school days in
> Columbus, I also went to work in the shops. Wilfred Gross of
> Columbus and I did a kind of brother-act on a very dreary machine
> called a bolt-cutter, where we both established records for diligence,
> devotion to duty and lust for hard labor that got us right out of there in
> about two months.

Johnson went to work as a reporter for the *Columbus Enquirer-Sun* in
1915. It was not a particularly striking debut in the world of journalism,
and not nearly as exciting as those pictures of Richard Harding Davis
had led him to believe. The first day he was on the job, the paper
suffered little harm since it assigned him to go on his daily rounds with
his departing predecessor, Mark Ethridge, later publisher of the *Louisville Courier-Journal*. They first went to the funeral parlors to get
information for the obituaries, then to the courthouse. Their final stop
that first day was at the private railroad car of the famous actor Sir
Johnston Forbes-Robertson and Lady Forbes-Robertson. The new reporter was so impressed with their glamor that he decided journalism was
indeed for him. Unfortunately, on his third day at the paper, when he
was assigned to cover a trial, he managed to get most of the information
wrong, which led the lawyers involved to threaten to sue the newspaper.
Johnson lasted six months on the *Enquirer-Sun* before he was fired.[4]

An older man who had encouraged Johnson as a writer in high school
told him there was a possibility of a job on the *Cleveland Plain-Dealer*
and gave him a letter of introduction to the editor. For Johnson, this was
a chance to get out of Columbus into the big world outside and he went to
Cleveland.

It was a disastrous move. The job he had been promised did not
materialize, and he ended up going to work weighing barbed wire in a
steel mill in Cleveland. He was so ignorant about living away from home
that he got a rented room on the other side of town from the steel mill,
which meant he had to get up at five in the morning to get to work. He did
not get any breakfast, and, unlike the other men in the mill, he did not
pack a lunch, so he ended up not eating anything until seven or eight at

night.[5] Just as he thought for sure that he was going to starve to death in Cleveland, he got a telegram from another friend offering him a job on the *Savannah Press*.

Johnson had been back in Georgia about six months when the call to colors came. The Georgia Hussars, officially Separate Troop A, Georgia Cavalry, the only troop in the U.S. Army 31st Division to retain its cavalry status, was going down to the Mexican border to repel Pancho Villa. Johnson joined right up, dreaming of adventure and thinking he would be outfitted in a coat with rows of buttons, long jack boots, and helmets that "made your head ache." Instead, he got the same uniform everyone else got: it didn't fit, and the spiral leggings kept getting untied and dragging after him in the dust.

After "Mexican Border Service, 1916-1917," the Hussars returned to Georgia in preparation for going overseas, but Johnson was sent to Louisville, Kentucky, for officer training. Assigned to an artillery battery, Lieutenant Johnson discovered that the battery clerk, a corporal named Steese, had been, in civilian life, an Assistant Night City Editor on *The New York Tribune*. As Johnson described it, "You never saw a Lieutenant suck up to a Corporal the way I sucked up to that Corporal. I wanted a job. He was very nice. I got out before him and he sent a note to the *Tribune*."

He had been commissioned in October 1918. In November, the war was over. By the end of the year, he was in New York and working for the *Tribune*.

He had finally escaped for good.

2

New York Columnist

New York City in the twenties was a legendary place in a legendary time. During the decade, everybody who was anybody was there sometime doing something: Texas Guinan was saying hello to the suckers, Eugene O'Neill was writing plays, Jimmy Walker was being Mayor, Coué was getting better every day in every way, Lucky Lindy was being a hero, Dorothy Parker was at the Algonquin Round Table making her not-so-gentle wisecracks in a gentle voice, and the newspapers were revelling in it all. So were most New Yorkers, then, as now, claiming New York City as the center of the world. But New York in the twenties was not the center of the country, let alone the world. It was on one side of a contest between the values of small-town America, which had dominated the country in the decades before the twenties, and the values of urban America, which would dominate the country in the decades after the twenties. In that decade, the clash of these two value systems, always a part of American life, flared into open warfare in which, as historian William Leuchtenberg says, "The provincialism of the city was arrayed against the provincialism of the country."[1]

As a refugee from the country living in and attracted to the city, Nunnally Johnson was aware, more intuitively than intellectually, of this conflict. By the time he was writing short stories, he often wrote about life in both, and he wrote about what happened when the two collided.[2] In one story, "New York—My Mammy," Johnson makes a sharply observed comparison between New York and the fictional Riverside and the mentalities of the citizens of both. The story begins with a young New York couple, Al and Roberta Kirkland, sadly awaiting the train that will take them "away—completely away—from New York City, and with the possible exception of death no greater calamity can blight a New Yorker's life." Al has been promoted to the job of assistant manager of his company's Riverside branch, and his relatives say of Riverside, "I was just wondering if it's the kind of place you could get your laundry done in. . . . I hear that once you get out of New York you can't tell." When Al and Roberta arrive in Riverside, they immediately suspect each act of Southern hospitality as an effort to con them. They begin to be taken with being awakened in the morning by mockingbirds and sitting out in the yard in the evening. Ultimately, the strain of such charms is too much for them. When two men on a passing train happen to drop off a New York newspaper, Al devours the headlines of gangland slayings, subway jams, heat waves, and the like. The couple eventually has to get back to New York.

Johnson shows an awareness in his stories of the glamor and excitement of life in New York, but he also seems appalled by the artificiality and phoniness beneath that glamor. For example, "It's in the Blood" deals with a rather dimwitted man named Moak whose only ability is grabbing souvenirs. He first comes to public attention when he steals a garter from a murderer being led off the jail. Moak becomes a national hero for the "Hartman garter caper." Johnson has one man say, "There is little comparison between Lindy and Moaky," meaning that Moaky is superior to Lindbergh in every way. Johnson is not only taking a sharp look at idolatry, but also at the attitude so prevalent in New York in the twenties that anything bigger or noisier or more daring was automatically better.

Nunnally Johnson had learned early in his days in New York that life in the big city was not as great as it was supposed to be. The job at the *Tribune* that he had so carefully coaxed out of Corporal Steese lasted six weeks. He had been hired because nearly all the male reporters were in the Army, and, as the "real reporters" came back from overseas, the latecomers were let go. Furthermore, he had been caught wrestling with one of the copy girls and had also accidentally thrown a match into a wastebasket and set the city room on fire.[3]

Johnson next found work on the *Brooklyn Eagle*, which was similar in style to a small town newspaper. He spent three years on the *Eagle*, but he was never very good at reporting. When he was sent out to cover a wedding he could not even locate the church. He once attempted to interview English author Margot Asquith, but, with her English accent and his Georgia accent, they were unable to understand each other. Johnson was sent to cover the death of Julius Caesar Coolidge, the father of Calvin Coolidge, and the story he sent back told in detail how the

elder Coolidge repeatedly sold his general store and then reclaimed it
each time in mortgage foreclosures. His managing editor later told
Johnson he kept that story to show new reporters as "the worst example of
judgment I've ever seen a newspaperman use."

Some stories did not turn out so badly. Since Johnson was a small-
town boy he was sent to cover the Scopes Monkey Trial in Dayton,
Tennessee, a classic confrontation between the small-town values of
William Jennings Bryan and the big-city values of Clarence Darrow.
Johnson got tired of the trial postponements and went down to visit his
parents in Columbus. He filed the last of his stories on the trial from
Columbus, and, when he returned to New York, he was told by his editor
that the last stories were the best he had ever done.

Johnson's social life in the early days in New York met with the same
general brand of success as his professional life. He was "jumping at
nearly every woman I'd see, the way you are when you get out of the
Army." One of the women he was jumping at was Alice Mason, the
attractive and outgoing editor of the *Junior Eagle,* a weekly insert section
in the *Brooklyn Eagle* for children. When he jumped, she caught him.
In late 1919, the *Eagle* carried this item about two of its employees:

> Miss Alice Love Mason, editor of the Junior Eagle, and Nunnally
> Johnson, a member of the news staff of the *Eagle,* were married at 5
> o'clock yesterday afternoon. . . .
> Miss Mason is the daughter of Mr. and Mrs. Charles Mason of 192
> Prospect Pl. She was educated in Brooklyn and Spring Valley, N.Y.
> She joined the *Eagle* staff after having been with the Hartford, Conn.,
> Times for several months. She came to the *Eagle* on March 30. . . .
> The marriage yesterday came as a surprise to most of the *Eagle*
> friends of the couple.

The marriage also came as a surprise to Johnson himself. He later
said, "I felt I had to get married. She wasn't pregnant, but she wanted to
get married and I was a nice Southern boy, and I couldn't think of a way
to get out of it. Going up the aisle I was still trying to think how to get out
of it and I couldn't."

Johnson was probably feeling instinctively what would soon become
very obvious, that he and Alice were a complete marital mismatch. He
had been attracted by her charm and her eccentricity, but it was that
very eccentricity, fascinating from a distance, that made her an inappropriate wife for Johnson. As much as he liked the exciting life of New
York, which Alice represented, his middle-class, small-town sense of
order needed a wife who could run a perfectly organized home. Alice was
simply incapable of it. She was later described by a relative as having

"that marvelous way of doing everything wrong." She was the sort of messy housekeeper who would dirty every pot in the kitchen making a sandwich. In addition, they were both too immature to adjust to each other's needs. They lived together for less than two years, had one daughter, Marjorie, then separated and were later divorced.[4]

After her divorce, Alice seemed to make a career out of her eccentricity. In addition to working at such mundane jobs as merchandising manager of Macy's, she also took it into her head, without the benefit of any sailing experience at all, to sail down the East Coast with a cat and a copy of the Rules of the Road as her only companions. She went aground in Savannah harbor, shooting off as a distress signal several rounds of her Very pistol; these were ignored by the Coast Guard because it was the Fourth of July. She spent some time in the Philippines where she became a good friend of a young Army officer named Dwight Eisenhower, for whom she later designed the first five-star insignia. She designed a successful line of costume jewelry and at one time set up an artists' colony somewhere in Mexico. As Roxie, a Johnson daughter by a later marriage, said, "My father wouldn't marry a dud."[5]

After Johnson was separated from his first wife, he was back in social circulation, now with a little more grace and just as much Southern charm. He was never a particularly handsome man, but, as a friend of his, Marian Spitzer Thompson, recalls, "He had a delightful pixie face with a manner to match . . . a guy who always created laughter and whom everybody loved on sight." His charm and wit were now mixed with caution. One evening he took to dinner a girl with whom he was having a casual romantic affair. During the dinner, he told her the romance was off. The girl began crying and asking, "How can you do this to me?" Finally she said to him, "How can you sit there wolfing down food when my life is crashing down around me?" Johnson's Southern gallantry rose to the occasion: "Honey, if I'd known you were going to feel this way, I'd have ordered something I didn't like."

Johnson was progressing professionally as well as socially. The management of the *Brooklyn Eagle* recognized that he was a better humorous and descriptive writer than a reporter, so he became a columnist. For three years he wrote "One Word After Another," a column done in the style of Franklin P. Adams's famous "The Conning Tower." It was filled with jokes, stories, humorous observations of the New York scene, and contributions from friends and readers. One of the contributors cost Johnson his job. He recalled,

> I turned up a child poet, a little girl named Nathalia Crane, and she was a marvel. She was eleven years old, and her verses were so charming and childish. My editor, for some reason, decided this child

was a fake and that William Rose Benet, Edwin Markham, Faith Baldwin, and a couple of others were writing this stuff and this kid was signing it. By now the kid had a volume of verse. This editor went to work as if he were exposing the Mafia. While on the front page he was exposing this kid, my column, which was on the back page of the first section, was promoting her. I was denying everything he said and describing him in rather rude terms. I didn't want to work for anybody that I didn't like, so I quit.

Johnson was by then a successful enough columnist to be hired by his former employer, now the *Herald-Tribune*. He did his "One Word After Another" column for the *Herald-Tribune* from 1924 to early 1927, then took the column to the *Evening Post*. His beat was New York City. Fifty years later he described New York in the Twenties as a "seedy heaven" and "a dreamland for newspapermen. They could keep a murder story going for days in the papers and it was all a lot of fun. That's gone and won't be back. Any ring of the phone in a newspaper office then meant excitement. Today you wouldn't want to answer it." He wrote about graft and crooked politicians. He helped organize the mythical American Royalist Party, dedicated to bringing back a king for America.

Along with journalists Frank Sullivan, Stanley Walker, and Joel Sayre, Johnson founded the Novel Nomenclature Club. Membership in the club was given to people with strange names. Each of the founders would keep a lookout in the newspapers for such real-life names as Hyacinth Ringrose, Jasper Spock, Miss Lois Trice, Fice Mork, Jr., and Phoebe B. Beebe. Johnson recalled, "You would read the obituary column in *The London Times* and find the death of Sir Richard Bastard. I daresay it was pronounced differently but it was spelled in the old way. Of course he became a member of our club. We put him in the records with a black border."

By the time Johnson gave up newspaper work in 1929, his skill as a humorous columnist was well-known. Commenting on Johnson's work in his "Beau Broadway" column, Walter Winchell wrote:

He invariably refused to be over-impressed by anything (I hope to read his comments on the events of the Last Great Day, to see whether Gabriel himself can awe Johnson), and he never tried to manufacture a jest where there was no jest to be manufactured. . . .

Best of all you could tell that never for a minute did Johnson consider himself a literary man. He knew damned good and well that he was a newspaperman as long as he wrote pieces for a newspaper, and he acted in print accordingly. This, though he was publishing mag stories all the time.[6]

For all of Winchell's approval, Johnson did not enjoy the highest status a wit in New York could have at that time. Because of his later reputation for wit in Hollywood, it has generally been assumed that he was part of the Algonquin Round Table. He attended a few sessions with the poet John V. A. Weaver, but was never asked to become a member, although as he later said, "I longed to have been." His wit, so dry and sharp, was never as savage or vindictive as that at the Algonquin Round Table, and the charter members of the group may not have known what to make of a man who could be funny and a gentleman at the same time.

As Winchell noted, Johnson began writing short stories while he was still a newspaperman. His first stories were written anonymously for *True Confessions*. In 1923 he began dating Marian Spitzer's roommate, Katharine Brody, a reporter who had written short stories for *The Smart Set*, a magazine that epitomized the cynical and sophisticated attitudes associated with New Yorkers. He wrote four stories, and Brody took them to the magazine. Three of the four were accepted. The fourth was turned down because it was "a newspaper story and the magazine does not accept newspaper stories."

Johnson wrote several other stories for *The Smart Set* before it folded, and he continued to write for *The Saturday Evening Post* until the early thirties. He had lived in the worlds of both publications. He had grown up in the kind of small town romanticized by the stories and pictures of the *Post*. He had left that world, but not without some small sense of guilt over his apparent betrayal of its values. He could lessen his guilt by romanticizing Riverside in his stories. With a few exceptions, Riverside is not used to provide any illumination of life in small-town America. The Riverside stories are slight, mildly amusing, sentimental comedies. The hero of many of the stories is Bascom McNutt, the soda jerk at the drug store, and his primary concern is inventing new sodas. At the same time, Johnson was attracted to, and living in, the exciting world of New York in the twenties, and he wrote about that world, too. Many of these stories, like some of the Riverside ones, tend to be overwritten. The *Post* required 5000 words and Johnson felt he was at his best at 3500 words. Johnson tended to take one joke and simply repeat it until he had the right number of words for a story.

Most of Johnson's short stories do not stand the test of time, but in the best of them there are clear signs of his improvement as a writer. He began with two formidable qualities: his powers of observation and his wit. His ability to see different things, or at least to see things differently, originally caused him some problems, as in his reportage on Coolidge's father, but it was an ability that served him well both as a columnist and as a writer of feature stories. What he saw differently was transmuted in his mind into a way of writing that was dry and amusing.

Johnson always had an orderly mind and his work on short stories gave him a chance to develop this sense of order as a literary skill. In "Ashes to Ashes," one of the first two stories that appeared in *The Smart Set*, the writing in the individual lines goes off on tangents and is often unclear. Even in the less successful later stories the writing is kept more fully under control.

Although there is occasionally some knowing observation of small-town types in the Riverside stories, there is less successful characterization in them than in the New York stories. This developing skill can be seen in his three stories about actors. In "The Actor," Reginald Peacock tells the narrator about a woman who has just come into the restaurant. She is Greta, his childhood sweetheart, who later married a man who has recently died. Reginald goes over to Greta and it is apparent they are both still in love with each other. Then Greta asks him what he has been doing the last ten years, and Reginald is so appalled that she does not know he is a famous actor, he leaves her on the spot. This final act, as well as his melodramatic recounting of their young love, reveals the enormous ego of an actor. In "An Artist Has His Pride," an out-of-work actor has a job in a haberdashery and he turns down parts in plays because they do not pay $90 a week, which is his set price. When he is promoted to a job in the store that pays $150 a week, he turns it down because he has just landed a part at $90 a week. Johnson's satire of the actor's ego is matched by an appreciation and reluctant admiration of his intense devotion to his craft.

It is difficult to have any admiration for Al Rose in "Pagliacci Blues." Rose is a mediocre vaudeville comedian who writes his own material. His wife leaves him for a singer-comic, but he is not so much bothered by that as by her leaving him for a man who cannot even get belly laughs, Al's measure of a performer. Al is depressed over this disaster, but he snaps out of it when he learns he is a hit in a new show, which, Johnson has carefully pointed out, has material Al did not write himself. We last see Al driving away from the theatre in a flashy new roadster with a huge Great Dane at his side, and he is laughing. Johnson accurately captures the dreariness, the crassness, and the sentimentality of Al Rose, and, at the same time, shows how he is so completely absorbed in show business that, in spite of his limitations, he could do nothing else.

Johnson was developing skills as a writer that would be particularly useful to him later as a screenwriter, and he was also beginning to be well-known. His stories were appearing regulary in *The Saturday Evening Post* and, by the later twenties, Johnson's name was listed on the cover along with such authors as James Gould Cozzens and John P. Marquand. He was a Famous Author.

In 1927, he married again. Her name was Marion Byrnes, and they had met when she was on the staff of the *Brooklyn Eagle*, which prompted Johnson's later comment that "marrying me was considered an occupational hazard for young girls working on the *Eagle*." She had grown up in New York City and attended Wellesley and Barnard before trying to get a job on a newspaper, which she thought was the way to begin a writing career. Through the efforts of her brother and a local politician, she ended up on the *Eagle*. She and Johnson had what she calls a "nodding acquaintance" for a year before he asked her out to dinner. They dated steadily for a period of two years, during which she left the *Eagle*, was the ghost writer of a novel, and even spent some time as a chorus girl in *Mayflowers*, a costume musical. When she and Johnson were finally married, she was an assistant editor on a magazine called *Success*.[7]

They started married life in a top-floor walk-up in a brownstone where Rockefeller Center now stands, from which they went out to the theatre, parties, and several nearby speakeasies. They soon began to branch out, having a house in Great Neck, Long Island, for the summers, building a house in Miami Beach for the winters, and taking trips to Europe from which Johnson sent back material for his column, now called "The Roving Reporter."

By late 1929, Johnson was making $1500 a story from *The Saturday Evening Post* and he was selling the magazine a story a month. He began to consider quitting his newspaper work and spending all his time doing short stories. It seemed financially feasible but it was very difficult to pull away from the security of newspaper work. He finally decided to make a try at it.

He could not have picked a worse time. He quit his newspaper job in November of 1929. The Depression was beginning, and the result for *The Saturday Evening Post* was that their advertisers were buying fewer and fewer advertisements. Over a period of three years, the pages in each issue of the *Post* dropped from 200 to 100. Instead of ten or twelve short stories each issue, there were now four. One of the writers who was cut back was Nunnally Johnson. Three of his stories were rejected by the *Post*, which meant the loss of three months' pay.

The publishing company of Doubleday, Doran tried to get him to write a novel and, to push him along, they brought out a volume of his collected short stories, *There Ought to Be a Law*. It did not sell particularly well, and, in any case, Johnson was wary of attempting a novel. He saw himself as a writer of light comedy, and, most recently, a writer whose light comedy was not selling. He was, after all, a young man who had only slightly more than a decade before come out of Georgia, and, unlike several other small-town boys who had come to the big city, he had not, and never would, become sophisticated. It was true that he had become slightly more knowledgeable about the world and slightly more polished, but he was still something of a small-town boy in the big city. He had changed, but he had not changed that much, and the effects of the Depression on him were telling. It shook his confidence in his abilities as a writer and convinced him he could not write anything as sustained as a novel.

In the spring of 1932, another form of escape presented itself. Johnson got an offer to go out to Hollywood and write for Paramount. The money was much less than he had heard other writers were getting, but he was feeling the financial pinch, especially now that Marion was pregnant with their daughter Nora. At Marion's urging, he took the offer of $300 a week. He borrowed money for the trip from his agent and a few other friends, and he and Marion took the train west.

3
First Films

Johnson's move to Hollywood in 1932 was not his first experience with the movies. He had sold a story, "Rough House Rosie," to Paramount and even though Johnson's name was on the credits for the 1927 release, his story suffered the fate of many others adapted into films. Johnson's story deals with a stuffy young Harvard man who falls in love with a showgirl, Rosie O'Reilly, and eventually decides not to marry her because of his fear of her toughness. In the film, about the only thing held over from the story is the character of Rosie, played by Clara Bow, who is now the leading character. Her boyfriend is a pug fighter who cannot keep his mind on his fighting because he is busy thinking about Rosie. She becomes a hit with her cabaret act, "Rough House Rosie and her Smooth Little Roughnecks." The fighter's manager tells him he has to get tough with Rosie, which he does in a dream sequence. Nunnally Johnson took the money and ran.

His next experience with the movies involved him with a young director, Frank Capra, who had risen from gag writer for Mack Sennett to writer and director for comic Harry Langdon. Langdon, after driving Capra off, had spread the word that Capra had had nothing to do with his success. Capra's agents, Edward and Morris Small, finally managed to get him a job directing a low-budget picture in New York. The story of the film (eventually called *For the Love of Mike*) was by John Moroso, and Johnson was called in to write scenes. Johnson said "Capra had a kind of a casual way of doing things. He would tell me, 'They find this baby, and leave it on the doorstep.' He would give a rough outline of what he wanted, and I would write it. Take a hack at it, anyway." They managed to stretch it to seven reels (seventy minutes), and the film was released in August 1927. Its only distinction was Claudette Colbert, in her first film after a successful stage appearance in *The Barker*. Johnson recalled, "It was such a real nothing. When it came out I snapped back to newspaper work, Claudette snapped back to the stage and Frank Capra snapped back to writing gags for Mack Sennett."[1] Shortly thereafter, Capra went to work at Columbia Pictures, and the rest, as they say, is history. His first big success was *It Happened One Night* in 1934, starring Claudette Colbert, who had vowed that *For the Love of Mike* would be her first and last film.[2]

Johnson's next brush with the movies came in the summer of 1927 when he was brought out to Hollywood under what was, in those days, referred to as the Paramount Fresh Air Fund for Reporters. Johnson prefers to call it the Mankiewicz Fund after its founder and driving force, Herman J. Mankiewicz (who later wrote, among other things, the original screenplay for *Citizen Kane*). Johnson said, "Mank was kind of paying off social obligations and everything else" by offering writing jobs to his friends and relatives (and telling each of them not to tell anybody else about it).

During Johnson's six weeks at Paramount in the summer of 1927, he did "almost nothing. A fellow took me into his office and he said, 'Look, here are our stars: Richard Dix, Adolphe Menjou, Richard Arlen. Now we want you to do this: pick out one of the stars and do a story for him.'" Johnson decided, for reasons nobody remembers, to try a story for Menjou. He may even have written part of it, but it wouldn't have been easy: he was given a large office, a secretary, lots of paper, but a typewriter without a ribbon in it. Mankiewicz later asked, "How long did it take you to find that out?"[3]

He spent as much time observing the Hollywood scene for his "Roving Reporter" column as he did writing for Paramount. In one column, he commented on the lavishness of a premiere, "How was I to know that it was only a Hollywood movie premiere? How was I to know it was just Buddy Charles Farrell arriving with Buddy Janet Gaynor? The way it looked to me, I thought the world was coming to an end."

So, in 1932, Johnson returned to Hollywood. He had heard stories of how writers were treated when they were brought out to Hollywood under contract. Dudley Nichols and Oliver Garrett had been put on the Twentieth Century Limited in their own drawing room full of fruit and liquor. In Chicago they were transferred by limousine to the Super Chief, and they were met in San Bernardino by another limousine that took them into Los Angeles.[4] Johnson later satirized this whole business in *Life Begins at Eight-Thirty*, when he has one character say, "The CLASS crowd—OUR sort—gets off at Pasadena. The best people—the REAL tops—get off at San Bernardino." Later, the same character says, "I was just wondering. Mightn't it be pretty effective if we got off, say, at Kansas City and took a taxi to Hollywood?"

There were no such elaborate arrangements for Johnson. He had to borrow money even to make the trip. All he had been promised was that, if he showed up at Paramount on a certain Monday morning, he could go to work. As he stepped off the train in Los Angeles, Marion asked Johnson, "Are you nervous?"

He replied, "No, not in the least."

"Why aren't you?"

He said, "I've been looking at pictures, and I wasn't impressed with the dialogue. I think I can do better."

Marion remembers that he paid attention to more than just the dialogue. "Nunnally had been studying movies for several years. We had gone to many. While I was caught up in the story, the romance, with tears, with fear, Nunnally was studying exits and entrances, build-up, story climax, hurdles, interruptions, let-downs, false motivations, and all of the many complexities that go into the making of a story in a magazine or on the screen."

Johnson started out as sort of a junior writer on three films at Paramount, although he did not receive screen credit for any of them. Mostly, he was just a wide-eyed newcomer who simply watched what was going on, which, at Paramount, was often rather strange. One day, the story editor who had brought Johnson out to Paramount, Merritt Hulburd sent Johnson over to the office of Harold Hurley, a producer of "B" pictures. When Johnson arrived he found director Henry Hathaway and another young writer, Joseph Mankiewicz. Hurley was explaining his idea of how the picture was going to be written. He outlined the story and then he assigned each of the characters to one of the five writers who were working on the picture. Each writer was to come up with dialogue for that character and then Hurley would put it all together into the final script. Both Mankiewicz and Johnson were completely baffled, but went off to do what they could. Johnson had been assigned a sailor with a parrot—a great advantage, since it allowed him to write dialogue between them. But no movie ever came out of this scheme.

Johnson's first screen credit at Paramount was for a Maurice Chevalier vehicle called *A Bedtime Story,* in which Chevalier plays an explorer who returns from Africa to discover a baby in the back seat of his car. He decides to bring it up himself and hires a nurse, played by Helen Twelvetrees. Naturally, Chevalier, Twelvetrees, and the baby end up as one happy family. Johnson's writing partner on the project was a Paramount veteran named Waldemar Young, who had written such films as *The Unholy Three* and Cecil B. DeMille's *The Sign of the Cross.* Johnson remembered him as a "wonderful old guy" who was "content to let me do the writing. He'd sit and we'd talk over the situation and he'd say, 'Well I think that would make a very good scene there. You want to try it?' I'd say, 'Yep,' and I'd try it."

Johnson and Young got along well; their biggest problem was their producer, Benjamin F. Glazer. Glazer often insisted on certain scenes in a picture, for example, a scene in a barber chair. In such a case, Glazer had a barber shop set he could sell to Paramount to include in the picture. Johnson and Young would cut the scene out and then go into a story conference with Glazer, who was not aware that they knew exactly why he wanted to put the scene back. He would give elaborate explanations of why that scene was crucial to the story and what a good scene it was. Both Johnson and Young knew the scene would go back into the picture, but they could not resist the opportunity to upset Glazer.

On Johnson's next film for Paramount, *Mama Loves Papa*, Johnson was assigned to work with Arthur Kober. There were attempts at Paramount and the other studios to turn writers into specific kinds of cogs in the moviemaking machine. Johnson was considered a dialogue man, while Kober was called a continuity man. According to Johnson, that meant Kober "every now and then wrote 'Cut,' and 'Fade in' or 'Fade out' or something like that." Johnson discovered that Kober was getting more money than he was, and so Johnson became determined to learn all the technical terms so he would not have to share the money with other writers who did just that sort of thing.

Mama Loves Papa was much closer than *Bedtime Story* to the kind of subject matter that Johnson had been doing for *The Saturday Evening Post*. The story was concocted by two other writers, Douglas MacLean and Keene Thompson, specifically as a vehicle for Charles Ruggles and Mary Boland. In the story, Jessie Todd (Boland) goes to a lecture about the ideal of success and tries to convince her husband, Wilbur (Ruggles), that, in order to become a success, he must act like one. She convinces him to wear a Prince Albert to work, and, everybody who sees him in his fancy clothes, thinks someone died. His boss lets him have the afternoon off to go to the funeral. Ruggles wanders past a playground where a group of ladies mistakes him for the commissioner of playgrounds, and, through a series of misunderstandings, he becomes the commissioner; this, in turn, leads him into a harmless flirtation with a local temptress, played by Lilyan Tashman. The tone is very much that of the domestic humor of the Riverside stories, even though the story is set in what looks like a fairly large city. Johnson was not yet well-known as a screenwriter, but his reputation as a short story writer and humor columnist was such that another columnist, Lee Shippey of the *Los Angeles Times*, noted at the time of the release that movie audiences should really pay more attention to the writers of movies, and that one of the reasons he went to see *Mama Loves Papa* was because he liked Johnson's brand of comedy.[5]

While he was working on "B" pictures for producer Harold Hurley, Johnson came down with appendicitis and was taken to the hospital. Because Johnson was so inexperienced and, at the same time, so conscientious, he began to get worried that they were paying him while he was in the hospital and not writing. He had been in the hospital about ten days when Merritt Hulburd came to see him, and in what Johnson described as "a burst of nobility" he told Hulburd, "Merritt, I would like you to understand that if you suspend me during this time I will understand it." Hulburd seemed rather embarrassed. He said, "I wouldn't tell you before because you've been quite ill. The minute the ambulance rolled out, Hurley chopped you off the payroll." Johnson was beginning to understand the ways of Hollywood, and said of Hurley it was "one of the few times in my life I hated anybody."

Just as Johnson was beginning to learn about the craft of writing for the movies, as much as he could under the rather chaotic conditions that existed at Paramount, he was also beginning to learn of the pressures of the motion picture business. He was working very hard and very long hours, and one of the releases was through drinking, which was probably inevitable when that many ex-reporters got together in one place. Johnson described Hollywood in an interview in 1934, "Hollywood is all right. I have a good time there. In fact, it is about the only place now where I can find my friends. They're all out there. A party looks like the old *Herald-Tribune* room. No, it looks more like a speakeasy."[6] Many years later, Johnson remarked, "I don't remember that we drank *that* much," but that seems to be because it did not take more than a few drinks to get Johnson very drunk, and he would retain no memory the following day of what had happened when he was drinking.[7] One of Johnson's writing and drinking companions of those days remembers that when Johnson was drunk he could be as "slippery as an eel. There was nothing to hold on to." On one occasion, it fell to this friend to take Johnson home after a drinking spree. The man poured him up to the door and rang the bell. Marion answered the door, looked at the limp form of Johnson and said, "Put him down on the couch." He did and Marion watched them; then she simply turned and went up to bed, leaving Johnson on the couch.

The pressures of working in Hollywood began to affect Johnson's marriage. In New York and Florida, he had spent a lot of time at home during the day, either writing or, particularly in Florida, fishing, playing tennis, and going to the races with Marion. Now he was working at the studio during the day and often drinking at night; when he came

home from work, he would be exhausted and withdrawn. At the same
time, Marion was feeling out of place. In New York, she had been active
as a reporter, editor, and even a chorus girl. She no longer had those jobs
and she felt the need for some kind of activity. Johnson described it,
"You see it coming. First they are taking night courses at UCLA. Or
joining the dramatic club. You know they're not sharing the interests of
the husband."[8] It was not that Marion did not want to share Johnson's
interests; it was more that Johnson made it difficult for her by his own
withdrawal when he was home. As Marion recalls the situation, "I felt
rejected. We seemed to be growing apart and I didn't know what to do
about it."[9]

He was undoubtedly driven by his compulsions about his own writing.
He wanted to write, and he wanted to work at it, and he wanted to be
good at it. As much fun and as entertaining as the work at Paramount
might have been, it still must have been in many ways a comedown from
the days in New York and on *The Saturday Evening Post*. Now he was
one more semi-anonymous screenwriter, and, in spite of the conviviality
of his writer friends at Paramount, he was worried about his craft,
particularly in view of the kinds of criticism many people made of writers
who had gone to Hollywood. Harold Ross, the editor of the *New Yorker*,
later singled out Johnson in a statement that was typical of the attitude of
East Coast literary types toward those writers who had gone to Hollywood. Ross said, "Johnson is also sickening from my standpoint, for he
had been sucking around the diamond merchants of Hollywood for the
last fifteen years and hasn't written anything. There is a misspent life."[10]

F. Scott Fitzgerald told Johnson the same thing even earlier. One
night, Fitzgerald and Sheilah Graham had to party to "celebrate"
Fitzgerald's being taken off a screenplay he had been working on. At the
end of the party, Fitzgerald suddenly pulled Johnson aside and took him
into the den. Fitzgerald locked the door and began telling Johnson to
leave town, that he had talent but that Hollywood would ruin it.
Fitzgerald went on for twenty-five minutes trying to convince Johnson to
give up Hollywood, while Johnson kept insisting that, since he was
making more money than he ever had before, he did not want to be
saved. With the help of Sheilah Graham and his wife, Johnson freed
himself from the clutches of Fitzgerald and left.[11]

Johnson, in the search for order in his own life, had found in writing a
way to organize and express his own approach to the world. Writing not
only satisfied his own desire for order, and at the same time his desire for
escape (into his own stories), but he knew he had the talent to satisfy
others with his writing. His faith in his talent, however, had been
strained by his later lack of success in selling his stories, by his

unwillingness to attempt a novel, and now by his only mild success at this new form, screenwriting. In 1932 he had, like millions of Americans before and since, escaped to the West. Now he was as far west as he could go. He had no other means of escape, so he withdrew into his drinking and into himself. The other compulsions, for order and for the expression of order, did not, however, go away.

4

Enter Zanuck

Darryl F. Zanuck came from Wahoo, Nebraska. At fourteen, he lied about his age, joined the Army, and eventually went overseas during World War I. After the war, Zanuck went to California, where he supported his attempts at writing short stories for the pulp magazines by taking such jobs as catching rivets at a shipyard at Long Beach. He started selling stories to the movies, and ended up as a screenwriter of sorts at Warner Brothers, a job he got primarily on the basis of his ability to act out Rin Tin Tin stories. Zanuck soon moved from just writing to "supervising," as producing was called in those days. Zanuck's supervisor status eventually turned into the job of head of production for all Warner films just at the time Warner Brothers decided to take an enormous gamble and interpolate several sound musical numbers into *The Jazz Singer*.

Zanuck was associated with a wide variety of pictures at Warner Brothers, most of them successful. He produced two of the best-known gangster pictures, *Little Caesar* and *Public Enemy*, and he did one of the first backstage musicals, *Forty-Second Street*. He started a series of pictures about social problems with the film *I Am a Fugitive from a Chain Gang*.

Zanuck departed from Warner Brothers in 1933. The Depression came late to Hollywood because of the beneficial impact of the introduction of sound pictures. In late 1932, along with the heads of the other studios, the New York executives of Warner Brothers had agreed to a 50 percent pay-cut for all employees. Zanuck was selected to tell the employees, and he was also empowered to tell them the date the pay cuts would be restored. In April 1933, when the time for the restoration of the cuts approached, Zanuck was told by Harry Warner that the studio had decided to extend them for another two weeks. Zanuck was furious and felt betrayed by the studio. He tore up his $5000 a week contract and resigned. Shortly thereafter, Zanuck was talking business with Joseph Schenck over breakfast at the Brown Derby.[1]

Schenck was one of the ugliest men in the motion picture business and also one of the most charming. He was also, in Nunnally Johnson's phrase, "the Joe DiMaggio of gamblers. . . . he had the heart of a lion . . . because it took the heart of a lion to lay a hundred thousand dollars on the table."[2]

Joseph Schenck and his brother Nicholas came to the United States from Russia either in the late 1880's or the early 1890's. They got into business as pharmacists and later owned a series of drug stores in the Bronx, from which they branched out into the operation of amusement parks. This in turn led them into the film business in connection with theatre owner Marcus Loew. Nicholas became the secretary of Loew's Consolidated and Joseph ran the company theatres. Nicholas eventually became the president of Loew's Incorporated which was to become the parent company of Metro-Goldwyn-Mayer, while Joseph left Loew's and became a producer, promoter, and financier. He started a company that made films starring his wife, Norma Talmadge, and he started another independent company for Buster Keaton, who happened to be married to Norma Talmadge's sister, Natalie. It was also Joseph Schenck who later convinced Keaton to give up the independent company and join Nicholas' company, MGM, which was the beginning of the end of Keaton's period of greatest creativity. Joseph Schenck was holding the job of president of United Artists in 1933 when he had breakfast with Darryl Zanuck at the Brown Derby.

By lunchtime, Zanuck and Schenck had agreed to form a new independent company which would release pictures through United Artists. The new company, Twentieth Century Pictures, was to have as its third partner William Goetz, Louis B. Mayer's son-in-law. Goetz had been a producer at MGM, Paramount, Fox, and RKO, and Mayer, vice-president in charge of production at MGM, had wanted to set Goetz up in business for himself. Mayer, probably with the help of Nicholas Schenck, convinced Joseph Schenck to take Goetz into the new company in return for which Mayer gave Schenck a check for $100,000 to help get the company off the ground. The new company had no studios, no equipment, and, most important of all, no stars. So Mayer also offered to make it easier to borrow such MGM stars as Wallace Beery, George Raft, and Clark Gable.

If the new company got its stars from MGM (in addition to such performers as George Arliss, Constance Bennett, and Loretta Young, whom Zanuck was able to convince to leave Warners), it still had to get equipment and studio space. They both were rented from the United

Artists (later the Goldwyn) studio on Santa Monica Boulevard in Hollywood. Johnson recalled, "They didn't own anything. They rented typewriters, they rented everything. They didn't own a chair over there." They
manned the rented typewriters with writers borrowed from MGM, such as
Bess Meredyth, and with other writers hired outright, such as Gene
Fowler and Nunnally Johnson.

Johnson never knew why Zanuck asked him to join the new company.
"I don't know how my name came up, but he made two or three efforts to
get me. He told my agent he wanted me to go to work for him. I don't
know why this was. I could hardly have impressed him in any way
because I hadn't done enough. I don't suppose I would have asked him
even if I'd thought about it even though I worked for him for twenty-odd
years."

Most likely, Zanuck had read Johnson's stories in *The Saturday
Evening Post* and thought of Johnson as a real writer. Zanuck had always
thought of himself as a writer, although he had never been as successful
at it as Johnson; writing pulp magazine stories and Rin Tin Tin movies
did not have quite the status of writing for the *Post*. Still, Zanuck
continued to think of himself as a writer, only now he was "writing" films
through other writers as well as through directors and actors. Zanuck
always emphasized the writing of the script as the basic element in the
making of a film. Thus, the major element in a Zanuck film was not a
lavish physical production, or a name director, or even big stars, but
rather a good story. To get good scripts out of good stories, Zanuck felt he
had to have good writers. Writers like Nunnally Johnson were crucial to
the way Zanuck was going to make movies.

If Johnson was important to Zanuck, Zanuck was even more important
to Johnson. First of all, Zanuck valued writers, which Paramount had
not. Secondly, screenwriting at Paramount had been uncontrolled chaos.
Zanuck provided the kind of order which Johnson was seeking and under
which Johnson functioned best. Zanuck's leadership pushed Johnson to
organize his own writing, both in terms of the style of the writing itself,
and in the way Johnson went about it. Zanuck's emphasis on the
narrative line in scripts provided a style through which Johnson could
express himself. Zanuck's story conferences were the way Johnson would
learn to write Zanuck's kind of scripts.

It was at Twentieth Century that Zanuck began to develop the story
conference method of dealing with writers. The story conferences were
shows in themselves, sometimes more entertaining than the films that
came out of them. Zanuck pantomimed, shouted, cursed, sang, danced,
and plotted with dazzling speed, giving out a hundred variations on both
plot and character while acting out everything. Ben Hecht said that

Zanuck was "sharp and quick and plotted at the top of his voice, like a man hollering for help."[3] Johnson agreed: "Zanuck was the master of the story conference, and I never realized how good he was until I worked with some other people. I know that he was a definite contributor to every picture that he ever had anything to do with."

Zanuck's story conferences were a long way from those of Benjamin Glazer at Paramount, but they were not without their moments of what critics might refer to as pure Hollywood. On one of the later pictures at Twentieth Century, *Cardinal Richelieu*, Johnson asked Zanuck to hire a friend of his, Cameron Rogers, who was an authority on the seventeenth century, the period the film dealt with. Johnson said "Cam was a very scholarly guy, and he knew the period the way Winchell knew Broadway. I remember at one of these story conferences he would just sit there looking popeyed at what Darryl was doing with history. Cam said, 'If you don't mind my saying so, Mr. Zanuck, I can't imagine any scholar accepting such a thing.' Christ, I think Darryl was going to put the Battle of Waterloo in there or something like that because it fit. Darryl thought about it for a few minutes and then he said, 'Aw, the hell with you. Nine out of ten people are going to think he's Rasputin anyway.' "

In the beginning, two things bothered Johnson about the story conferences. The first was that they were held late at night. Zanuck was a night person and usually would not arrive at the studio until eleven in the morning. He would hold conferences with executives and other personnel during the day, and then after dinner would view rushes, rough cuts, and completed pictures—from his own studio and others. He would not get around to story conferences until ten or eleven at night, and frequently the conferences would go on for three or four hours.

The other thing that bothered Johnson was the large number of people who attended these conferences. First of all, there were Johnson, Zanuck, and Zanuck's secretary, who had the unenviable job of taking down in note form what was said and done and typing it up in some way that made sense to everybody the next morning. In addition, there were William Goetz and former actor Raymond Griffith, whom Zanuck had taken on as a production supervisor. Griffith's career as an actor was virtually ruined by sound films since he had lost his voice as a young man and could speak only in a whisper. Both Goetz and Griffith were listed as associate producers and were so jealous of each other's position that Zanuck had to put both their names on each picture to convince each of them that neither one had higher status than the other. Zanuck also had a number of hangers-on, yes-men, and cronies who sat in on story conferences in the early years. One of these was an old-time director by the name of Al Green, and Johnson could not figure out exactly what his function was at these story conferences. Finally one night, when Zanuck was driving Johnson home, Johnson said, "Look, most of those guys there, I know what they're doing, but what about that fellow Green?"

Zanuck laughed and said, "You notice every now and then I'd say to Al, 'What do you think of that, Al?' And Al would answer. I'm just trying to find out if it was clear to Al. If it's clear to Al, it'll be clear to everybody in the United States."

The first picture Johnson was assigned to was an unacknowledged steal from the film Alfred Lunt and Lynn Fontanne had done two years before of Ferenc Molnar's play *The Guardsman*. In that film, Lunt and Fontanne are actors married to each other, and he tests her faithfulness by attempting to seduce her while in the disguise of a Russian officer. Johnson and Zanuck changed the story around by having it deal with a female singer, Helen, who is trying to convince her husband that she still has talent. Her old partner in a sister-act, who is now the sensational French star Raquel, talks her into pretending to be Raquel in a new show in New York. The picture was called *Moulin Rouge*, (not to be confused with the later picture of the same name about Toulouse-Lautrec).

Pictures were sometimes conceived at Twentieth Century in rather casual ways. Johnson had seen the 1929 version of *Bulldog Drummond* with Ronald Colman in the lead and had been fascinated by the character Drummond. Johnson was talking with Zanuck one day about how much he had liked it, and Zanuck said, "Jesus, let's make another one and get Ronnie to play it." So they did, calling it *Bulldog Drummond Strikes Back*.

Johnson whipped up the script, which has fun with the whole genre of mystery films. At one point, when a woman who is about to explain the mystery faints, Drummond says, "Splendid! Splendid! I was afraid for a moment we were going to find out what this show is all about."

Johnson also managed to pick up some extra money working for Samuel Goldwyn on the side. Goldwyn asked Zanuck if he could borrow Johnson to work on an Eddie Cantor musical he was doing. Zanuck told him that Johnson had a vacation coming up and that he could hire him to work during that vacation. This was not exactly what Goldwyn had in mind, since he had hoped to borrow Johnson at his Twentieth Century salary. Johnson was not particularly interested in doing the Cantor picture, so, for having to work during his vacation, he asked what he thought was an excessive amount of money. Much to his surprise, Goldwyn paid it. He did so little work on the movie, *Roman Scandals*, that he received no screen credit. The following year, he went back and worked on another Cantor picture for Goldwyn, *Kid Millions*. Johnson said, "I did all the writing. I'm always very insistent on that," and maintained that the other two writers, Nat Perrin and Arthur Sheekman, simply "were good in thinking up funny stuff and gags and scenes, particularly for Cantor." Since the entire script is "funny stuff and gags and scenes, particularly for Cantor," with very little story line, it is unclear what Johnson's contribution was. There is certainly no evidence of the Johnson wit in the gags, which ran to tired old Broadway wheezes like "A wedding is a funeral where you smell your own flowers." Johnson was better off with Zanuck.

Johnson did get along well with Goldwyn, which may be attributed to Johnson's feeling that Goldwyn had much the same kind of instincts about pictures that Zanuck did. Johnson said:

Goldwyn kept very close to the picture. He would read the stuff and his comments were all pretty good. He was an instinctive man about pictures, as if he had some kind of Geiger counter in his head—like Zanuck. I always thought Zanuck had a Geiger counter in his head. Zanuck would read a script and the minute it got dull or didn't move or went off the track—tick-tick-tick! He'd go back two or three pages and figure out where the movement stopped or went wrong. When you came in to talk to him he knew exactly where it wasn't moving right. Goldwyn had some of that, but Goldwyn left a good deal of it to directors. Darryl was not like that. Darryl's idea was to get a script and call in the director. The director was then not only permitted, but expected, to make his contributions, but it all had to be on paper before it went on the set. And Darryl had to okay it. There was none of this the-director-takes-charge while Zanuck was making a picture. Zanuck was in charge. Another one I did with Zanuck was *The Man Who Broke the Bank at Monte Carlo* with a director named Steve Roberts, who'd been working at Paramount where the director was a kind of king. I remember sitting with Zanuck and Steve. Steve in his airy fashion said, "I'll tell you what I'll do. I'll read the script over the weekend and kick it around." You'd have thought he insulted Darryl's mother. Darryl said, "What do you mean, kick it around?" Steve was so startled. Darryl said, "Don't kick anything around. Now if you've got some suggestions, I'll be very happy to listen to them. But don't kick things around here." Steve had never been spoken to like that at Paramount.

When George Arliss was at Warner Brothers, he had often suggested to Zanuck making a film from a play by George Westley about the Rothschild banking empire. The play, identified in the credits of the film *The House of Rothschild* as an "unproduced play," is more a bad attempt at writing a screenplay. There are suggestions in it for cinematic devices, but the plot sprawls through scene after scene. It is obviously the character of Nathan Rothschild that appealed to Arliss. Nathan does not show up until the second act, when he immediately solves everybody's problems, only to be faced, in the third act, with different troubles, which he solves with equal brilliance. In mid-1933, Zanuck had Sam Mintz and Maude Howell, an Arliss collaborator, prepare an outline. They focused the action on Nathan and did away with several extraneous plots. In September, Arliss made a number of suggestions, including adding the role of Mayer Rothschild, the father of Nathan and his brothers. This gave Arliss two roles to play. Maude Howell prepared another outline incorporating Arliss' suggestions and, in the process, making the plot more complicated. In mid-September, Zanuck called Johnson in and began to talk about the Rothschild project. After a while, Johnson said, "Are you sure you know what I do? I write low comedy, and this is a dramatic story. All my characters are liable to fall into flour barrels and things like that." Zanuck nevertheless encouraged him to work on the project.

Johnson and Maude Howell wrote a treatment based on her outlines. Johnson straightened out the story line and developed the story in major sequences. He was by then working, not from Westley's play, but from Maude Howell's outlines and Arliss's notes, which were in turn based on a recently published book, *The Rise of the House of Rothschild*. Johnson then wrote the screenplay.

One of the problems was the major theme: how the sons of Mayer Rothschild overcame the strong anti-Semitic feeling of their time (the late eighteenth and early nineteenth century). The script does not skirt the issue. The opening shot of the script and the film is the closing of the ghetto at the curfew hour, with the local police putting up a heavy chain to barricade the entrance. Later in the picture, the villain, Ledrantz, is given a vicious anti-Semitic speech which was, of course, then topped by Nathan's speech. Joseph Schenck, who virtually never read scripts, read the script for this film, and expressed his anxiety to Zanuck about Ledrantz's speech. Zanuck, thinking that Schenck perhaps erroneously assumed, as many people did, that Zanuck was Jewish and was offended by the speech, started to say something and Schenck quickly cut him off by explaining, "Oh no, not like that. I'm afraid people will cheer."

Johnson found writing for Arliss worrisome in another way. He liked to write by acting out each part. On the first Eddie Cantor picture, it took him a whole day to learn to imitate Cantor. He found Arliss even more difficult: "It held me up trying to get that lip right. . . . Very difficult, yes, but I finally got the technique."[4] Johnson described Arliss as "a gentle, nice man, but very imposing. I mean, it was like the King of England was working around with you."

Arliss was not any easier on Zanuck. Arliss was to play both Mayer and Nathan Rothschild, and he mentioned to Zanuck that Nathan Rothschild had been a good friend of Disraeli's. Zanuck managed to dissuade Arliss from having Disraeli written into the script so he could play three parts instead of two.

The House of Rothschild was released in March, 1934, and became the biggest hit the new company had. The picture went on to be named as one of the best of the year by both *The New York Times* and *The New York News*. The National Board of Review picked it as the second best picture of the year, and the Screen Writer's Guild picked Johnson's screenplay as one of the six best of the year. Lewis Jacobs has pointed out in *The Rise of the American Film* that "the integrity of bankers in national and international dealings was eulogized in *The House of Rothschild,*" which suggests that perhaps Zanuck and Schenck were trying to curry favor with the bankers for their new company. There seems to be no other evidence this was their motivation. What is perhaps unusual is that a film which could be interpreted as praising bankers could be such a success in the middle of the Depression.

A major portion of the success of the film in its time was due to Johnson's script. It was certainly the best he had done up to that time. There is a narrative drive to the story that seems to have come from the Zanuck-Johnson collaboration in their story conferences. Certainly the story line is both more believable and more efficiently told than in any of Johnson's previous scripts. Individual scenes show a high degree of human sensitivity. After the opening sequence, Johnson shows the family of Mayer Rothschild, particularly the five young sons who are imitating their father and his work as a money changer. The scene establishes very carefully the humanity of the family, which probably was enormously helpful in making the film a success with the non-Jewish audience in America. Ironically, it was this same sequence, taken out of context, that was used in an anti-Semitic 1940 Nazi "documentary," *Der ewige Jude (The Eternal Jew)*, to suggest the beginning of the financial "empire" of the Jews.

Johnson did get in some comedy, although not of the flour-barrel kind, particularly in the scene with Nathan and the Duke of Wellington, played in a cameo by C. Aubrey Smith with an emphasis on the duke's crankiness and his snuff. Johnson also could not resist having Nathan say to his daughter, who informs him that the Gentile she wants to marry is not after her money, that he is pleased since "So many Gentiles have that terrible grasping spirit. All they ever seem to think of is . . . money, money, money."

Johnson's touch can also be seen in the choice of characterization, particularly in Hannah, the wife of Nathan Rothschild. Granted that the part was written specifically for George Arliss's wife, Hannah is still one of the earliest examples of a particular piece of characterization that Johnson was to return to time and again in his scripts. While Nathan is out-maneuvering Napoleon in the banking houses, Hannah is the epitome of the good and faithful wife, supporting her husband in everything he does. When he goes off to the Exchange on the day of the Battle of Waterloo, he forgets the flower which he always wears in his lapel, and she sends it via messenger so that he is reassured at the proper moment.

If the beginnings of Johnson's style as a screenwriter are evident not only in the structure of the story and the individual scenes but also in the humanity with which the characters are written, there is at least one element that was not handled in what was becoming Johnson's style. This is the characterization of the villain Ledrantz, who is still given the standard, stock, melodramatic characterization, without the redeeming quality of some kind of understandable motivation. Ledrantz's villainy is only an expression of his anti-Semitic feelings, which, in turn, are given no particular motivation.

The film holds up remarkably well and is still entertaining. Arliss, C. Aubrey Smith, and Boris Karloff as Ledrantz, are enjoyable to watch, and the plotting, particularly since it has been fleshed out with the human touches Johnson provided, seems less obvious and melodramatic than many similar historical pictures of the time. The opening sequences in particular seem powerful, as does the scene in which Nathan tells his daughter that he cannot permit her to marry a Gentile because of the way he has been treated.

The House of Rothschild was not only a financial success for Twentieth Century but also a personal success for Nunnally Johnson. He had been known primarily as a humorous writer of short stories, one of many writers who had drifted out to Hollywood to pick up some of the money that was being thrown at writers, but now he had succeeded in writing a first-rate dramatic script for a film that had been a hit. He was beginning to establish himself as a screenwriter, and he was aware of that, as indicated by what happened on the next picture he wrote—another biographical picture for George Arliss, this one about Cardinal Richelieu.

Johnson and Cameron Rogers adapted the nineteenth century Edward Bulwer-Lytton play about Richelieu, and, when the picture got into production, Johnson heard that Arliss was rewriting the script. Johnson went in to see Zanuck and asked that his name be taken off the picture. Zanuck automatically assumed that Johnson had heard that the picture was not going well and would probably be a flop.

Johnson said this was not so. He told Zanuck, "I don't know how it's going. I'm told that Mr. Arliss is rewriting stuff on the backs of menus and things, and I don't want credit if it's so good and I don't want to get blamed if it's so bad. I'd just as soon withdraw." Zanuck agreed, understanding that Johnson had pride in his craft.

5
Rewriting Faulkner

In 1931, a combination of the telephone company, Wall Street brokerage firms, and several New York banking houses became so upset by William Fox's disregard for their financial manipulations and by his attempt to dominate the production of sound motion pictures through his German Tri-Ergon patents that they drove his Fox Film Corporation into receivership. The banking houses which had worked so hard to take over Fox's company arranged for the corporation to be run by executives selected by themselves. These executives, unfortunately, had no idea how to run a film studio, and, by 1935, it was worse off than it had ever been under Fox. Fox, at least, had been a showman. The businessmen who ran the studio in the early thirties, while moderately skilled in business, had neither the show-business background, the skill, nor the chutzpah to make the decisions necessary to make pictures. In 1935, Sidney Kent, president of Fox, was looking for a way to increase the company's earning power. His eye fell on Twentieth Century Pictures. Fox, with all its studios, distribution exchanges, and theatres had a net worth of $36 million, but an earning power during the previous year of only $1.8 million, while Twentieth Century Pictures had an earning power of $1.7 million on assets of only $4 million. Emissaries having been sent, complicated negotiations ensued, various stock deals were worked out, and Schenck, Zanuck, and Goetz moved Twentieth Century Pictures out of their rented offices and into the Movietone City William Fox had built in Westwood in 1928.[1]

For Nunnally Johnson, the big change at first seemed to be that, instead of a rented typewriter, he now had one of the company's own.

The first picture Johnson wrote at Twentieth Century-Fox was *The Prisoner of Shark Island*. Zanuck called Johnson into his office one day and handed him a short magazine clipping about Dr. Samuel Mudd, the doctor who had set John Wilkes Booth's broken leg after the assassination of Lincoln. Dr. Mudd had been convicted as part of the assassination conspiracy even though the evidence against him was extremely circumstantial. Zanuck asked Johnson, "Does this sound like a picture to you?"

Johnson said, "It might."

Zanuck said, "Why don't you look into it and see if we can get something?"[2] Johnson took the clipping and went to a book he had read several years before: Lloyd Lewis's *Myths After Lincoln*. The book contained a number of stories about Booth and some material about Dr. Mudd. Johnson became fascinated with the story and went deeper into Dr. Mudd's case. He got a copy of the court transcript of the conspiracy trial from Washington. Johnson came to the conclusion that Dr. Mudd was "a man who was accidentally dragged into this thing and the trial had brought in a kind of Scottish verdict, 'Not proven, but just for the hell of it, we'll give him six years for being around there.' "

Johnson's screenplay for *The Prisoner of Shark Island* contains one ingredient familiar from *The House of Rothschild* and another that is a definite improvement on the earlier script. Dr. Mudd and Nathan Rothschild are both married men, like nearly all the heroes of Johnson's scripts and unlike the heroes of many other commercial films. Peggy Mudd is similar in characterization to Hannah Rothschild. Both women stand by and support their husbands no matter what difficulties they get into. While Hannah's activities are on the order of seeing that Nathan has a flower in his lapel every day, Peggy takes a much more active role. She tries to get Dr. Mudd's conviction overturned, and it is she who comes up with the plan for his escape from prison. When asked why he was attracted to such a characterization of the wife, particularly in *The Prisoner of Shark Island,* Johnson modestly replied, "I don't think it's attraction. It was lack of imagination. Standard equipment is called for in that situation. I didn't have the inspiration to give her any other character. I don't know that any other character would be any better. After all, it was his story, and if he'd had a wife with any strength or particular individuality, the story might not have gone the same way." Johnson's reply is an indication of his lack of self-consciousness as a writer. He was creating this kind of character out of a conviction both of his own and of his audience. Later this characterization changes both for Johnson and his audience.

In this script Johnson has also begun to go beyond the stock villain characterization he gave Ledrantz in *The House of Rothschild. The Prisoner of Shark Island* shows the first example of what would be a distinct pattern in Johnson's future scripts, his ability to be scrupulously fair to people on all sides of a conflict. Early in the script, the assistant secretary of war is talking to members of the court who are going to try the conspiracy case. The assistant secretary's motivation is made clear when he says, at the beginning of the scene, that the country is in turmoil because of the assassination, and they have to be "hard" to save the country. A writer with less empathy for his characters would simply make the plot point that the assistant secretary was telling them to be hard, but Johnson has made the man's motivation clear. In a like manner, when Dr. Mudd is sent to prison, he is tormented by a guard whose actions are well motivated by several lines that show how upset he was at the death of Lincoln.

Zanuck assigned John Ford to direct *The Prisoner of Shark Island*. It was the first of three films Johnson and Ford did together. Johnson had met Ford a year or so before at a small gathering. Johnson recalled,

> I had done a script called *The Man Who Broke the Bank at Monte Carlo*. I had handed it in. I didn't know it had been offered to Ford. Somebody at this party began talking about "directorial touches," a favorite cliché of critics who hadn't the faintest idea of what they were talking about.
>
> John said he'd read a script he liked very much. "I'll tell you a thing in it that would be attributed to the director." Without looking at me and with a complete deadpan, he described a scene I had written, something with a wagon wheel passing over a flower. I recognized it and then he looked at me and grinned. "Don't you think that will be called a director's touch Mr. Johnson?"
>
> I said, "I don't know who it's going to be attributed to, but I wrote it."
>
> He said, "I know."
>
> So he was quite aware of that, at least in those days. I don't think John ever claimed anything that wasn't his, but John has been the beneficiary of more gifts by critics than any man I know.[3]

One of the gifts critics usually give to Ford is the opening of *The Prisoner of Shark Island*. The first scene shows Lincoln, after the end of the war, asking the band to play "Dixie." The sequence comes from the Lloyd Lewis book that Johnson used as the basis for the script, and Johnson took it over *in toto*. The reason most critics credit this sequence to Ford, however, is because of a similar sequence in a Ford picture made three years later, *Young Mr. Lincoln,* in which the young Lincoln is shown playing "Dixie" on a harmonica. When another character asks what tune he's playing, Lincoln says he doesn't know the name of it, but thinks it's rather catchy. This is not John Ford stealing from himself as much as it is one good screenwriter, Lamar Trotti, stealing from another, Nunnally Johnson.

This is not to say there are not true "directorial touches" in *The Prisoner of Shark Island*. After Lincoln is shot, a curtain is drawn between Lincoln and the camera, giving the scene the aura of a tintype which suggests the end of an era. The drawing of the curtain is not in the script, nor is another interesting visual touch. When the audience is first introduced to Dr. Mudd's father, he is seen giving a harsh speech condemning the North. In the script, it is immediately obvious he is talking to his granddaughter, but, in the film, the camera starts out on him and then pulls back to reveal the granddaughter, which suggests, in a humorous way, his senility by showing him making such a fiery speech to a child.

When Ford started filming *The Prisoner of Shark Island*, his first picture specifically for Zanuck, there were expectations on the lot that Zanuck and Ford would tangle, and they eventually did. Warner Baxter started to play the part of Dr. Mudd with a thick Southern accent, which grated on Johnson's Southern nerves. Johnson went to Ford and said, "Can't you tell Warner to speak normally? Southerners don't know they've got an accent to begin with until they hear somebody mocking it, and then they get their backs up."

Ford replied that he had spoken to him about it, but, as Johnson said, "Baxter had an ego about equal to Ford's and he kept on using the accent." Johnson saw Zanuck one day at the rushes and asked him what he thought of the accent. Zanuck said it was God-awful and asked if he had spoken to Ford about it. Johnson said he had, but that Baxter had kept using it. So they went down to the set. Johnson described it:

> Darryl called Ford over and we went down to the end of the stage. Darryl said "What about this accent that Baxter's using?"
> Ford said, "Well, what about it?"
> Darryl said, "Well, I think it's bad. I think it's giving a bad effect. Have you spoken to him about it?"
> John said, "Yes."
> Darryl said, "Well, can't you do anything with him about it?"
> Ford said, "Now if you're not satisfied with the way I . . ." I never saw anything like it. Zanuck said, "Are you threatening me? Are you threatening me you'll walk off this set? Don't ever threaten me. I throw fellas off this set. They don't quit on me." I never saw a thing like this. I was embarrassed. I thought Zanuck was going to punch him in the nose. Ford had him outweighed by forty or fifty pounds. I was glad to get away from there. I just didn't want to witness this sort of thing. Not that John didn't survive it. It happened a few months later I got on John's boat, and around the boat were Gene Markey and two or three other fellows. Markey said, "How'd you get along with Darryl?"
> Ford didn't realize that the only person who was a witness happened

to be sitting there. He said to Gene, "Oh, well, we had a little meeting. We had a little discussion. There's been no trouble since." Then he looked up and saw I was listening and said, "You were there, Nunnally."

I said, "I remember," but I didn't make a point of it.

Needless to say, Baxter did not use an accent in the picture.

In spite of the confrontation between Ford and Zanuck, *The Prisoner of Shark Island* turned out to be a very substantial picture. Ford's skill with actors is very evident, particularly in those sequences where Johnson had provided realistic motivation for the characters. On the other hand, because Ford was not as skilled in dealing with the relationships between men and women, the scenes with Dr. Mudd and his wife do not have the impact on the screen they do in the script. Fortunately, these scenes do not take up too much time in the film and are overshadowed by the drive Ford maintains in the rest of the picture.

There was a greater change than just getting his own typewriter in store for Johnson at Twentieth Century-Fox. At Twentieth Century, Zanuck had been in charge of a company making between ten and fifteen pictures a year. Since one of the purposes of the merger was to increase the use of the production facilities at the Westwood lot and thereby provide products for the Fox theatres, Zanuck found himself producing fifty-eight pictures in the first year after the merger. Zanuck would continue to retain control over all the pictures being made by the company, but he felt that he did not have the time to personally supervise each production. Therefore, Zanuck decided to expand the system of associate producers he had used at Twentieth Century. Previously Zanuck had been able to get along with only Raymond Griffith and William Goetz, but now he needed other qualified people. Johnson was one he asked to become an associate producer.

Zanuck did not ask Johnson to exercise the same kind of control over the productions that he himself held. He was looking not for a replacement for himself, but rather for a person to act as his representative on the productions and to bring back to him those questions or problems on which he had to make decisions. Zanuck felt Johnson could fill that role because he had come to trust Johnson's skill and judgment. While Zanuck still had to have lengthy story conferences with most of the other writers on the lot, he did not with Johnson. Zanuck and Johnson would discuss story ideas, decide on one that Johnson liked, and then Johnson would go off to write a first draft. Zanuck would then look at the first and subsequent drafts and make suggestions and changes, but he knew that Johnson was experienced enough by that time to turn in a first draft that could be developed into a final script. Johnson's scripts, unlike those of many other writers, did not have to be scrapped completely. Zanuck felt that Johnson's experience could be used in guiding other writers in the preparation of scripts.

Johnson accepted the new title of associate producer. As he later put it, "I suppose I took it because Zanuck asked me to and if he'd asked me to jump off the bridge I'd have done it. I had a great regard for him." He also expected that he would have a little more control over the pictures, "and of course, being a producer sounded as if I had more control. I didn't really have a great deal more control, because Darryl at that time was in charge of everything. He even had to okay the hairdresser going to work on the leading lady."

One of the first films that Johnson supervised was a little picture very quickly put together called *The Country Doctor*. It was nominally the story of Dr. Defoe, the doctor for the Dionne Quintuplets, and it was rushed into production to take advantage of the publicity surrounding the birth of the quintuplets. The story was taken from a series of newspaper articles by Charles Blake, and was developed into a screenplay by Johnson, Sonya Levien, and the director, Henry King. King and Sonya Levien talked over the plot lines in Johnson's office until one day King said, "I think Sonya and I ought to just go away and write up what we have." Johnson agreed heartily. As King says he realized later, "He just wanted us to get out of his office and stop bothering him."[4] Johnson was discovering there were drawbacks to being a producer.

Henry King had been assigned to *The Country Doctor* by Zanuck as something of a test.[5] King had been a very successful director, particularly with such silent classics as *Tol'able David, Stella Dallas*, and *The Winning of Barbara Worth*. In 1930, he had joined the Fox Corporation and directed several outstanding sound films for the studio, such as the 1933 version of *State Fair* with Will Rogers. When the merger between Fox and Twentieth Century took place, several people told Zanuck that King was too slow a director and ought to be fired. Zanuck assigned King to do *The Country Doctor*, which, because of the enormous publicity about the quintuplets, had to be brought in quickly. King finished the picture several days early, thus helping to insure his twenty-plus years as Zanuck's number one director—including several Nunnally Johnson screenplays.

Both Zanuck and Johnson continued to look for stories, books, plays, and even vague ideas that could be used as the basis for a picture. Two vague ideas turned out fairly well. One day, Johnson got it into his head that he would like to see Shirley Temple, whom the new company had inherited from the Fox Corporation, play the part of Little Eva in *Uncle Tom's Cabin*. Johnson and the two screenwriters on the project, Arthur Sheekman and Nat Perrin, did not want to do yet another remake of the Harriet Beecher Stowe book, so they came up with a story about a little street performer, played by Shirley, who is taken away from her "perfesser," a scrubbed-up Fagin played by Frank Morgan. She is adopted by a well-to-do lady, but eventually runs away and rejoins the "perfesser" and his acting company, thus getting to finish off the picture by playing Little Eva in a melodramatic stage production of *Uncle Tom's Cabin*. Johnson and the writers called this script *The Bowery Princess*, but, as soon as it was announced for production under that title, the studio was flooded with letters complaining that sweet little Shirley Temple should not be connected with anything that even suggested the sordidness of the Bowery. The name of the picture was changed to *Dimples*.

Another vague idea that turned out well was one to do with a musical set in New York in the twenties. Johnson wanted to hear some of the songs from the period, so he took over the project and wrote it. Since one of his assignments as a reporter had been covering Nicky Arnstein's arrest, he based the script on the marriage of Arnstein and Fanny Brice. To fatten out the plot, Johnson wrote in a part for Al Jolson, who sang whatever songs Alice Faye in the Fanny Brice part did not get to sing. Because the film was very obviously based on real people, the main titles for the film, instead of having the standard disclaimer about the characters being fictitious in very small print, had it in big letters on a title card all by itself. This precaution did not prevent most of the principals involved from threatening to sue.[6] Their prices for not taking legal action were very reasonable, and *Rose of Washington Square* became one of the most successful musicals Fox produced.

Johnson occasionally turned down material sent to him by Zanuck. One day, Johnson got the synopsis of a new novel. Since it was about his home state of Georgia during the Civil War, he opened the synopsis with interest. He was immediately put off by the name of the heroine, Scarlett O'Hara, and was completely discouraged by the name of the hero, Rhett Butler. He closed the synopsis, sent it back, and told Zanuck he did not think any story with character names like that could be taken seriously.[7]

Johnson also refused to write *The Story of Alexander Graham Bell*. He hated the telephone and would have no part in its glorification. He told interviewer Eileen Creelman how he got out of the job, "I suggested to Darryl that after the usual funeral oration—we always have a funeral oration, you know, in a screen biography—that we have a short epilogue with Edgar Kennedy. This would show the telephone today, with Kennedy asleep in bed. The telephone rings. Kennedy awakes, startled, answers the telephone, and says, 'Wrong number.' The picture would close with Kennedy doing one of those slow burns."[8]

Zanuck turned down a book Johnson brought to him, *Paths of Glory*, a bitter anti-war novel by Humphrey Cobb. Johnson wanted to do it as a film, but Zanuck explained that, since the story showed the French generals in a bad light, the picture would have been banned in Europe (as indeed it was until 1975, after it had been made in 1957 by Stanley Kubrick). Not only would that one picture have been banned, Zanuck explained, but so would all the pictures produced by Fox and possibly the other film companies as well. As a sort of a consolation prize, Zanuck assigned Johnson to produce another World War I picture which was finally called *The Road to Glory*. (The title was probably to convince people they were going to see something as hard-hitting as *Paths of Glory* without the company actually delivering it.) The idea behind making the picture was to remake a French picture, *Croix de Bois*, which Fox had bought several years before. The Fox company had already used some of the battle scenes two years before in *The World Moves On*, and now the new company was going to use the story as well as the battle scenes. Howard Hawks was to direct the picture, and one of the writers Hawks wanted on the picture was William Faulkner.

Faulkner used to come out to Hollywood from time to time to make a little money writing screenplays. When he arrived at Fox on this trip, he came to see Johnson. As soon as he was shown into Johnson's office and was seated, Faulkner produced an unopened bottle of whiskey and offered Johnson a drink. Johnson had his secretary bring in two glasses. Faulkner started to open the bottle and cut his thumb severely. Johnson offered to call the studio infirmary, but Faulkner declined. Faulkner simply moved Johnson's wastebasket next to his chair and let the blood drip into it as he drank and talked to Johnson.[9] Johnson's story conferences were not as high-pressure as Zanuck's.

Johnson asked Zanuck if it would be all right to put another screenwriter on with Faulkner. Zanuck agreed, and they put Joel Sayre on the picture. Sayre was a newspaperman and a friend of both Johnson and Faulkner. Johnson recalled what happened, "This resulted in two being drunk instead of just one. Bill was a real classy bottle man, and Joel was not far behind him. I don't suppose there were forty lines that Bill wrote that we could use, and I don't think he cared much. Sayre wrote a good deal of it, and I think I rewrote most of it, mainly because they were writing interminable scenes and it had to be edited."

After the picture came out, a young man from Tennessee sued Twentieth Century-Fox for plagiarism. The man had been in the Army and was therefore a hero, particularly to his lawyer. The lawyer indicated that the case was one of a big ruthless company trying to cheat a war hero. Johnson remembered the situation:

> On the face of it you would have said the script being written by William Faulkner, Joel Sayre, and myself, another old-timer,

wouldn't have to fall back on something from a boy from Tennessee, but for some reason Fox decided to fight it. Or else they wouldn't settle. It became clear what had happened. In those days, companies would give out copies of the script to some fan magazines, which would dramatize the story. The boy had gotten a copy of this and copied out some of the dialogue, and sent it to Fox, and they sent it back, because they didn't open unsolicited stuff. He claimed that they had opened it, and pinched his dialogue. For one thing, he had about six lines of dialogue from the script in succession, word for word. Now that's not chance. Two lines, yes, three lines, maybe, but you can't go six. Chance doesn't go that far. Anyway, he fought this thing. They came out here and took depositions. I was on the chair for a day and a half. Zanuck had to leave the studio and come over to fight this thing. By then we'd all scattered and so the lawyer and the young soldier went down to Oxford, Mississippi, where they had to wait three days, until Bill sobered up, to get his deposition. Then they went to Philadelphia, where Joel was on a newspaper, and I had no doubt that they had to wait a day or two for Joel. The outcome of the thing was something perfectly extraordinary: when the thing was all laid out in front of the judge, the judge not only threw the case out, but he recommended to the Bar Association that they disbar this lawyer. The judge thought that the lawyer had really nudged the boy into it with the idea that they could collect a lot of dough. That was *The Road to Glory*.[10]

Johnson was listed in the credits as the associate producer of a number of other films he did not write, but he never saw most of them. He finally came to regard his work as a producer of other writers' scripts as a complete fiasco. He felt he was totally unable to tell people how to write. He got so discouraged, he went into see Zanuck and told him, "I'd better quit."

Zanuck asked, "What's the matter?"

"I can't produce. I've got a script on my desk right now and I physically cannot open that thing. I know the script's not good. I don't know what to do about it, because I cannot tell this fellow exactly what to do. It's not fair to the other writer. And I can't do them all by myself. I can't do all that work."

Zanuck said, "Why don't you be like Ray Griffith?"

"What do you mean?"

"Ray doesn't know a God damned thing about what a script's doing. He just looks at it and says in that growly voice of his, 'Not right. Not right.' The writer doesn't know. Ray says, 'Try again.' And the writer goes on trying. Ray certainly is not going to worry himself to death about this thing. I know I worry like hell. You really want to quit?"

Johnson said, "I do."

"Why don't you take a vacation?"

Johnson agreed to do that. He had been spending so much time and energy trying to produce other writers' scripts that his own writing had suffered. His scripts had become tight and mechanical. He needed time away from the studio to sort himself out. Zanuck could be a producer for other writers, but Johnson could not.

He had put so much compulsive energy into his writing and his attempts at being a producer that his marriage to Marion had finally broken under the strain. The divorce was final, and Marion had left to go back to New York. Because Marion had been much better suited to him than had Alice, and because the marriage had lasted as long as it did, Johnson was particularly despondent over the divorce. He decided to go down to Miami Beach for a few weeks.

He had been in Miami about a month when Zanuck called and said, "Look, would it be all right if you just produce the pictures you write yourself?"

Johnson asked, "Would that just consist of picking the story, casting, going through the routine of production?"

"Yes."

Johnson said, "I daresay I could do that." So he came back.

Young Nunnally playing cowboy; obviously a forerunner of *Jesse James*.

Mr. and Mrs. James N. Johnson and their two sons; Patrick is on the left, Nunnally on the right.

Nunnally selling *The Saturday Evening Post* in Columbus Georgia a few years before he started writing for it. He is second from the right on the bottom row.

Nunnally Johnson waiting to become a Lieutenant.

Johnson at the time of his arrival in Hollywood.

Nunnally and Marion Johnson.

Johnson, John Steinbeck, and Irving Pichel, the director of *The Moon is Down*.

Dorris Bowdon at the time she was a contract player at 20th Century-Fox.

In his office at 20th Century-Fox. The desk was really that well organized.

Johnson's office at home. Behind the curtains is a breathtaking view, but when he was writing he kept the curtains closed so as not to be distracted. (Photo: George R. Szanik)

The man on the left is Herman J. Mankiewicz, the founder of the Mankiewicz Fresh Air Fund for Reporters, which brought Johnson out to Hollywood. The other two people are Margaret Sullavan and David O. Selznick.

6

Jesse James

Nunnally Johnson came back to write one of the most relentlessly entertaining movies ever made. It is also typical of a major studio production of the thirties and forties, both in how it was made and in how it related to its audience.

Johnson had been trying for years to get Zanuck to make a picture about Jesse James.[1] When Johnson first proposed the idea, Zanuck suggested it to the New York executives of the company. He reported their reaction to Johnson: the picture would only make money in "Missouri, Kansas, and parts of southern Illinois." Still, Johnson was enthusiastic, and Zanuck let him have other writers to work on treatments of the subject. In March 1936, Sheilah Graham announced in her column that Johnson was beginning research on Jesse James. That column produced stacks of letters from people in the Missouri and Kansas area who knew Jesse James, or had relatives who knew Jesse James, or had relatives who were robbed by Jesse James, or had guns from the period, or had written a song about Missouri. Somebody out there was interested. Most of this unsolicited information was ignored, except for the news that a newspaper writer named Rosalind Shaeffer was writing a biography of Jesse James with the assistance of Jesse's granddaughter, Jo Frances James. Shaeffer and James were paid for their research, and although little of it was used in the final film, both women received screen credit for "historical data."

When he was still a boy in Georgia, Johnson had first become interested in Jesse James. Young Nunnally and his friends repeatedly saw the Jewel Kelly Stock Company perform an old melodrama called *The James Boys in Missouri,* with the middle-aged, pot-bellied Jewel Kelly as Jesse. Johnson particularly remembered the impact of the final scene of the play. Jesse is taking down a sampler from the wall, and the little boys in the audience, who knew the play by heart, were so involved in the situation that they were screaming for Jesse to watch out for "that dirty little coward," Bob Ford, who shot Jesse in the back. As Johnson remembered it years later, Jesse/Jewel "turned around, looked for a soft place to fall, and hit the ground."

The first treatment was written in March 1936 by Johnson and a junior writer named Curtis Kenyon. They took over the ending of the play, but the story line was rambling and episodic, and the idea languished on the shelf for over a year. In March 1937, still under Johnson's supervision, Johnson's friend Gene Fowler and another junior writer, Hal Long, wrote another treatment which began to deal with a problem the Kenyon treatment had not entirely solved. The real Jesse James rode with the notorious Quantrill's Raiders in the Civil War while he was still in his teens, and he had simply never stopped being an outlaw. To help make the James boys sympathetic, Kenyon had introduced a newspaper editor, Major John Edwards, who wrote editorials defending the James boys. Edwards had existed in real life and had written an editorial for the Sedalia *Democrat* in 1881 condemning in colorful language what he considered the murder of Jesse James. The Edwards character did not completely succeed in making the James boys sympathetic, so the emphasis was now put on how the arrival of the railroad cheated many families out of their land. The James boys' train-robbing then becomes simple revenge.

In April, Fowler and Long did another treatment. Jesse had been, in earlier treatments, in love with Zerelda, the daughter of Major Edwards, and she, in turn, was in love with Will Wallace, the local politician. In the April treatment, Will (whose last name was now Wright) puts Zerelda, or Zee, in jail in an attempt to capture Jesse. Members of Jesse's gang dress up as women in a funeral procession and rescue Zee from jail. Most of the plot points were carried over into treatments done in May by Fowler and Long. Zanuck, however, found the story line unclear and without the human values that would make it more than just an ordinary western. Zanuck made several suggestions, among them that, instead of Zee being put in jail, Jesse should give himself up and then discover that, because of the railroad's political power, he will be unable to get a fair trial. Zanuck also suggested a funeral oration to be given by Major Edwards similar to the editorial the real Major Edwards had written.

Johnson took over the writing of the project himself and, by the end of June 1937, he had written the first twenty-nine pages of a treatment. Johnson's treatment took many of the incidents of the earlier treatments, but put them into a straighter narrative line. Johnson did not complete the treatment at that time, and the project lapsed while he went to Miami for his vacation.

When Johnson returned from Florida, he suggested to Zanuck they reactivate the project. According to Zanuck's contract, he had complete authority over what pictures were to be made, but in practice there were frequent maneuverings between Zanuck and New York. Zanuck was by now tired of the project and repeated what the executives in New York had told him about how badly they thought the picture would do. Johnson, rested after his vacation and anxious to get back on the project said, "Why the hell do you have to listen to those guys? They ain't got no crystal ball." The appeal to Zanuck's contractual authority worked, and Johnson finished the treatment he had started the year before.

Johnson's 28 March 1938 treatment finally solved the middle section of the story. Johnson borrowed from another play, a French swashbuckler called *The Purple Mask* that he had probably seen in New York in the twenties, when Leo Dietrichstein had played in it. In the play, the hero, Rene, who has taken over after the Purple Mask has supposedly been killed, announces that, to prove that he is still alive, he will kidnap the prefect of police at midnight. The prefect laughs it off at first, then doubles the guard, and is, of course, kidnapped. Johnson changed this slightly. Jesse has surrendered with Will Wright's assurance of a fair trial. When Jesse discovers the railroad is going to have him hung, Frank James sends word that, if Jesse is not out by midnight, he will come in to get him. McCoy, the president of the railroad, tries to laugh this off, but he finally selects a posse to hunt down Frank, inadvertently picking two of Jesse's gang for the posse. They bring Frank in, and they all take Jesse out. Johnson says, "You just can't give up that stuff. You've got to do a little pinching now and then." Johnson did add an original touch at the end, although it was one that Zanuck only reluctantly let remain in the script. After Frank and Jesse escape, McCoy sends a group of soldiers after them. As the soldiers gain on Frank and Jesse, the outlaws take money out of their saddlebags and throw it at their pursuers, who stop to pick it up, allowing Jesse and Frank to escape.[2]

Zanuck told Johnson to do a script from the treatment, and, in a little over six weeks, Johnson completed the 182-page first draft, the longest script he had done up to that time. Unlike Johnson's work just before his vacation, there is nothing mechanical about *Jesse James*. Johnson has added enormously to the smooth flowing story line of the treatment in his energetic handling of the characters and the individual scenes. Jesse is a good boy gone bad and obviously enjoying it very much. Frank is dry in his humor and steady in his loyalties. Jesse's wife, Zee, is a typical Johnson heroine, loving and devoted, but she also serves as the voice of conscience for Jesse. One of Johnson's most interesting embellishments is the newspaper editor, whose name was changed from John Edwards to Rufus Cobb. Johnson has the character continually writing editorials in which only the subject is changed, from railroad presidents to dentists to lawyers, as the sentiment remains: "If we are ever to have law and order in the West, the first thing we must do is take out all the (railroad presidents, etc.) and shoot them down like dogs."

Johnson also provided strong bits for minor characters. In the jail-break sequence, a continual reminder that Frank is "set in his ways" is provided by a country bumpkin guard. Again, in a meeting in Jesse's hideout just before the gang's final bank robbery, one of the gang accuses Jesse of having become mean-tempered. Johnson, in the writing of the scene, makes it clear that the man is not a coward and still likes Jesse; he is worried about him as a friend. The dignity of the man is upheld in a quick, precise, and sympathetic characterization.

The script is full of exciting action. The first train robbery is an almost perfectly constructed sequence, moving swiftly from the civilized cele-bration of the first train leaving the town through the robbery itself to the train coming into a chaotic station the next morning. The jailbreak sequence provides the action in the middle of the film, and the climactic sequence is the Northfield Minnesota raid.

Johnson's script is a glamorization of Jesse James, but it comes out of Johnson's own feeling for the material, rather than any cynical attempt to manipulate the audience, which is not to say that Johnson did not want to entertain the audience the same way he had been entertained as a child. Johnson's feelings about Jesse coincided with the feelings of the audi-ences of the time. They had seen and accepted the glamorization of outlaws and gangsters, not only in films, but in real life. The thirties' equivalents of Jesse James were just as much folk heroes in their time as Jesse had been for an earlier generation. Johnson's sense of the appeal of the outlaws is what underlies his vision of Jesse, and he understood that appeal because that was what had drawn him to the stage melodrama. Johnson puts that appeal into words in Major Cobb's eulogy for Jesse that ends the picture. The eulogy is similar in tone, but not in specific language, to John Edwards' editorial "The Killing of Jesse James." Major Cobb says:

There ain't no question about it. Jesse was an outlaw, a bandit, a criminal. Even those that loved him ain't got no answer for that. But we ain't ashamed of him. I don't know why, but I don't think even America is ashamed of Jesse James. Maybe it was because he was bold and lawless like we all of us like to be sometimes. Maybe it's because we understand a little that he wasn't altogether to blame for what his times made him. Maybe it's because for ten years he licked the tar out of five states. Or maybe it's because he was so good at what he was doing. I don't know. All I do know is that he was one of the dog-gonedest, gol-dangedest, dad-blamedest buckaroos that ever rode across these United States of America.

Johnson showed the script to Henry King and suggested he might like to direct it. Johnson went to King not only because he was a successful director, but because Johnson instinctively understood that King was right for the material. King was particularly skilled in showing exact physical details of small-town American life, and he managed to get sensitive preformances from the actors.

King read the script and immediately told Zanuck he wanted to direct it. Zanuck said, "Why do you want to do this? You've been making pictures that make money all over the world," and he repeated what "New York" had said about the picture only making money in Kansas, Missouri, and parts of southern Illinois. King insisted, and Zanuck finally agreed to let him direct it.

Zanuck now realized that two of his top craftsmen were firmly committed. He put it on the schedule as one of his personal productions and let them have the top male star at Fox, Tyrone Power, to play Jesse. The rest of the cast was filled with such reliable character actors as Henry Hull, John Carradine, Brian Donlevy, Donald Meek, and Slim Summerville. The one part that seemed to defy casting was Frank James. Johnson had earlier suggested only half-facetiously to Henry King that he, Johnson, play the part. King began to feel that the only actor he could see in the part was Henry Fonda, but he was afraid to mention Fonda's name to Zanuck. When Zanuck and Twentieth Century had come to Fox there were two pictures with Fonda completed by Fox. Zanuck, in looking at the pictures at the time, had decided that Fonda would never be a star and indicated that he never wanted him to be used in a Twentieth Century-Fox picture again. King finally said to Zanuck and Johnson, "There is only one actor I can see playing Frank James. There is only one actor I can see getting his mouth around those words." Johnson sat up expectant.

Zanuck asked, "Who's that?"

King hesitated. "Henry Fonda." Johnson slouched back down.

Zanuck was silent. He turned to Lew Schreiber, his assistant, and said, "See if Fonda is available." He was, and he got the part.

Johnson became associate producer on the picture, Zanuck left on safari in Africa, and King took off in his private plane to search for locations for the picture. He found the small town of Pineville, Missouri, took pictures of it, and returned to the studio. Before Zanuck had left, he had tentatively ordered that *Jesse James* should be made in Northern California, since he did not approve of long location trips, which tended to result in productions going over their budgets. When King got back from Missouri, he showed his pictures to William Darling, the art director for the picture, and William Goetz, who was running the studio in Zanuck's absence. They all agreed that it would be cheaper to use the perfect locations King had found, which included many buildings from the period which were still standing and could be used in the picture. Goetz decided to let the film be made in Missouri. When Zanuck returned from safari, he was furious that his instructions had been disobeyed, but he realized that, by then, it would cost even more to change the plans that had been made. He let the filming proceed in Missouri.

Shooting began in Missouri in August 1938, but was hampered by large numbers of visitors who came to view a movie being made about their local hero. As the shooting progressed, it became apparent that the location trip was going to cost more than had been budgeted for, and there were people back at the studio who urged Zanuck to stop the production completely. Zanuck refused, but sent a second unit under the direction of Otto Brower out to Missouri to do several of the action sequences that remained to be filmed.

King and the first unit returned to California to film the interiors and the climactic Northfield robbery, which was to be done on a standing outdoor set. King was shooting interiors one day when he suddenly began to feel dizzy. A doctor was called in and discovered that a seemingly minor fall King had taken off a camera truck in Missouri had, in fact, given him a concussion, which would put him out of action for the remaining shooting days. Zanuck and Johnson got Irving Cummings, who had directed several Shirley Temple pictures and later *The Story of Alexander Graham Bell*, to finish the picture.

The picture was cut together in late 1938. When Zanuck saw it, he was still worried. Now his concern was for Tyrone Power. He was afraid it would end his career to have him killed off in the picture, even with Major Cobb's eulogy. Zanuck did not feel the eulogy was enough to offset Power's death. He had Johnson write another scene, which King shot, in which Zee, Will Wright, and Jesse's son are together and Zee says, "He was our best friend . . . when you love somebody, they never die." This ending was tried but fell flat. Zanuck considered other possibilities, but the final ending was Jesse's death and the eulogy.

Jesse James opened in January, 1939, to almost unanimous rave reviews. The *New York Times* said it was "the best screen entertainment of the year"—at least as of 13 January. A number of women's clubs complained that the picture glamorized Jesse too much.[3] The picture was one of the most successful Twentieth Century-Fox had made until that time and for many years thereafter. The picture did nothing to hurt Tyrone Power's career, and, in spite of the original objection of the New York office, it made as much money in Europe as it did in the United States.

There are a number of reasons for the picture's success. The script is almost perfectly constructed in dramatic terms. Henry King has called it "the most perfect script I ever directed." Also noteworthy are King's pacing and his use of the visual richness of the Missouri countryside. While Tyrone Power is nominally the star of *Jesse James*, it is Fonda who walks off with the picture. This is partly because of Johnson's lines and the tough, laconic character Johnson gave to Frank James, but a great deal of the impact of the character comes from the way Fonda "gets his mouth around the words." This picture convinced Zanuck that Fonda could be a star in films, as he became in such later Fox films as *Young Mr. Lincoln* and the sequel to *Jesse James*, *The Return of Frank James*.

It was Henry King's habit to fly around the country as each picture was being released and talk to the heads of the local distribution offices of Twentieth Century-Fox about the picture. While King was going around for the picture he did after *Jesse James*, he flew into New Orleans. One of the first things the exchange manager asked King was, "When are we going to see *The Return of Frank James?*" King told him there was no sequel planned, and the manager said, "There has to be. The people here are screaming for Frank James to come back and kill Bob Ford for what he did to Jesse." The manager told King that people had come into the theatres to see *Jesse James* who had never seen a movie before and did not even know the theatre seats folded down; they sat on the floor through several showings. King dutifully took all this information back to Zanuck. Zanuck laughed and threatened to throw him out of his office for suggesting a sequel. King was not too surprised a few months later to open up a trade paper and read an announcement by Zanuck of the forthcoming production of *The Return of Frank James*.

Johnson was approached by Zanuck to write *The Return of Frank James*, but he refused, as he did several other times in his career when asked to do sequels for pictures he had written. Johnson said, "I knew if a picture was successful enough to warrant making a sequel, the sequel was not going to be better than the first one. I wouldn't do it with Frank James, though there was enough material for it." The writer assigned to *The Return of Frank James* was Sam Hellman. Although Hellman borrowed the Johnson-created characters of Frank James and Major Cobb, he turned in a straight revenge tale in which Frank James hunts down Bob Ford and his sidekicks. Johnson was surprised that it was given to German director Fritz Lang to direct and imagined that he directed it "wearing a western hat and a monocle." Although *The Return of Frank James* is inferior to *Jesse James*, it has received greater critical study, primarily because of Lang's reputation.

On the "B" picture level, *Jesse James* spawned a number of cheap westerns such as *Jesse James Rides Again* (a 1947 Republic serial), *I Shot Jesse James* (1948), *The Return of Jesse James* (1950) which used Johnson's story structure and the presence of Henry Hull as Frank Younger, *Jesse James Versus the Daltons* (1954), and even *Jesse James Meets Frankenstein's Daughter* (1966). On the "A" picture level, *Jesse James* was remade in 1957 by Twentieth Century-Fox as *The True Story of Jesse James*. According to the credits, the 1957 version was "based on" the script by Johnson, but there is very little evidence of it in the film. Not only has the entire story construction of *Jesse James* been dismantled, but all the richness of texture in both the dialogue and characterization has been eliminated. *The True Story of Jesse James*, which is even less the true story than was Johnson's picture, is a pale and unsuccessful copy of the original, although it has been examined in detail because of the reputation of its director, Nicholas Ray. A number of the things that critics admire as Ray's touches are merely watered-down elements of Johnson's original script.

Jesse James is large-scale, popular, glamorous entertainment. Its entertainment value comes not from the dominant vision of one man, but from the variety of elements within the picture. Johnson provided the initial drive to get the project off the ground, as well as the framework and dialogue of the completed script, and, for this reason, *Jesse James* can be considered more "his" than King's or Zanuck's, but it is also true that the picture "belongs" to all of them. Each of these men, as well as the actors, contributed to the film, and each of those contributions provides an element in the texture of the film as a whole. An audience can enjoy Johnson's dialogue, or Fonda's delivery, or King's staging within the scenery, or all of those things. The multiplicity of talents involved may, if those talents are working together as they are in *Jesse James*, provide an aesthetic experience different from that provided by a work of art created by one artist. This kind of collaboration could also create a deeper kind of experience, as in *The Grapes of Wrath*.

7

The Grapes of Wrath

According to his own account, Darryl Zanuck was in New York one day in 1939 and he ran into Winthrop Aldrich. Aldrich was then chairman of the board of the Chase National Bank, which, since 1931, had been one of the controlling financial interests of Fox. Zanuck had already purchased the film rights of *The Grapes of Wrath*, and he had been told by many people that, in view of the novel's none-too-generous comments on banks, he would not be able to get money from the Chase Bank to make the picture. Zanuck rather cautiously mentioned to Aldrich that he had bought the book. Aldrich said his wife had read the book and had insisted he read it. Aldrich had read it and loved it. Zanuck got the money to make the picture.[1]

When Zanuck had been at Warner Brothers he had developed a policy of making what he called "pictures torn from today's headlines." After the formation of Twentieth Century Pictures, Zanuck had generally avoided that kind of picture as he did in the four years he had been at Twentieth Century-Fox. There were probably two reasons. First, he was in charge of building up a studio that had been close to bankruptcy, and he had to make pictures that would be fairly certain financial successes. By 1939, the studio was in a good financial position, and he may have felt that he could return to the type of pictures he had done before. Secondly, and probably just as important to Zanuck as the first reason, he had not found any story material of that type which he wanted to do. Zanuck's primary artistic concern was not with political and social comment in his films. He was interested in good stories, and he saw in *The Grapes of Wrath* a story to which he felt he wanted to devote the energies and resources of the studio, and he wanted it told dramatically on the screen. He picked Nunnally Johnson to write the screenplay.[2]

Johnson, like Zanuck, was a storyteller rather than a pamphleteer. Politically, Johnson was a Southern Democrat, liberalized to a degree by his years as a newspaperman in New York City. He thought of politics and politicians, if he thought of them at all, only as possible material for a story to tell, either comically, as in his 1947 movie *The Senator Was Indiscreet*, or seriously as in *The Grapes of Wrath*. He had no interest in political action, since his way of approaching the world was through the telling of stories. While he was sympathetic to the ideas in *The Grapes of Wrath*, he was more sympathetic to the people. It is possible to look with irony on a screenwriter earning over $100,000 a year writing a script for a film, to be financed by a large bank, about poor people, but Johnson did not see it that way. Part of his stock in trade as a writer was his empathy with the characters he was writing about, and that was the focus of his concern in writing the screenplay for *The Grapes of Wrath*.

This is not to say that he was unaware of the social and political aspects of the material. While he found the book relatively easy to adapt, the problem he faced in doing the script was his awareness of the importance of the material he was dealing with, both in terms of its literary richness and its political overtones. The book was much longer and more complex than anything Johnson had ever adapted before. It was a five-hundred-page epic that carried the Joad family from their Oklahoma farm across the Southwest into California and through experiences at various ranches, government camps, and Hoovervilles. In addition to a large number of incidents, John Steinbeck used a variety of stylistic devices in telling his story. Under the narrative line of the book, there is a subtext of biological imagery by which Steinbeck establishes his characters as part of the natural order of things. Steinbeck also included a series of interchapters in which he deals, sometimes in very abstract terms, with the larger political and social questions. By use of these interchapters, Steinbeck was able to place the story of the Joads against a broader background of the times.

To begin his work, Johnson read the book through several times. Finally, the outline became clear to him. To Johnson, the basic story was about "what an act of nature did to a great segment of helpless people and how they reacted. They all became involved in this act of nature that threw them out of their homes and filled them full of hope and drove them west to the land of Canaan." Johnson began to see the outline of the screenplay. Zanuck apparently gave Johnson very few specific instructions. They discussed what Johnson was doing, but Johnson did no treatment. Zanuck did want the film to start off the same way as the book, with Tom Joad walking down the road. Johnson wrote in 1939, "Beyond that, his instructions were simply that I get as much of the book as I could into the screenplay." During the two months that it took Johnson to do the first draft, Zanuck called him from time to time to check if certain scenes that stuck in Zanuck's mind were in the script.

Zanuck's comments on Johnson's first draft of the script were likewise limited. In his 19 July story conference notes, Zanuck says the script is excellent but "there are several places where we can heighten the drama and suspense." The most detailed suggestion Zanuck made concerned the arrival of the Joads at the Hooverville. In the first draft, Johnson simply cut from the family looking out at the lush Tehachapi Valley to the Joads at the camp. Zanuck wrote in the margin of the script, "The first visualization the people told the truth—no milk and honey. Very emotional—realization—all this and for what?" According to the conference notes, Zanuck suggested a scene in town before going out to the camp and then the arrival at the camp. Johnson wrote both scenes, and John Ford, the director assigned to the picture, had the inspiration of shooting the arrival from the Joads' point of view. The camera moves into the camp, allowing the audience to experience it as the family does. The effect of this traveling shot, after the relatively static camera set-ups in the rest of the film, is still one of the most stunning moments in the film and an example of the results of the collaboration of Johnson, Zanuck, and Ford.

One of Johnson's first concerns when he was assigned to do the adaptation was that he would not do anything that would upset Steinbeck. Johnson went to Pare Lorentz, the famous documentary film maker, who, he knew, was a friend of Steinbeck's. Johnson told him he had a few things that he was concerned about. He said, "I don't like to consult Steinbeck, because for one thing, he'll say, 'Look, that's your job,' but on the other hand, I'd hate to do something which would seem to him to violate what he was trying to say in his story."

Lorentz did not share Johnson's doubts. He told Johnson, "If it doesn't violate the book, do whatever you want to do that you think's best. I'll promise you that John won't object, because he knows enough to know that this is another medium." Johnson was considerably relieved, and he did talk to Steinbeck about the project, which was the beginning of a lifetime friendship between the two men. A few years after *The Grapes of Wrath* was released, Johnson was beginning to adapt another Steinbeck novel, *The Moon Is Down*, and he met with Steinbeck. Johnson asked him if he had any suggestions for him. Steinbeck said, "Yeah. Tamper with it."

After Johnson talked to Steinbeck, he did not hesitate to "switch things around, but I had to preserve the things I thought were pertinent and important. I did what I thought was most effective for the medium." He dropped the biological imagery completely, but he kept parts of the interchapters. Johnson took material from them and integrated it into the narrative line of the script. In one of the interchapters, chapter five, there is an essay on how the tractors came to drive the farmers off the land which Johnson transposed in the film into part of the flashback in which Muley tells about losing his land. Muley's explanation is thus elaborated on and dramatized as it is not done in the book. In another interchapter, chapter fifteen, an unnamed family stops at a roadside diner to try to buy a loaf of bread. The waitress does not want to sell the bread, but is told to do so by the cook. The children of the family ask the price of the candy on display and the waitress, seeing how much they want it, tells them it is two-for-a-penny. The children buy the candy and after the family leaves a truck driver who has been eating in the diner says to the waitress, "Those weren't two-for-a-penny—them's a nickel a piece." In the screenplay Johnson transformed the family into the Joads. Johnson's feeling on using parts of the interchapters in his script was, "The book's all mine to choose from now. I can use any part of it I want."

Johnson and Zanuck did make a major change in the overall structure. In the novel, the episode in which the Joad family takes refuge in a clean, well-run government camp is followed by episodes in which they work as strike-breakers at the Hooper Ranch and are forced out of a boxcar camp by a flood. In the screenplay, the flood sequence is dropped altogether, and the government camp episode is put at the end, after the episode at Hooper Ranch (renamed Keen Ranch in the film). The result, as George Bluestone points out in his book, *Novels Into Film,* is to change the shape of the material from a parabola to an ascending straight line. A number of critics of the film, e.g. Arthur Knight in his *The Liveliest Art,* have objected to this change on the grounds that it gives the film an optimistic ending to what is a rather depressing story. The change was made not solely to provide a "happy ending," but because it seemed to Johnson "dramatically right." He felt that adding more depressing detail after the government camp episode would cause the audience to say, "The hell with this. This is just needlessly harrowing," and give up on the picture. Johnson wanted to hold the audience to the end.

Johnson felt, however, that he could not leave the Joads at the government camp at the very end of the film. They would have to be moving on, because, just as it would not have been "dramatically right" to leave the audience on a completely depressing note, it would also have been wrong to leave them on a completely positive note. Johnson had to come up with a closing scene that would capture the spirit of the picture. During his readings of the novel, Johnson had been struck by a line that Ma Joad spoke in chapter twenty, a little more than half-way through the book: "We're the people—we go on." Johnson said, "I knew I was going to use that at the end because that's all you could do. Once you found that line, you said, 'Nothing can top this. Nothing is more beautifully

understated than that kind of noble fact.' " When Johnson met with
Steinbeck in New York before writing the script, he raised the possibility
of using those lines as the ending. Steinbeck approved and said he had
considered ending the book on those lines.[3] Johnson did more than just
use those lines. He built up an entire scene to go with them, using both
material from the book and material he wrote himself to make it work
dramatically.

An examination in detail of how that scene is constructed gives some
idea of Johnson's skill. The scene is set in the front seat of the truck just
after the Joads have left the government camp. Pa Joad and Al, a
younger son, are excited about the work they think they're going to get.
Ma reminds them that there might not be any work: "We ain't got it till
we get it." Al grins and asks Ma, "What's the matter, Ma? Gettin'
scared?" Ma replies, in a speech that is not in the book,

> No. Ain't never gonna be scared no more. I was, though. For a
> while I thought we was beat—GOOD an' beat. Looked like we didn't
> have nothin' in the world but enemies—wasn't nobody frien'ly any-
> more. It made me feel bad an' scared too—like we was lost . . . an'
> nobody cared.

Al, still in high spirits, says, "Watch me pass this Chevy," and then Pa
says, "You the one that keeps us goin', Ma. I ain't no good anymore, an'
I know it. Seems like I spen' all my time these days a-thinkin' how it
use-ta be—thinkin' of home—an' I ain't never gonna see it no more."
The first line of that speech, "You the one that keeps us goin', Ma," is not
from the novel, although the rest of the speech is. By adding that line,
Johnson has done two things. He has given the dramatic motivation for
Ma's speeches that follow, and he has expressed his own view of the
world in which the man should be the strong, active member of the
family and the wife the helpmate. In this scene, Pa admits what is to him
(and to Johnson) defeat by telling Ma that she, not him, is the one who
has kept the family going. This puts the dramatic emphasis on what Ma
then says and why she says it. Ma's next speech, which comes almost
directly after Pa's lines in the book, is:

> Woman can change better'n a man. Man lives in jerks—baby born,
> or somebody else dies, that's a jerk—gets a farm, or loses one, an'
> that's a jerk. With a woman it's all one flow, like a stream, little
> eddies, little waterfalls, but the river it goes right on. Woman looks at
> it like that.

Johnson follows this speech from the script with a comic counterpoint

line for Al, referring to another jalopy, "Look at that ol' coffeepot steam!"
Pa is more thoughtful about what Ma says, and he comments, "Maybe,
but we shore takin' a beatin'," which provides the transition from Ma's
"Woman can change" speech, which is from chapter twenty-eight in the
novel, to her final speech, which is from chapter twenty. Ma says,

> I know. Maybe that makes us tough. Rich fellas come up an' they
> die, an' their kids ain't no good, an' they die out. But we keep
> a-comin'. We're the people that live. Can't nobody wipe us out. Can't
> nobody lick us. We'll go on forever, Pa. We're the people.

Many critics have taken Ma's final speech out of the context of the
scene and quoted it as an example of "Hollywood liberalism" at its
worst.[4] Although Johnson is also guilty of taking the speeches out of their
context in the novel, he has developed for them a scene structure that
makes them work in dramatic terms, rather than as just a "liberal"
message. Johnson begins with a statement by Ma of how defeated they all
were, which is followed by Pa's statement of defeat, which leads to Ma's
reassurance of Pa in her generalizations about the differences between
men and women, and from there Johnson goes up to Ma's generalizations
about the poor. The sequence has a rising dramatic structure as written
and as played in the film. The rising power of the final scene matches the
kind of rising dramatic structure that Johnson had given to the script by
the rearrangements of the events in the story.

The final scene of the script has been controversial in another way. In
Mel Gussow's biography of Darryl F. Zanuck, *Don't Say Yes until I
Finish Talking*, Gussow claims that Zanuck wrote the final scene of the
screenplay, and that, furthermore, the scene was not in the book.
Technically, the whole scene was not in the book, but, as has been
pointed out, Johnson borrowed from two different places in the book in
writing the scene. Johnson's touch is evident in his construction of the
scene and in the line he added to Pa's speech, "You the one that keeps us
goin', Ma," which uses a negative variation of a standard Johnson theme.

Although Gussow does not say where he got his information, it appears
to have come from Zanuck himself. What Zanuck is probably remembering is the original controversy over which ending was to be used.
Johnson has said that he knew from before starting the script that he was
going to use Ma's speech at the end, and he wrote the ending as it now
stands (with the exceptions of Al's lines, which have been cut) as part of
his original script. In Johnson's mind, there was no doubt that that scene
was to be the final one in the film. In the minds of Zanuck and John Ford,
there was some question. In the copy of the script used by the
cinematographer of the picture, Gregg Toland, the final scene does not

appear. Instead, the scene before it ends and is followed by a note: "The ending of the picture has not been decided upon and you will be given it when the film is in production."[5]

Johnson's third wife, Dorris Bowdon Johnson, who played Rosasharon in the picture, remembers that the actors were never given full scripts for the film but mimeographed "sides," with only their lines of dialogue on them. Dorris remembers Ford used to tell her that they were going to use the original ending of the book, which may have been what Ford wanted to do, or, more likely, one of Ford's jokes. The final scene of the book is one in which Rosasharon, whose baby has died, nurses an old derelict with the milk from her breasts, and it is difficult to imagine any way it might have been done in a Hollywood film in 1940. Furthermore, the ending of the book was the one element that nearly all the critics agreed upon as being wrong and out of key with the rest of the novel.

Ford indicated to Peter Bogdanovich (in Bogdanovich's book *John Ford*) that he wanted to end the film with Tom Joad leaving the family, which does occur just before the last scene in the film. Ford filmed a shot (not in the script) of Tom walking up a hill, which gives the film a feeling of a premature ending. Johnson was never approached to write any ending other than the one in the truck which appears in the film. Johnson's comment on Gussow's statement that Zanuck wrote the scene was simply, "Oh, by now Darryl probably thinks he did write it."

The production of *The Grapes of Wrath* was smothered in secrecy. When Otto Brower was sent to Texas and Oklahoma to shoot the second unit sequences of the cars and trucks on the road, the studio announced the unit was shooting an innocuous comedy entitled *Highway 66*. (While Brower was filming on the road, he tried to get real "Oakies" to stop long enough to appear in sequences of the film, but they were all in too much of a hurry to get to California to stop.)[6] Zanuck is reported to have received some 15,000 letters while the film was in production, all but a few of them saying he could not possibly make the film because of the relationship between the film industry and big business.[7] Most of the pressure on Zanuck not to make the film seemed to come from other people in the industry who were afraid of some kind of retaliation against the industry.[8] As Johnson said, "The movies have always been filmed with the fear of ghosts." Steinbeck read newspaper reports that Fox had bought the book to keep it off the screen. He wrote to Johnson about this, noting that he thought Warner Brothers had probably started the rumors. Johnson, writing at the time in *Photoplay*, said "Nothing improves Zanuck's disposition like a good stiff rumor that he'll never do it. His spirits rise, soft drinks flow like water in his office, and it is a first-rate time to hit him for a raise or a vacation." Johnson quoted Zanuck as saying, "Show me a man that can prove that I spent $70,000 in order to shelve it and I'll make a picture about him."

A large number of the supposedly exterior shots were in fact filmed on the sound stages at the Fox studios in Westwood. Unlike Henry King, who wanted to go on location for everything, Ford was perfectly willing to shoot in a studio since it gave him a greater control over the elements of the production, particularly the lighting. The man specifically in charge of the lighting for Ford was the cameraman, Gregg Toland, who was generally considered one of the most distinguished cinematographers in Hollywood. Toland was particularly skilled in the sculptural use of light, and, as a result, the film is beautifully shadowed and very richly textured visually, which corresponds to the richness of characterization of the script.

While Ford had the very considerable help of Toland on the photography of the film, the credit for the handling of the actors belongs entirely to John Ford. Ford took a very large cast and got from them some of the best performances of their careers. Zanuck was by then convinced of Henry Fonda's stature as a screen actor. When Fonda indicated he wanted the part of Tom Joad, Zanuck let him have it only on the condition he sign a seven-year contract with the studio. Fonda wanted the part so much that he signed, and, although he later regretted the contract, he did not regret playing Tom Joad.[9] As Fonda played him, the character can be seen as continuing in the line of characters that Fonda played in *You Only Live Once* three years before, and in *Jesse James* the year before: tough, solid men of integrity who find themselves on the wrong side of the law.

Perhaps the best remembered performer in the film was Jane Darwell, who, as Ma Joad, won an Academy Award for best performance by an actress in a supporting role. This was in spite of the fact that she did not match the physical description of Steinbeck's Ma Joad, who was thin and gaunt. John Carradine as Casy, the preacher who lost the call, and John Qualen as Muley, were on the same high level.

Zanuck had the practice of taking films out to be sneak-previewed to get audience reactions to them. After the previews, Zanuck and the rest of the production team would come back to the studio and discuss what was to be cut. *The Grapes of Wrath* was previewed with an audience that had just seen a Bob Hope comedy and they did not respond to the film the way Zanuck thought they should. In fact, they hated it. According to Johnson, Zanuck and his assistants went back to the studio and preparations were made to run the film again. The group sat in the studio projection room waiting for Zanuck to give the signal to start the film. He smoked one of his very long cigars. He finally put out the remains of the cigar and said, "That's one audience. Friday night. Full of kids. They don't give a God damn about Oakies. The wrong audience. Who the hell booked it to sneak there? Tell him if he does that again, don't come back. If I don't know more than that stupid audience, I don't deserve to be running a studio. The picture will go out as is."[10]

Johnson did not approve of the way Zanuck arranged the New York opening of the picture. Zanuck invited important members of the film industry, the banking and brokerage businesses, and the New York society world. According to Zanuck as quoted by Gussow, this audience "loved" the picture. According to Johnson, who was sitting in the balcony, the audience on the main floor slept and belched through most of the film, having come from a big dinner given by the company before the screening. As Johnson remembered it, the most enthusiastic response to the film came from the newspaper people sitting in the balcony. Johnson was so appalled by the reaction of the audience on the main floor that he left the theatre for most of the showing, returning at the end of the picture. John Ford, who did not attend the premiere, heard only that Johnson had walked out. Ford sent Johnson a scathing note for having been so "disgusted" with the picture he walked out. Johnson wrote back to Ford explaining what the premiere was like, and later he received an apology from Ford who had in the meantime heard Johnson's report of the premiere confirmed by others.

What Zanuck was trying to do with that premiere was, consciously or not, very shrewd. He knew that the film, like the book, would be controversial, so he was doing as much as he could to get the film accepted. By taking the Establishment into his confidence, Zanuck was trying to protect his investment. However, he may also have taken away from the impact the film might have had; he might have lulled audiences into seeing it as less than revolutionary and simply a reasonably accurate picture of the "Oakie" situation without accepting the implications of what the film said about the culpability of the Establishment in creating that situation. What moved the audiences then in the film, and what still moves audiences seeing the film now, is the human rather than the political qualities of the story.

Frank Capra, in his autobiography *The Name Above the Title*, puts forth the theory that, for a film to be artistically successful, it must be made under the total control of one man and one man alone. That theory cannot account for *The Grapes of Wrath*. It is too much a collaboration. John Steinbeck's book provides the story material, the major themes, and most of the dialogue: the outlines and limits of the film. Darryl Zanuck had to decide that there would be a film—with the support of Winthrop Aldrich. Nunnally Johnson did the specific, detailed work of adapting a 500-page book into a 148-page screenplay, and John Ford controlled all the physical elements of the production. Among those elements, Gregg Toland's cinematography sets the visual style. Each of the actors brings a presence which helps to make the performances work both individually and, under Ford's orchestration, as a collective whole.

It would be easy to say, as some might, that *The Grapes of Wrath* is a work of art and *Jesse James* is not because John Ford is a better director than Henry King. Ford is a better director than King, but this by itself does not make the difference between the two films. The difference begins with the basic material, and, perhaps more importantly, the difference in attitude toward that material. Johnson's intention in *Jesse James* was to create a rousing melodrama, and the film has a richly textured surface. However, Steinbeck's conception of *The Grapes of Wrath* was deeper, and Johnson, as a screenwriter, had enough honesty and integrity, as well as skill, to carry over Steinbeck's attitude into the script. In *The Grapes of Wrath*, a number of the same people who worked on *Jesse James* are at work again, but the depth of the material demands more of them. The system that was created to make purely entertainment films like *Jesse James* was flexible enough not only to permit them to make a *Grapes of Wrath*, but solid enough to force them to do the best they were capable of in such a film.

8

About Directors

Tobacco Road began as a novel by Erskine Caldwell, but later achieved great notoriety on the stage. Adapted by Jack Kirkland, the play opened in December 1933 to generally bad notices, but went on to run for a record 3,182 performances. When Johnson was given the assignment of adapting the play for the screen, he went to see it in New York.[1] He was puzzled by the play's success, which he thought based on an element that did not justify it. At one point in the play, the Sister Bessie remarks to Jeeter Lester that he would lust after his daughter Ellie Mae if she did not have a harelip. Nothing more is made of this in the play, but in 1933 this was apparently enough of a suggestion of incest to give the play the reputation of "being dirty." Johnson felt people were going to see the play for that reason. To Johnson, what was interesting was the rich regional humor from Caldwell's book, and it was with the intent of reclaiming that humor that Johnson went to work on the screenplay.

Although the screenplay is nominally adapted from the play, Johnson worked as much from the book as the play. In the movie, the dramatic center consists of the attempts by Jeeter to get money to stay on his farm, which is important in the novel but only a minor subplot in the play. Johnson replaced the melodrama of the play with Caldwell's expression of love for the land, which makes Jeeter less comically absurd in the film than in the play.

Ford's direction suggests some of that attachment for the land in the last sequence, in which Jeeter and his wife, Ada, leave the farm on the way to the poorhouse. These scenes have a feeling similar to *The Grapes of Wrath*, but what in Johnson's screenplay is gentle, rural comedy becomes, on the screen, a kind of maniacal farce in which the actors push the comedy too hard, trying to make it wilder than written. The most painful example is the performance of William Tracy as Jeeter's son, Dude. As Caldwell and Johnson wrote him, Dude is a simple country boy with a one-track mind: he wants an automobile and he is willing to do anything to get it. As Tracy plays Dude, he is a shrieking madman, lashing out at anybody who stands in his way. Considering the kind of control Ford has over actors in other films, it must be assumed he permitted and even encouraged Tracy to play the part that way.

Johnson was appalled at what he saw on the screen, but he could not get Ford to change his direction of the performances. Johnson recalled, "Ford was much too powerful for me, and it was just as if I were talking to him in Greek. To him, a low, illiterate Georgia cracker and a low, illiterate Irishman were identical. They reacted the same way. Since he didn't know anything about crackers, except me, and he did know about the Irish, he simply changed them all into Irishmen. The whole thing was a calamity, which was a disappointment to me, because I thought it was an awfully good story."

When Johnson refers to Ford as being too powerful, he is not talking about Ford's personality or political position at the studio. He is talking about the kind of power any director has once production has begun on a picture. Johnson said, "Once the picture is on the set and the director's in charge, it's out of your hands. There's nothing you can do about it any more. You can say, 'Look, this is going too far,' but you have no control. The producer has no control, and the writer has no control. It's in the hands of the director. You can't change things like that. You just have to trust to luck and trust to your judgment in the director. He has one way of directing a picture. If he understands it, he'll do it right. Unfortunately, if he doesn't understand, nothing you say will ever make any alteration in the thing."

Johnson could complain to Zanuck about the way directors were shooting his material, but without much success. Zanuck explained to Johnson, "On the set the director has 90 percent control. You may be able to persuade him to do this or that, but only within 10 percent. The rest of it he's going to do it his way." Once, when Johnson came to Zanuck to complain about a director, Zanuck told him, "Before you begin to beef, take a look at it and think about it. Is his alteration better than yours?" Johnson remembered his reaction, "It didn't occur to me that such a thing could be possible. But I saw what he meant. It was true. He might be doing a better scene than I'd written, but I know what the scene looks like when I wrote it."

Examples of the kind of alterations that Johnson objected to but which might have helped the picture can be found in the film he wrote the year following *Tobacco Road*. *Roxie Hart* was based on Maurine Watkins' 1926 play *Chicago*, and the spirit of Johnson's screenplay is so close to that of *The Front Page* that the script has sometimes erroneously been

credited to Johnson's friend Ben Hecht, the coauthor of *The Front Page*.
The director of the film was veteran William Wellman, who had earned
the nickname "Wild Bill." As soon as Wellman started the picture,
Johnson began to feel he was directing it too broadly. Wellman had
Ginger Rogers, who was playing Roxie, chew gum incessantly through
the picture, which Johnson felt was too easy a way to characterize the
girl. In Johnson's screenplay, the lawyer who was Roxie's "simple,
barefoot mouthpiece" is described as being disheveled and as having his
hair rumpled when he is talking to the jury, but Wellman took it one step
further and had Adolphe Menjou make a deliberate gesture of rumpling
his hair before he goes into the courtroom. In the script, the judge is
described as being very dignified and baffled by the intrusion of the
press, particularly the photographers, although he later jumps up to get
into every picture. Wellman had the judge getting into every picture from
the start.

Because of what Johnson felt were Wellman's violations of the tone of
his script, Johnson never particularly liked the film. He was one of the
few people who does not. As the picture now stands, the energetic
vulgarity of Wellman's direction catches the spirit of Chicago of the
twenties and becomes part of the celebration of that spirit in the picture.
It is possible that if the picture had been directed the way Johnson saw
it, it would have been a more unified picture, but it is difficult to imagine
it being a more entertaining one.

In addition to directors changing Johnson's intentions, it was also
possible for directors to ignore them. After Johnson left Twentieth
Century-Fox in 1943 and was at International Pictures, he wrote the
screenplay for a picture called *Woman in the Window*. The story was
a psychological study of a man who accidentally kills someone. To
contrast with the dramatic tension of the story, Johnson put several witty
touches in the screenplay. Some of these added to the tension. In one
sequence, the hero, played by Edward G. Robinson, is taking the body
of the man he has killed out to the country to dump it. He has the body in
the back of his car, and, when he stops at the toll booth on the turnpike,
he is delayed because he drops the coin on the road. Several lines are
intended as comic relief. When the boy scout who discovers the body is
being interviewed in a newsreel he explains that with the reward money
he is going to "send my brother to a good school, and I'm going to
Harvard." When Robinson is listening to the radio for news of the police
investigation, he must first listen to a dreadful commercial.

The director hired to film *Woman in the Window* was Fritz Lang.
In Johnson's view, Lang was a completely humorless man. Johnson
recalled, "He offered various suggestions that were so corny that I

thought he must be joking. He wasn't. We had one scene where Robinson, with the body in the car, came to a red light and stopped. Suddenly there was a motorcycle cop beside him. Fritz, somewhere in his past, had heard the story of the man who went to call on J. P. Morgan, Sr., and was advised not to look at Morgan's nose. Morgan had a fat, ugly nose and he was very sensitive about it. The visitor was so intent on not calling attention to it that he lost track of things and said, 'I'll tell you this, Mr. Nose.' Fritz told this very old story and said, 'Wouldn't it be funny if the cop looked in there and asked why he was so nervous. Then Eddie could answer in the same way, 'I'm a murderer.' "[2]

Johnson kept this out, and Lang directed the story with his usual emphasis on the psychological aspects of the story. Lang creates tremendous tension during the film, and the Johnson lines are still in the film, but they are not played with a feeling for the humor in them. The boy scout says his line about Harvard as if it were a piece of exposition. The commercial on the radio seems an intrusion rather than a comic relief. The comic touches that were supposed to add to the tension do so, but without being in any way comic. What Lang did was simply emphasize the elements of the script he sympathized with and ignore those that he did not. The film is successful artistically because Johnson's skill in writing the dramatic scenes is matched by Lang's direction of them, but there are still several awkward moments in the film when Lang is ignoring what seems obviously a part of the script. These moments are unsettling in an entirely different way than Lang and Johnson intended the film to be.

When Johnson was at International, he did two pictures with Gary Cooper, the second of which was a comic western, *Along Came Jones*. The director hired for the picture was Stuart Heisler, whom Johnson described as "one of the two or three directors I ever had any genuine antipathy for." Johnson, as the acting producer of the picture, began to notice that the rushes he was seeing had very little of the spirit of the script. Johnson asked Heisler why he was shooting the scenes that way. Heisler replied, "I like to make a contribution to the picture."

Johnson said, "Naturally. But if it's contrary to the spirit of the picture, why do you think that's a contribution?"

Heisler replied, "John Ford makes a contribution."

"Yes he does, but the contribution is generally in the spirit of the picture." Johnson later said about Heisler, "He wasn't John Ford, but he was imitating John Ford and he was imitating him in all the wrong places."[3]

Johnson became so discouraged that he told an interviewer from *Life* and *Time* that Heisler's chief contribution seemed to be that he kept the actors from going home before six o'clock. In the tradition of the Luce publications, this was misquoted as if Johnson had said this about all directors. The membership of the Screen Director's Guild was upset, as director John Cromwell informed Johnson in a letter, and Johnson replied that "I regret the whole episode. I regret the necessity of having to defend myself against a statement which I never made; but I am fully aware of its effect on those with whom I have worked but also on those with whom I might like to work in the future."[4] Mervyn LeRoy, who later became a good friend of Johnson's, got up at a meeting of the Screen Director's Guild and made a resolution that no director ever work with Johnson again. The resolution was seconded by Edmund Goulding, which did not stop Goulding from directing a Johnson picture a few years later.[5] When Johnson inquired lightly if the resolution was still in effect, Goulding dismissed it and his part in it with an airy wave and the comment, "I was dead drunk, old chum, dead drunk."[6]

Johnson's general feelings about directors are only a little more charitable than his particular feeling about Heisler. He said, "The director deserves little more credit than, say, the engineer who brings the Twentieth Century Limited from Chicago to New York. There's very little he can do except stay on the track and come into New York. He didn't create the track. He had no choice about which way he was going."[7] Part of the reason for Johnson's apparent dismissal of the director is because he was, as he described himself, a "pro-writer fellow," and he wanted to emphasize the value of the work a screenwriter does on a script.

The two primary elements the director works with are the actors and the camera. The director controls the pacing of the actors. If the director is doing a good job, then he is guiding the actors within the rhythm of the dialogue and characterization set down in the script, and the result, as with Ford's direction of *The Grapes of Wrath*, is a combination of script and performance working together in a unified way. When the director does not work with the natural guidelines of the script, as with Ford's direction of *Tobacco Road*, the film suffers from internal contradictions (which may be harmful to the film, or may give the film an interesting tension).

The director, in theory at least, says, "Put the camera here." John Ford, although he is reputed never to have looked through the viewfinder, had an almost unerring instinct for selecting exactly the right angle on the scene and the right camera distance from the actors. Henry King is skilled at picking a camera angle or a camera movement that fits the tone of the scene and unobtrusively tells the story. Fritz Lang's composition within the frame suggests the psychological pressures on characters within his films. There are other directors who hardly concern themselves at all with the placement of the camera.

In addition to the two major elements of the actors and the camera, the director also has to maintain control over the physical production of the film, and this involves hundreds of small decisions that must be made immediately. The job of directing a film requires enormous concentration and discipline, and it is easy to lose both in the daily activity. It is no wonder that Samuel Goldwyn once observed, "If a director doesn't lose more than five or ten percent of the script, I think he's doing good. Some director can add five or ten percent; those are the great ones. But the others are just the fellows who make the run with a capful of marbles and only lose a few on the way."[8]

The director who lost the fewest marbles on any of the projects he worked on with Johnson was Henry King. King came from the kind of small town Southern background that Johnson did, and he shared the same set of values as Johnson. In *Jesse James*, Johnson's vision, often humorous, of small-town life in the nineteenth-century America is expressed in the ways the local people feel about the railroad and Jesse; these values, expressed in the writing, are matched by King's sense of place, which sets those people against the real backgrounds of Missouri.

King directed two films Johnson produced alone, *The Country Doctor* in 1935 and *The Gunfighter* in 1950. In the former, the feeling for humanity of the characters is carried through by King's direction, particularly the handling of the relationship between the doctor and the nurse, who are shown to be in love without ever having a love scene. In *The Gunfighter*, the formally structured story is played out against the accumulation of very realistic detail, which gives the picture an authenticity that reinforces the reexamination of the myth of the gunfighter. The only King-Johnson collaboration to lose money, and one of the few films of either man to do so, *Chad Hanna*, has the rambunctious, rustic humor of *Jesse James*, but it does not have as strong and melodramatic a story line. This is perhaps why it was not financially successful when first released, but *Chad Hanna* holds up much better than most films of the period, including several of Johnson's, and is a thoroughly charming movie, especially in its scenes of nineteenth-century circus life.

If Henry King was the director who most consistently handled Johnson's material to his satisfaction, there were other directors who "added" to his scripts. Among the later films, Henry Hathaway gave a strong sense of energy and drive to the opening sequence (an attack on Rommel's headquarters) in *The Desert Fox*. George Roy Hill added considerably to *The World of Henry Orient*, not only in the staging of the scenes, but also by shooting material not in the script.

However, most of the directors Johnson worked with did not add noticeably to the films, but simply shot the scripts. In 1943, Johnson adapted Arnold Bennett's novel *Buried Alive*, which was filmed under the title *Holy Matrimony*. He had read the book some fifteen years before and "was sore as hell that such a splendid comedy idea hadn't been mine." He had seen a play version of the story, but had not liked it very much, so he was pleased to have a chance to do it when Julian Johnson, the story editor at Fox, suggested the book to him as a possible vehicle for Monty Woolley. The story is a warm, domestic comedy about a publicity-shy artist, played by Woolley, who pretends his dead servant was himself. He takes the identity of the servant, marries a woman from a small British village, and begins painting again. His new wife, played by British music hall performers Gracie Fields, stands by him when he is accused of forging paintings by the supposedly dead artist.

The direction of *Holy Matrimony* was assigned to John Stahl, who was primarily noted for such thirties' soap operas as *Back Street*, *Imitation of Life*, and *Magnificent Obsession*. Stahl did add a few directorial touches, but made no major addition to the screenplay. His direction does bring out the charm of the relationship of the couple Johnson captures in his script.

Jean Negulesco directed four of Johnson's scripts, *Three Came Home*, *The Mudlark*, *Phone Call from a Stranger*, and *How to Marry a Millionaire*. The results were uneven. Negulesco was good at staging particular scenes, such as the Australian prisoners gathering at the barbed wire fence in *Three Came Home*, but he often paid very little attention to individual actors. Alec Guinness in *The Mudlark* and Sessue Hayakawa in *Three Came Home* give outstanding performances, but often the supporting players are weak.

Irving Pichel, a former actor, directed four Johnson scripts, and on three of them—*The Pied Piper*, *The Moon Is Down*, and *Life Begins at Eight Thirty*—the performances communicate the same human warmth as the scripts. Pichel's fourth picture was *Mr. Peabody and the Mermaid*, a romantic fantasy, and his direction is too heavy-handed and realistic for the material. Other directors also lost qualities in Johnson's films. Negulesco's direction of *Phone Call from a Stranger* is flabby and Henry Koster, whose direction of *My Cousin Rachel* is competent, manages to squeeze all the loose charm out of Johnson's script for *Mr. Hobbs Takes a Vacation*. Johnson's friend, George S. Kaufman, who had some skill as a stage director, directed *The Senator Was Indiscreet* as though it was a stage play, and the result was a film that seems labored and artificial.

One of the directors who filmed several of Johnson's later scripts and who, on occasion, dropped several marbles was Nunnally Johnson. He began directing in 1953, did eight pictures, and then returned to screenwriting. There is a professional competence even in the worst of the films he directed, but he was simply never as dedicated to directing as he was to screenwriting. He was, like Jesse James, good at what he did, and he knew it. He was as strong-willed about his work as Zanuck was about his, or John Ford and Henry King were about theirs. Underneath Johnson's charm and good manners, he was tough-minded and not without his own share of ego. Zanuck once described Johnson: "Nunnally was brutally frank, a Rock of Gibraltar."

In 1942, Johnson had prepared the script for *The Pied Piper,* which, before it was assigned to his friend Irving Pichel, had been assigned to another director. This director had not talked to Johnson about the project until shortly before production was to begin. He came into Johnson's office with an idea. At one point in the story, Monty Woolley was to spend a night in the barn. The director said, "We'll have Woolley be a pipe smoker, and as he wakes up in the morning he gets out his pipe and fills it and lights it and discovers he's filled it with manure."

Johnson said, "Wait right here for a minute."

Johnson went down the hall to Zanuck's office and told him what the director proposed. Johnson said, "This is the first idea that this man has offered about the script, the only idea so far. I'd like it made clear that if there's any shit in this picture, I'm going to put it in."[9]

Zanuck laughed. And replaced the director. With Nunnally Johnson.

Johnson insisted that he did not want to be a director at the time and that Zanuck assigned him as a co-director with Irving Pichel because he, Zanuck, was not convinced that Pichel could do the picture. Fritz Lang, who knew Johnson at the time, said that he thought Johnson did want to be a director then.[10] Pete Martin, in writing an article about Johnson for *The Saturday Evening Post* in 1946, came to the same conclusion.[11] Certainly whatever enthusiasm Johnson may have had for directing quickly vanished. He was only too happy to leave decisions about the cast, particularly the little children on whom the story centered, to Pichel. Johnson later said that when he tried to co-direct *The Pied Piper* he was "bored stiff."

9
Middle Class

F. Scott Fitzgerald was wrong. Hollywood did not destroy Nunnally Johnson's talent as a writer. Fitzgerald was caught up, both in his own life and in his thinking, in the conventional view of what happens to a writer in Hollywood. The standard myth was, and to a large extent still is, that those who come to write films are inevitably corrupted and/or destroyed as writers. Like most myths, it is only partly true. There are other patterns for writers in Hollywood to follow. Some, like Faulkner, simply used Hollywood for their own financial gain and were not destroyed as writers. Others might have been corrupted or destroyed wherever they worked. There are a few like Johnson, Sidney Buchman, Casey Robinson, and others who, by a combination of attitudes and skills, became masters of the new craft of screenwriting. Johnson's talents for narrative structure, for lively dialogue, and for empathy with his characters were suited for the writing of films. Under Zanuck's guidance as a story editor, Johnson was able to develop as a writer doing the kind of scripts Zanuck preferred. One can come to the conclusion that, in the set-up at Twentieth Century-Fox, Johnson was able to perfect his particular talents more effectively than he would have as a short story writer or a novelist.

Fitzgerald worked as a screenwriter, on the whole unsuccessfully, at various times in his career. As Aaron Latham has observed in *Crazy Sundays*, near the end of his life he was only beginning to develop some skill at it. The last screen project Fitzgerald worked on was an adaptation of Emlyn Williams' *The Light of Heart*, and his 1940 script was not used when the picture was made in 1942 as *Life Begins at Eight-thirty*. The screenplay was by Nunnally Johnson. Fitzgerald's script is darker, Johnson's more sentimental. Fitzgerald's story and scene construction are competent but not unique, and his writing is tired and heavy, while

96

Johnson's script has the smoothness and grace one normally associates with Fitzgerald's prose.

Johnson developed his craft of screenwriting to such a degree that he seldom went through more than two, or at the most three, drafts of a script. His average time was ten weeks; other writers took four to six months, and they would often end up with unshootable scripts. Johnson's scripts worked dramatically, and they nearly all made money. No wonder Abel Green, the editor of *Variety*, said, "The answer to every producer's prayer is Nunnally Johnson."[1] No wonder Johnson was the fourth highest paid producer at Fox in 1939, only Zanuck, Sol Wurtzel, and Harry Joe Brown made more than the $119,166 Johnson got.[2] To a studio head like Zanuck, who had to turn out fifty to sixty pictures a year, a Nunnally Johnson was a necessity.

But it was much more than skill that made Johnson valuable. To begin to understand the professional relationship between Zanuck and Johnson, one must start with the fact that, in spite of large differences in individual personalities, the two men basically shared the same system of middle class values. So did many of the people working at Twentieth Century-Fox. Of the six major creators at Fox over a long period of time—Zanuck, Johnson, John Ford, Henry King, Philip Dunne, and Lamar Trotti—all but Dunne came from the same kind of small-town, middle-class background.

There were several values stressed within this value system. There was a major emphasis on the emotional unit of the family. There was the belief that the small town was better than the big city, although the big city could be exciting and wicked. The rich were not much good, the poor could be honorable and honest, although occasionally dumb, and the best people were those who upheld the middle class values, whether they were rich, poor, or middle class. The system also, of course, promoted the work ethic. Because it was in the middle, the system embraced values held by both the rich and the poor. Therefore, the system at times seemed contradictory, unless one accepted the idea that such opposing values were simply the positive and negative sides of the same system. If there was an emphasis on the family, there was also an emphasis on the individual hero who, at times, had to go against the will of the other members of the family. The family did not withdraw its emotional support of him during his adventures. Opposed to the work ethic, there was also a belief in adventure and escapism, and it was this belief upon which Johnson and Zanuck based not only many of their films, but also, in somewhat different ways, their lives.

Both men, at an early age, escaped from the small towns they were brought up in, ending up, in the twenties, in big cities, Johnson in New

York and Zanuck in Los Angeles. Both were trying to escape not only from the small towns themselves, but from small town values. They brought these values with them, reinforced by their own drives against those values. If they were escaping from the small towns of their youth, they were also bringing a nostalgic picture of those towns with them. If they were escaping from their families, they were bringing their need for families of their own. And, if they were escaping from the ethic of conventional work, they would still find themselves compulsive about the unconventional kind of work they became engaged in.

Within that work their values show up clearly. The view of the family as the strong emotional unit is, of course, at the heart of the film version of *The Grapes of Wrath* even more than in the novel. Nearly all of Nunnally Johnson's heroes are married men, and men who enjoy being married. In picture after picture of Johnson's, one theme is the happy marriage. Sometimes it is a minor theme, as in *Jesse James* and *Prisoner of Shark Island*, but often it is a major one, as in *Holy Matrimony* and *Wife, Husband and Friend*.

Johnson's films are filled with people from small towns, as in *Prisoner of Shark Island, Jesse James, Chad Hanna, The Moon Is Down*, and *Holy Matrimony*, while both *The Grapes of Wrath* and *Tobacco Road* deal with farm people. If the rural eccentricities of some of the citizens of small towns are occasionally held up for humor, the idea of the small town community as a possible negative force is never more than hinted at.

The big city, whether it is New York in *Rose of Washington Square* or Chicago in *Roxie Hart*, is seen as a place of danger and sin—gambling in the former and murder in the latter. In *Roxie Hart*, when Roxie's father, a country type, comes back from the phone to tell his wife that Roxie has been charged with murder and is probably going to be hung, the wife's reply is, "What did I tell you?" She knew that sort of thing would happen to Roxie when she went away to the big city.

The few rich people in Johnson's films are portrayed as unpleasant. McCoy, the owner of the railroad in *Jesse James*, is a cowardly, dishonest man who goes back on his word. The opera lovers in *Wife, Husband and Friend* are presented as snobs, as are Oxford, the art dealer, and Lady Vale, his customer, in *Holy Matrimony*. The poor, in *The Grapes of Wrath* most obviously but also in the opening of *Jesse James*, are presented as noble souls. The nobility of the Joad family seems to stem from the fact that the family members want to work; i.e., they accept the work ethic of the middle class, and they move on at the end of the picture because they would rather get work than sit around being taken care of in a government camp. The poor in *Tobacco Road* are being made fun of primarily because they do not want to work. Jeeter Lester is constantly putting off actually going to work while he tries to think up various schemes to get money without working for it. The work ethic is also used as something of an excuse for Jesse James, since Major Cobb suggests in the eulogy at the end of the picture that one of the reasons America is not ashamed of Jesse is "because he was so good at what he was doing."

If America was not ashamed of Jesse, it was also because, at least in Johnson's version, he was a full-fledged hero, "one of the dog-gonedest, gol-dangedest, dad-blamedest buckaroos that ever rode across these United States of America." Tom Joad, if not quite so flamboyant as Jesse, is still in the same heroic mold, as is the Monty Woolley character in *The Pied Piper* who leads a group of children to safety out of occupied France. They are middle-class heroes, not in the sense of their actual status in life, but in terms of their values. The portraits of these heroes are part of the escapist approach these films present to their middle class audiences: by suggesting that the ordinary man can become heroic, Johnson's films present a slightly romanticized view of life that emphasizes escape through adventure, but, at the same time, ties that adventurousness to a very real and concrete world. It is a delicate balance. The glamorized adventures of Jesse James are photographed against real Missouri locations, or the real unemployment problems of the migrant workers are photographed in the artificial lighting of Gregg Toland.

It is this very balance in Johnson's films between reality and the dream that causes audiences to connect with the films. The realistic mode of the films, whether in the situations or the photographic reality with which the details are presented, makes references for audiences to the reality of everyday life. The fantasy side of Johnson's films is the romanticization of the middle-class values which subtly distorts those values and, at the same time, makes them entertaining in Johnson's dramatic contexts. This romanticization on Johnson's part (and Zanuck's) was not a conscious process; they were not pandering to their audiences. The process was completely unconscious and all the more powerful for that, since it influenced every aspect of the story material they dealt with and became deeply embedded in that material. Because the values they were promoting were so deeply a part of them and, at the same time, so deeply a part of their audiences, their films affected their audiences and became more than just an amusement.

10
A Family of His Own

If Zanuck had suggested the meeting of Dorris Bowdon and Nunnally Johnson as a scene in a story conference, Johnson probably would have asked Zanuck if he "could work on it a little bit" back at his office. He would have written a much more believable scene.[1]

Zanuck and Johnson were at the top of the executive hierarchy at Fox, and Dorris Bowdon was at the bottom of the actors' list. The youngest of seven children, she always wanted to be an actress. Her mother, a believer in the power of education, had encouraged her to go to college. Dorris was performing in a play at Louisiana State University when she was seen by a talent scout for Fox. Shortly before Christmas, 1937, she got a letter from the studio asking her to come out to Hollywood for a screen test. She was put under contract as a "stock girl," an actress doing extra work and small parts. She was treated the way stock girls were, which is to say, badly. One day, she was appearing in a crowd scene, and the assistant director, instead of asking people to move into the proper places, started shoving them. She hit him back. In spite of that, she did manage to get a medium-sized part in a "B" picture, *Down on the Farm*, but, by mid-1938, she was disappointed in her lack of progress and was feeling homesick. She had a friend in the publicity department, and she asked him if there was a publicity tour she could make that would take her near her home in Tennessee. The friend noted that the studio was going to make *Jesse James* in Missouri, and he suggested that she see the producer about a part in it. Dorris went up to Nunnally Johnson's office.

By this time Johnson's divorce from Marion was final. He was single again, although he was finding bachelorhood something of a strain. He said, "Being unmarried is exhausting. It's not the sexual activity, it's the social activity. Being unmarried in Hollywood is like trying to live in a

Holiday Inn." In fact, he was spending a lot of time at a restaurant run by a friend of his, Dave Chasen. Chasen was a former vaudeville comedian with a reputation for being one of the greatest freeloaders in town. He had borrowed so much so often from another of Johnson's friends, Harold Ross, the editor of *The New Yorker*, that Ross's accountant suggested that, if Chasen were involved in some kind of business, Ross could write off the loans as a business expense. Chasen opened a restaurant under the name of the Southern Barbeque Pit, but, in spite of the patronage of Johnson, Frank Capra, and Ross (when he was in Hollywood), the restaurant only became a success several years later after the name was changed to Chasen's.

It was through Johnson's friendships with Chasen and Ross, in the days between Marion and Dorris, that he became involved in a situation that was as near as he ever got to a Hollywood orgy. Whenever Ross would come out to the West Coast, the three of them would get together. One evening, Chasen called to say Ross was there, and Johnson went over to the restaurant. He discovered the two men and a blonde girl that he had never met before. When the restaurant closed for the night, it was decided they would all go to Johnson's apartment for a drink. As they came into the patio of the apartment house, the girl noticed the swimming pool and suggested they go for a nude swim. They all agreed, and she was the first one out of her clothes and into the pool. Johnson stripped and jumped into the water. He and the girl were swimming around when, Johnson said, "We looked at the side of the pool, and there were Ross and Chasen, fully-clothed, walking up and down by the side of the pool, talking about parsley, or something about the restaurant. I said to her, 'I don't think this is sweeping the country,' and we decided to get out. Of course I let her go first. She got out and got dressed and then I did. I didn't think anything more about it. I just thought she was a girl Chasen had got for Ross for the evening. Ross called me the next day and told me she was his fiancée."

Dorothy McBrayer, Johnson's secretary, had standing orders that he was not to be bothered by any starlets. When Dorris came into the office, McBrayer told her that Johnson was out. Not recognizing the standard brush-off, Dorris replied, "I'll wait," and she sat down in the outer office. After an hour, McBrayer went in and told him about the girl outside. Johnson said he would get rid of her. He told McBrayer to send the girl in, and then come in a few minutes later to say that Zanuck was waiting for him.

Dorris was ushered into Johnson's office, and she began to tell him her story. She was immediately taken with his kindness and good manners, especially after the way she had been treated by the other people in the studio. For his part, he was immediately taken with her beauty, although he said later, "I don't think it was because she was southern. I have a prejudice against southern women." When the secretary came in and announced that Zanuck wanted him, Johnson said airily, "Tell Mr. Zanuck to wait." Dorris was overwhelmed.

They began dating but were both wary of marriage. In spite of his dissatisfaction with the excesses of bachelor life, Johnson was not in any hurry to get married again. Johnson was not the sort of person who ever thought he would be married more than once, and yet, by this time, he had already had two unsuccessful marriages. The failure of the second marriage had been particularly upsetting, especially because of what he felt was the hurt suffered by Nora, his daughter from that marriage. The second marriage, he realized, might possibly have lasted. Johnson and Marion had been well suited to each other and were still friends after the divorce.

Dorris was also hesitant about getting married. She saw the guilt that Johnson felt about the break-up of his marriage, and she was well aware of the difference between their ages. She also did not want to give up her career. She was finally beginning to get good roles. She had a small part in *Young Mr. Lincoln* and a larger part in *Drums along the Mohawk*, both directed by John Ford. While she was doing the latter picture, Dorris learned that Zanuck had given her the part of Rosasharon in *The Grapes of Wrath*. She was fascinated with the part and tried to talk to Ford about it. Ford told her to keep her mind on the picture they were doing.

When Johnson finished writing the screenplay for *The Grapes of Wrath*, he told Dorris, "I don't want to get married and you are the type of girl that fellows marry. I am going to remove myself from the area of danger." He went to New York, leaving Dorris to face John Ford and the production of *The Grapes of Wrath*.

Her ego was fragile and easily put off balance by Ford's more sadistic moments with actors. One Friday afternoon, they were filming the square-dance scene. It had been a happy day for Dorris; her scenes went well. When the scene of Tom Joad dancing with Ma and singing "Red River Valley" was finished, Dorris applauded. Ford yelled, "Who did that?"

There was quiet on the set. Dorris replied, "I did."

Ford came over to her. "You amateur. You dumb amateur. Don't you know enough to know it's wrong to applaud?" As Dorris remembers it, what hurt was that she knew that she really was an amateur, and that Ford, with his particular insight into people, had hit her where she was most vulnerable.

She cried all weekend, emotionally demolished by being so put down by Ford. On Monday morning, Ford saw her on the set and noticed her puffy eyes. He asked "What's the matter?" as if he knew and were apologizing. She said it was her love life. Ford kidded her about it, but it was kidding with an edge. Johnson and Ford were never particularly close personal friends, and Dorris thought later that Ford, like a number of other targets of Johnson's wit, was trying to get to him through her.

In January 1940, Johnson was in New York, living with his daughter from his first marriage, Marjorie. Dorris was sent east by Twentieth Century-Fox for the premiere of *The Grapes of Wrath*, and, if Johnson thought New York City was out of the area of danger, he was wrong.

Nunnally Johnson and Dorris Bowdon were married 4 February 1940 in the Nyack-on-the-Hudson home of Charles MacArthur and Helen Hayes. The wedding party at the MacArthur home consisted of twenty-seven friends of Johnson and no friends of Dorris. Johnson's friends at the wedding were, in Dorris's words, "like a solid flank on the other side." They had known Johnson since his days in New York, and most of them had known, if not the first Mrs. Johnson, then at least the second. After the wedding dinner, the guests drifted to the bar, and, as the liquor flowed, each of Johnson's friends took Dorris aside to tell her what her role should be and what a great man Johnson was. Each of them, not noticing what the others had told her, repeated the same advice, that Johnson was the victim of two failed marriages and that she, Dorris, had to make sure this one was successful. She began to feel a strong sense of self-pity and terror at the idea of marriage. Her doubts were not helped when Johnson occasionally referred to her as "Marion" during the early months of their marriage. Still, there was Johnson's charm, and he was just as aware of the effort that would be involved in making this marriage work as Dorris was.

The Johnsons spent the first six months of their married life in New York. MacArthur and Johnson were writing a play entitled at various times *Stag at Bay* or *Melancholy Dane*. They had tried to collaborate once before, in the twenties. They had worked on a play in every saloon in New York, and, as Johnson described it, "We had three wonderful acts, but unfortunately they had no relation to each other." Their new effort seemed to hold more promise. The idea was to take a John Barrymore-type actor and have him visit his daughter at a private school where he falls in love with the girl's gym teacher. It never did get a production on Broadway, although Johnson was continually returning to work on it whenever he was not working on a screenplay. In the sixties, Johnson turned it into a screenplay, changing the lead from a John Barrymore-type actor to a John Huston-type film director. It still did not sell. In a note on the project, Johnson commented, "When a story is rejected periodically over a period of twenty-five years, it stands to reason that nobody wants it. This is the sort of thing that ages a writer before his time."[2]

The Johnsons returned to California in the summer of 1940, and, in addition to working on screenplays, Johnson had become a columnist for a well-known newspaper called *PM*. Johnson had been writing letters to one of the editors, Cecelia Ager, about Hollywood and its eccentricities. Ager suggested that Johnson write on a regular basis for publication. From August to December of 1940, Johnson turned out five-hundred word letters each week. They were similar in tone to his old Roving Reporter columns from Hollywood, except now he was writing as an insider. In one column, he says that it used to be easy to write an epic—you just had people going West and that made it automatically an epic—but it isn't that easy any more. In another, he spends half the column talking about the "almost hysterical demonstrations" that swept the country during National Alexander Korda Week, supposedly a week to honor the British producer, who had come to Hollywood with his wife, Merle Oberon. Johnson suggests that in Hollywood the celebrations were rather subdued; however, in grade schools, papers were read on "What Alexander Korda Means To Me," and "The Boy Korda," and, in upper grades, on "Korda: Man or Myth." He further insists that everyone was giving each other the pleasant greeting, "Merry Alexander Korda Week and a Happy Merle Oberon to You."

While Johnson was back at work writing, Dorris was uncertain about returning to work as an actress. She had done a small picture, *Heil Jennie*, and she was now concerned with setting up a house. She did test for a part in *Chad Hanna*, and, although she never saw the test, she felt she did not do well in it. Even so, the way she found out she lost the part was a blow to her vanity both as an actress and as a wife. She and Johnson were having lunch in the Fox commissary a week after the test, and suddenly Johnson said, "I guess I had better go over and congratulate Linda Darnell on getting the part." Johnson insisted it had been Zanuck's decision, and Dorris got some consolation from the fact that the picture was one of the few financially unsuccessful pictures Johnson made at Fox. *Chad Hanna* became a family joke over the years, with Dorris and the children referring to Johnson in grandoise Hollywood terms as "The man who gave you *Chad Hanna*."

Dorris took time off from work to have their first child, Christie, in 1942, and then returned to acting in 1943 in *The Moon Is Down*. She played the wife of a Norwegian villager who is killed when the Nazis invade and occupy the town. A lonely German lieutenant attempts to seduce her and she kills him with a pair of scissors after seeming to give in to him. The role was the biggest and best part she ever had, and she was more than equal to it, managing a gamut of emotional shifts from fear to resignation to coyness to emotional upset to numbness. Dorris particularly remembers one day of filming when everything went right, not only technically, but emotionally. She calls it "the most exhilarating day of my life," and for years that day seemed to haunt her as the kind of potential satisfaction she had given up.

The interest that finally came to occupy most of her time and energy was her assumption of the management of the financial affairs of the family. As long as he had a well-organized home, Johnson did not particularly care what happened with the rest of the money he made. Dorris began a program of investments. There was a shopping center development in Utah that took twenty years to turn a profit, and there were some citrus groves in Florida and California that may eventually also be profitable. There were also cattle farms in Alabama and Mississippi, and, perhaps the most profitable of all, an open field across from what is now Ontario Motor Speedway where Johnson children and grandchildren were known to supplement their allowances on race days by parking cars in the field. There was also an investment in a hydroponic gardening process, the only result of which was an oversized cucumber that lived in the refrigerator for a year or so. In spite of the occasional setbacks, Dorris' investments ultimately brought more money in than Johnson's earnings as a screenwriter, since the tax laws are more favorable to investors than to people earning high salaries.

There were now three children, Christie, Roxie, and Scott, and Dorris was concerned that Johnson was not spending enough time with them. She soon saw how compulsive he was about his work, writing seven days a week, and she felt that he was shortchanging the family. She knew that he was not doing it on purpose and was not even aware of it, because, when she mentioned it to him, she says he expressed "mild astonishment." She felt somewhat guilty about bothering him with it in view of the money he was providing for the family. She often thought that they would be better off if he did not work as hard and earned less. She once told him, "If only you made $100 a week, we might have a little more time with you."

Ironically, the children do not remember feeling he was not around. They often felt that they saw more of him than they did of her. Since he had to be at the studio early, or wanted to be to get to work, he had breakfast with the children and drove them to school, while Dorris did not get up until later. The children remember being read to by Johnson and he took Scott to the Coliseum to see the Rams play. All three felt the advantages of having a father who worked at a movie studio. Johnson had the Fox prop department paint a football helmet with a Rams design as a present for Scott, who, before such things were sold, wanted such a helmet very much. Scott also managed to get several of the Army props from the battle scenes in *The Man in the Grey Flannel Suit,* while Roxie saw a large doll one day while visiting the studio and Johnson brought it home for her. Unfortunately, it was too big to be played with, so it took up an extended residence on a chair in the dining room. There was also a large Christmas tree every year with an equally large pile of presents under it, some from relatives, some from friends, and many from a variety of people trying to curry favor with Johnson.

Dorris need not have worried about Johnson being a good father. He was a man devoted to the idea of family, not only in his films but in his life. One of the reasons for Dorris's success as his wife was her ability, like that of Ma Joad, to hold the family together in spite of the pressure put on it and on her. Dorris recognized that Johnson's sense of family loyalty included his ex-wives and the children of those marriages. He continued to pay alimony to his first wife until 1972, and, whenever he was in New York, he would have dinner with Marion, discussing their daughter, Nora. Dorris, with her strong and complex personality, was able to structure all the elements of Johnson's families into a loose confederation, with Johnson at the center.

Dorris could, with some difficulty, occasionally talk him into weekend vacations in Palm Springs. He would never argue about it with her, but, once they got there, he would stand around, in Dorris's words, "looking long-suffering." Dorris says, "It took me years to define the real essence of a writer: he is compulsive and he works alone. And that puts pressure on the wife of a writer. I felt isolated, and I felt a need to communicate. Nunnally is not like that. For him, communication is telling an amusing anecdote." At the same time, she felt the necessity of protecting Johnson from intrusion on the isolation necessary for his creativity. She might want to escape to Palm Springs, but he escaped to his typewriter, living in the world of the story he was working on. Often she would hear him talking to the typewriter as he worked.

Pamela Mason once said the Johnsons' marriage had to be one of the happiest in Hollywood because Johnson was one of the wittiest men in town. Dorris agrees. At dinner parties she found herself impatient with dull people who would not give Johnson a chance to talk, and she was equally impatient when cornered by women who wanted to talk about "women's things." She would rather have listened to Johnson. Even in a group of famous and talented people, he tended to set the mood of the party, since all the others were expecting him to say something funny.

His wit could get him into trouble, since nearly every witticism ended

up in the newspapers. One evening, at a party, the woman sitting next to
him, knowing that he was from Georgia and was working on the script for
Tobacco Road, asked him if he was from the Tobacco Road area.
Johnson recalled,

"I don't think she meant to be anything more than clumsily funny,
and my answer was kind of automatically clumsy. I said, 'Oh no.
Where I came from we referred to those people as the country club
set.' There are sometimes lines that are so quotable they are quoted
over and over and over again. It seemed to me that Bennett Cerf must
have reprinted this one forty times, as if he'd never heard it before.
In those days I subscribed to a clipping bureau and every time he
reprinted it, and another column would do it, I'd get 25 columns at
ten cents apiece with this same joke. I must have had 500 or 600
clippings, if I'd have saved them, with this same Goddamned joke in
it. At the same time, Erskine Caldwell was getting it from his clipping
bureau. He said, 'You're costing me all of my royalties for saying a
thing like that.' "[3]

Johnson's reputation as a wit-about-town extended beyond one-line
wisecracks. When Chasen's installed new facilities in the men's room,
Johnson thought the occasion called for a Hollywood premier. He and his
friends arranged for four search lights in front of the restaurant, and sent
out engraved invitations specifying formal dress for the introduction of
what the invitation noted in French was the new *salle de bain.*

Then there was the "Louella Parsons affair." The situation began in
late 1938 or early 1939. *The Saturday Evening Post* had intended to do
an article on Darryl Zanuck for some time, but the article had not
appeared. Since Johnson had once worked for the *Post* and knew the
current editor, Wesley Stout, it was suggested Johnson write to Stout to
encourage the Zanuck article. Johnson did, and Stout wrote back that he
was interested in publishing an article on Louella Parsons, who, at that
time, was the most powerful of the gossip columnists in Hollywood. Stout
was under the impression that Johnson was doing an article on Parsons
for one of the Luce publications. Then, in March 1939, somewhat to
Stout's amazement, he received a manuscript of an article on Parsons
written by another writer, Thomas Wood.[4] Wood had originally written
the article with the hope of selling it to *The New Yorker,* but it was turned
down there. Robert Benchley suggested the *Post.* The *Post* bought the
article and Wood has described his impression of what happened next:

They eventually sent it to Nunnally Johnson for checking. And
Johnson, who was a screenwriter, treated the manuscript like
screenwriters treated other material. He started to fiddle around with

it. He showed it to some columnists, and the first thing I knew everyone was under the impression he was the author. My name was on it, but the impression was that what I'd written wasn't good enough to be published and Johnson had come in and saved it.[5]

In fact, Stout bought the manuscript with the understanding that it would be rewritten, or at least this is what he told Johnson. Stout specifically asked Johnson to rewrite the material with the understanding that Johnson's name not appear as the author.

Johnson did completely rewrite the material, although he used most of Wood's facts as well as some original research of his own. In Johnson's rewriting, the emphasis shifted from Wood's research to Johnson's wit. He noted that "in her own field, where bad writing is as natural and as common as breathing, Louella's stands out like an asthmatic's gasps," and he wrote that she is "about twenty minutes late mentally from the time she rises until the time she reaches her bed again." He also commented on her "gay illiteracies," a term she used as the basis for the title of her 1944 autobiography, *The Gay Illiterate*.

Parsons' immediate response was not so flattering. The article appeared under Wood's by-line in *The Saturday Evening Post* of 15 July 1939, and, in a letter dated 19 July, Parsons threatened to sue the *Post*, a threat that was not carried out. In her letter, all the items marked as the basis for her suit are lines that Johnson had written. Johnson's authorship was not long a secret. On 20 July, Leonard Lyons announced on his radio program that Johnson was in fact the author of the article.

Johnson and Parsons eventually made up. At the 1945 Academy Awards dinner, they met, and Louella offered to forgive and forget. As Johnson put it, they had about eighteen drinks and the whole thing was over. At the same party, people were being called up to the stage and asked to say a few words. Parsons turned to Johnson and said, "Do me a favor and write something that will make me famous." William Goetz, sitting next to them, said drily, "He's already done that." As Johnson described the situation, "It looked for a minute as though the fat was in the fire, or vice versa. But lately Louella has gone out of her way to be nice to my scripts. Actually she is a big-hearted woman who winces when people don't like her. The trouble is, having her wince at you is like backing into a buzzsaw."[6]

If Louella could not get to Johnson directly, she found she could do it indirectly. A few years after the article came out, Louella wrote in a column, "I saw Dorris Bowdon at a party for the first time since she married Nunnally Johnson. She used to be so pretty."[7]

If their marriage changed Dorris from a young and unsophisticated actress to the complete wife, it also had an effect on Johnson. Many people who knew Johnson well comment on how unaware of people's feelings he could be, and, while this was true, he could on other occasions be extremely aware. Before Johnson and Dorris were married, they had long discussions about the problems they might face, and, in the early years of the marriage, Dorris found Johnson very tolerant of her seeming lack of sophistication. He also appreciated the situation Dorris found herself in, particularly when she gave up her acting career. He told her at one point, "I can give you everything but an identity of your own." That she had to work out for herself, which she did by making a career of being his wife, and she was probably more successful at that than she would have been had she remained an actress. Through his awareness of her, he became more sensitive to the characterization of women, the examination of character, and the concept of marriage in his writing.

In Johnson's films in the first part of his career, the heroine is characterized as the loyal, supporting wife of the hero. The marriage of the hero and the heroine is usually a subplot rather than the main plot. This pattern of the marriages in the earlier Johnson films is almost dream-like, a type of wish fulfillment, perhaps because of Johnson's inability to find that kind of marriage in his real life. After the first few years of Johnson's marriage to Dorris, the pattern in his films begins to change to a more mature examination of more realistic marriages. The main plots of the latter films, particularly in the fifties, begin to center on the marriages themselves, and, at the same time, Johnson moves toward examining his characters in greater depth and complexity, particularly the women. Dorris had gotten to Johnson where he lived—in his work.

11

A 20th Century-Fox Dropout

When someone complained that Johnson was getting more money than Shakespeare did, the answer was that Shakespeare did not have Johnny Hyde as his agent. Johnson's lack of interest in the details of contracts can be seen in his description of the activities of Hyde and Abe Lastfogel (of the William Morris Agency) on his behalf during the Fox years: "At the end of three years, it always seemed to me three men would come around: Abe Lastfogel, Johnny Hyde, and another little short fellow. These three little men would run back and forth between my office and Darryl's office and then they'd say, 'It's all set. Three years. Four years.' Whatever the hell it was."

Dorris, with her growing interest in handling the money Johnson brought in, was often shocked at his relative lack of concern about it. She remembers particularly a luncheon meeting she attended with Johnson and his agents and business managers. The details of an important new contract were being worked out, and, just as the final arrangements were being discussed, Johnson got up from the table, excused himself, and announced that he had to get back to the script he was working on. He left Dorris, the agents, and the managers to finish the negotiations.

It was Johnny Hyde who came up with the proposal for Johnson to leave Twentieth Century-Fox. His feeling was that Johnson could not get any more money out of Fox, which was not entirely true. Johnson was being offered a new contract that would have paid him $4500 a week, not for the standard forty weeks a year, but for fifty-two weeks a year, with six weeks paid vacation each year.[1] The problem Hyde saw was that the income was taxable as salary. He suggested to Johnson trying to find a setup where Johnson would be part of the company that made the pictures and could, therefore, take more of his money home.

110

If it had simply been a question of money, Johnson might not have left Fox. He had, in his ten years with Zanuck, risen to the top of his profession, but, because he was at the top, he felt he had gone as far as he could with Fox. His working relationship with Zanuck was as good as it could have been, but, at the same time, Johnson saw that while working with Zanuck he would never have complete independence. Johnson just felt that there might be more excitement and greater stimulation in making pictures on his own.

Johnson went in to talk about the situation with Zanuck, and he recalled Zanuck's reaction:

> He didn't want to let anybody go that was of use to him, and he just couldn't get it into his mind at first that I was leaving without some kind of a clear reason, that something had happened that made me mad. They had offered me everything in this new contract. He said, "Isn't that enough?"
>
> I said, "Yes, I'm not complaining about that, but I would be getting as far as I can with Twentieth Century-Fox. I remember when you left Warner Brothers. They said you left because Warner's wouldn't restore the pay cut during the Depression.
>
> He said, "Yeah."
>
> I said, "Is that the only reason?"
>
> Zanuck laughed. He said, "Well, to tell you the truth, I knew I never would see Zanuck-Warner Brothers over that studio."
>
> I said, "That's more or less than the way it is with me. I don't want to go on here for another ten years and be presented with a fitted weekend case for loyalty to the firm." I think he accepted it.[2]

What upset Zanuck more than anything else was that, in looking around for somebody for Johnson to team up with, Johnny Hyde had arranged for him to be part of a new company being formed by William Goetz. When Zanuck came back from his stint with the U.S. Army Signal Corps during the war, Fox was divided into two opposing camps, those who stood with Zanuck and those who stood with Goetz, who had been supervising the studio productions while Zanuck was gone. Johnson was not particularly aware of the politics since he did not have enough interest to become involved.

Zanuck accused Johnson of plotting with Goetz and Johnson replied, "I wouldn't do a thing like that, Darryl, and I wouldn't, I couldn't and I didn't." Johnson said,

> I hadn't even seen Goetz for six months when this thing came up. Goetz left there before I did. I told Darryl, "I didn't even know he was

leaving, and I had no intention of leaving." Well, he was mollified, but he couldn't resist one final needle. He had sent copies of scripts out to people that might make suggestions for revisions. When I was leaving him he said, "You know, this last script of yours, *The Keys of the Kingdom,* has quite a few major criticisms about it." He picked it up. Well, there always are, somewhere, but on this particular one there wasn't a one. "Aw hell," he said, "They're around here somewhere." He was in there fighting to the last.

Goetz was about the last person Johnson would have thought of plotting with. Johnson said, "It never occurred to me. I didn't think Goetz had any talent. I wasn't particularly fond of him. And if somebody had told me then, 'You are going to be a partner of Bill Goetz,' I would have said, 'You must be out of your mind.' "3

Hyde had got Johnson involved in a new company called International, being founded by Goetz and a well-known and wealthy lawyer named Leo Spitz. Goetz, of course, had a record as a producer at Fox, but, as Johnson said, "I must say it was not based on a rock foundation." Johnson later wrote of Spitz, whom he liked very much, "He is a very wary, cautious man, and primarily a box office and business man. He is almost unbearably conservative in his estimates of pictures and the business that they will do, and I value his opinion on such things."4

For Johnson, it was rather like starting all over again, since the new company did not own any studios or office space and rented everything, as Twentieth Century had done in 1933, from what was now the Samuel Goldwyn lot. Johnson says, "We went straight back to Goldwyn's lot, rented exactly the same offices, same chairs, same typewriters, and made some successful pictures."

For his first film at the new company, *Casanova Brown,* Johnson went back to a play he had seen in New York in the Twenties called *The Little Accident* based on a book written by Floyd Dell entitled *Bachelor Father.* The idea behind the book is that certain women might not be psychologically equipped for motherhood and should, in that case, be willing to give up their babies to the fathers to raise. The thesis is put forth in a comic story of a young man, who steals his own illegitimate child and tries to take care of it.

In spite of having left a major studio so he could have more independence in his work, Johnson still found himself hemmed in by the commercial requirements of the business. He found it necessary to change the plot line so that, instead of fathering an illegitimate child, the hero had been married to the mother for only the length of time required to conceive the child. Yet the opening sequences are still set up so that it appears that the child is illegitimate. The movie thus seems more daring than it ultimately is, a point James Agee made in his review of the picture in *The Nation*.

Fortunately, Johnson secured the services of Gary Cooper for the title role in *Casanova Brown*, and, as a result, the film is the only one of Johnson's works where the film is clearly superior to the script, in that it holds together in a way that the script does not. As Cooper plays the opening scenes of the film, he makes it clear that his concern is based on a matter of personal integrity, that he wants to do whatever the right thing is. His performance helps the script even more in the later portion of the film when he steals the baby. It is not clear in the script why he does it, but, with Cooper's image of moral sincerity, an audience watching the picture never doubts that he is doing the right thing.

If Johnson hedged a bit on the premise for his first picture for International, he hedged even more on the ending for the second film, *Woman in the Window*. The story deals with a man named Richard Wanley, who, while his wife is out of town, meets another woman. Before anything has taken place between them, a former boy friend arrives at her apartment and threatens her. Wanley kills him in a fight and dumps the body in the country, but he and the woman are blackmailed by the dead man's former bodyguard. In the end, Wanley is driven to suicide just as the police kill the bodyguard in a shootout, believing him to be the killer. The problem that immediately came up was how to get around the problem of the suicide, a story "solution" discouraged by the Production Code. Goetz insisted that the story be revealed at the end to be a dream. Johnson felt that kind of ending was a cheat, but Goetz was insistent, and Fritz Lang, the director, agreed with Goetz.[5] Nearly every review of the picture commented negatively on the ending, a fact that did not keep the picture from being a success.

Johnson managed to keep some of the production money on *Woman in the Window* in the family. His eldest daughter, Marjorie, who had started in the business as story reader at Fox in the early forties, had become interested in editing, because, as she said, "That's where they made movies."[6] Johnson was not trying to push her into the business, but, when she inquired about the possibility of working on the picture, he sent her around to the editor, Gene Fowler, Jr., who was the son of writer Gene Fowler, an old friend of Johnson's. As Johnson told it, three things happened to Marjorie: "She fell in love, she made money, and she found a job." She worked as Fowler's assistant on the picture and eventually married him. When he was drafted to make documentary films for the U.S. Army in the middle of production of the picture, she took over as the cutter on the film.

Shortly thereafter, Marjorie went down on the set, dressed in slacks and pigtails, which made her look even younger than she was. Edward G. Robinson struck up a conversation with her, and, when she told him that she was editing the picture, he said, "That's marvelous. How long have you been an editor?" When she replied, "Three weeks," he blanched and went off to talk to Fritz Lang about it. Lang managed to cool him off. Later, when Lang had some difficulty with her, Johnson simply told him, "If she's not O.K., fire her." She stayed on, and, in years to come, she became one of the best and busiest editors in Hollywood.

For Johnson's next picture at International, *Along Came Jones*, he gave up the role of producer to someone even less suited to the job than he was, Gary Cooper. The notion of Cooper's producing struck Johnson as funny. He wrote in *Photoplay:* "Until Gary Cooper came along, nobody in Hollywood ever thought of a tall producer. The very notion had the ring of a paradox, like a gloomy fat girl, or a comedian who smokes cigarettes." As Johnson said, "Well, old Coop wasn't going to do much producing, but he sat in." One day, the costume designer brought in designs for several costume changes for the female star, Loretta Young. The character she played was a farm girl in the old West, and Cooper was appalled that these costumes were going to cost something like $175 each. Cooper said, "Why don't we just send her down to Sears Roebuck to pick out the kind of stuff a farm girl would be wearing then?" Johnson asked him, "Would you like to tell Loretta that?"

Cooper said, "O.K., O.K.," and, in Johnson's words, "That was the last producing effort he made."

Johnson recalls the other problem he had with Cooper on the picture:

In the middle of the picture, the production manager came to me one day and said, "We're running behind on money and on time. Every day we're a little bit more in the red." I said, "Why do you think this is?" He said, "Cooper. He's not prepared when he comes in. He doesn't get his lines the night before. He's learning them on the set. He's not a fast study. We have to have a lot of takes." I said, "Why don't you tell him?" The production manager said, "Well, uh . . ." and I saw what he meant. What he was saying was, "You tell him. He's the star. He's the producer. Tell him."

I didn't want to, but I said, "All right, I'll tell him," though I didn't know how because I was as uneasy about this as he was, but I finally went out to Cooper's dressing room. I reminded him that he was the producer of the company and I said, "Do you know we are behind, running in the red? All on account of one actor." Very innocently. He tried to think of who it was, I was sure he was thinking of the others. I said, "He's not ready with his stuff and he's having to have more takes." He said, "Who is he?" I said, "You." and I walked on out. I'd never stay and argue with a star about this matter. Now he never got mad, but I didn't know him too well. It's awfully hard to go to a big star like that, and he was my boss too, and say, "You're screwing things up." After that he picked up. He realized it then. He was a nice man.

Along Came Jones was based on a western story by Alan LeMay, and, in adapting it to the screen, Johnson emphasized the comedy aspects of the story, in which Cooper is a bumbling cowboy who is constantly mistaken for a mean killer. This emphasis on comedy bothered Cooper's friend, Cecil B. DeMille, who called Cooper the day after the picture opened. He told Cooper, "You have just done the most foolish thing you have ever done in your life. I don't know how you could have done it because you may have committed professional suicide."

Cooper replied, "What do you mean?"

DeMille answered, "Your image to the public is a competent fighter and horseman, and in this picture you've made yourself a clown. They'll never take you again."[7] Two years later, Cooper starred in DeMille's *Unconquered*, and, eight years later, Cooper won an Academy Award for *High Noon*. Johnson commented, "So much for DeMille's opinion."

Along Came Jones is probably the weakest of the three pictures Johnson did for International, and not all of that weakness can be traced to Stuart Heisler's direction. The story line gets excessively complicated and overplotted, with five different groups of good guys or bad guys chasing Melody Jones at one point. The writing within the individual scenes is not as sharp as Johnson's writing usually is either, and some scenes are repetitive in a way that Johnson's scripts had not been since his very early days in Hollywood.

A part of the problem was that Johnson was missing the kind of creative input that he had received from Zanuck. Goetz was not able to perform the same kind of function that Zanuck had. Johnson described Goetz's work: "Bill wasn't a picture maker in the sense that Zanuck was. He didn't get into the contents of the script. I guess he just wanted to see them keep moving and come out happy at the end. He did fancy himself for making up titles, which seems to me a rather hollow distinction, but he named both *Casanova Brown* and *Along Came Jones*. That was the extent of his production supervision, that and the ending for *Woman in the Window*."

Another part of the problem was in the paradox that Johnson represented. He had become part of International because he wanted to be free of Zanuck's control and do something different in films. At the same time, he still retained and was guided by his own set of values, which had made him so valuable to Zanuck. These same values were the reason Johnny Hyde was able to arrange an independent production deal for him. The people putting up the money understood that Johnson would be making films like *Casanova Brown, Woman in the Window,* and *Along Came Jones,* films that, while independent, were not too independent, and therefore not too uncommercial. They understood that Johnson would not make a film that would upset people to the degree that it would not be able to get bookings and make money. They were, however, wrong.

12

Mr. Johnson Was Indiscreet

The situation was familiar. Over at the Goldwyn lot on Santa Monica Boulevard was this little company that was making a number of pictures that were doing big business. On the other hand, there was this big company that had a lot of studio space, but had not been able to turn out enough successful pictures. The little company this time was International and the big company was Universal, with studios on the other side of the Hollywood Hills. Emissaries having been sent, complicated negotiations ensued, various stock deals were worked out, and Spitz and Goetz moved International out of their rented offices and over the hills to Universal. International did not have quite enough clout to insist on top billing, as Twentieth Century had, so the new company was called Universal-International.

For Nunnally Johnson, this move meant he had a better office, "That's about the only change I could see. By then we already owned our own second-hand typewriters."[1]

Johnson was also of the opinion that Johnny Hyde had this outcome in mind from the beginning when he set Johnson up in International. If Hyde had not originally had the idea, he soon began to develop it after the establishment of International. Hyde and Johnson were discovering that the United States government, or at least the Department of Internal Revenue, did not consider talent in quite the same category as cash. When the ownership of the films at International were established, Spitz and Goetz arranged for the financing. Since Johnson's contribution to the films was "only" with his talent, the government did not consider his part ownership as an investment, and Johnson did not get the favorable tax advantage he and Hyde had hoped for, while Goetz and Spitz did because of their financial investment. Johnson was no better off monetarily than he had been at Fox.

Johnson's first picture for Universal-International was *The Dark Mirror*. It is a superbly plotted thriller about twin sisters, one of whom is a murderess. The story line and the dramatic pressure are as carefully laid out as in *Woman in the Window*, but without the latter picture's weak ending. *The Dark Mirror* also benefits from a striking performance by Olivia de Havilland in a dual role as the two sisters, which was made possible by a series of excellent special effects shots in which the two sisters appear to be in the same frame.

Johnson had been looking around for some time for a political story to do, and, as was the case with *The Grapes of Wrath*, he was more interested in the story than in the politics. Unlike many Hollywood writers, Johnson was not involved in practical politics of any sort. He was not a joiner, but an observer from a distance. He did not join the political groups, front and otherwise, that several Hollywood personalities did. His lack of interest in politics was also one explanation—along with his age, the fact that he'd already done one stretch in the army, and his status as a newly married husband—for his not volunteering for some sort of service during World War II.

Johnson finally found a story about politics that he thought would make an interesting film. It was a story by Edwin Lanham about a United States Senator who gets it into his head that he should be President. The only problem is that he is thoroughly incompetent. That is easily solved when he reveals that he has been keeping a detailed diary about the activities not only of himself, but also of all his friends. In late 1946, Johnson wrote to George S. Kaufman about it:

> I have tremendous high hopes for this story and I believe it can be such a series of firecrackers as has never been done in pictures. Political firecrackers. I know of no other picture that has ever spoken out and jeered and taunted the idiocies of an American statesman as this one could . . .[2]

Johnson was at the time trying to get Kaufman to direct the picture. They had been friends for a number of years, and, shortly before, they had collaborated on a stage musical, *Park Avenue*. The show died a quick death, but Johnson had been pleased to have the "education and privilege" of working with Kaufman, and he saw the Senator story as the perfect vehicle for Kaufman, a noted stage director, to make his debut as a film director. Kaufman had had some experience as a screenwriter in the twenties and thirties, mostly writing for the Marx Brothers, but he had not directed a film before. Johnson was persistent, and Kaufman finally agreed to direct the picture, although, up to two months before production was to begin, Johnson was afraid he would back out.

Johnson did not start out to write the screenplay for *The Senator Was*

Indiscreet. Instead, he hired his old friend, former drinking companion, and occasional coauthor, Charlie MacArthur. MacArthur got to work on the script and almost immediately began to drive Johnson crazy with suggestions for changes. Johnson recalled, "I asked Ben Hecht, 'How the hell did you ever get Charlie to stop altering things?' He said, 'I just watched for an opportunity and when he got enough pages, I took it out of the typewriter, went off and fixed it myself.' " Johnson, out of the force of his old habit of having to write the final draft, started working behind MacArthur, cutting and rewriting.

When the MacArthur script and the Johnson edited version of it were finished, they were mailed off to Kaufman, who asked his friend, playwright Marc Connelly, to come in and work on it a bit. MacArthur heard about this by accident and was upset by the report, but Johnson assured him that Connelly was not rewriting the script, simply polishing it. When the revised pages began to flow back to Johnson, he saw that Connelly was making structural changes. Now that the shoe was on the other foot, he was upset, and he finally, after much polite maneuvering with Kaufman, got Kaufman to stop both himself and Connelly from making any more revisions. About the only first class wit who is not known to have made a contribution to the script was Herman J. Mankiewicz, although, in one note to Johnson, Kaufman suggested putting Mankiewicz on for a week, simply to get "eleven great jokes."

Kaufman had expressed considerable concern about the technical problems of directing a picture, and, in a letter three months before production began, Johnson outlined possible ways of working. The method Kaufman elected to use was to rehearse each scene without any regard for the camera, simply moving the actors around the set, and then having the cameraman and cutter come in and figure out how best to shoot the scene. Johnson assigned Gene Fowler, Jr., the associate producer on the picture and a film editor himself, to help Kaufman line up the shots. When Kaufman had directed in the theatre, he would not watch the stage action, but would walk back and forth in the back of the theatre, listening to the dialogue. Fowler remembers that Kaufman worked in essentially the same way during the production of the film. Fowler says, "I would set up the shots and Kaufman would not even look at the actors. He would turn his back on them and just listen to the dialogue. He would approve a shot if the dialogue was O.K. even if the actors had been standing on their heads. I could have pointed the camera at the ceiling for all he knew." After he had been on the picture for some time, Johnson asked him, "Do you find it difficult directing a picture after the stage?" Kaufman, who was irritated by the long waits for relighting the sets, said, "The only problem is staying awake."

Unfortunately, Kaufman's lack of interest and lack of skill at film direction is very evident in the picture. The script does have some funny lines and satirical points in it, but everything is played at fever pitch, which might have worked well on the stage, but does not on the screen. The jokes might have been funny if they had not been so overemphasized.

As the script was being completed, there were complaints from Joseph Breen, administrator of the Motion Picture Code. He was upset over what he thought was too rough a portrait of the Senator, particularly in view of what he considered to be industry policy of avoiding comment on politicians. Certain elements of the script, such as the amount of drinking done by the Senator, were cut down, and the MPAA finally approved the picture.

After the picture was completed, Leo Spitz continued to worry about it. Johnson wrote to Kaufman in October about the troubles:

> Leo Spitz's worries about the picture were so cloudy and ghostly that I had a hard time finding arguments in reply. They had something to do with our attacking political parties which, as an old politician, he regards as governmental institutions, and our implications that the electorate of this country was a mass jerk. He seemed to feel that an audience would take this as a personal affront. As you can see, this sort of dialetic was difficult to cope with. Goetz was a good deal less disturbed.
>
> Without going into details, I could find nothing to say in reply to these mumbles and so contented myself with sulking. I just sat and waited. So long as he had the ball, let him carry it. At the end of two of these long sessions of silence, nothing was decided.
>
> Finally I went to Goetz and told him . . . I felt very strongly about this interference with the picture. Yesterday afternoon the three of us had another talk, quite pleasant, and Leo said, very well, he had this belief but that if I felt otherwise, it was still my picture and go ahead and do with it as I wished. So I said thank you and left.[3]

What Spitz, Goetz, and Breen were worried about was the gathering storm of the House Un-American Activities Committee. In March 1947, while the picture was still being written, the Committee had begun its investigations of Communist influence in the motion picture industry. The centerpiece of the hearings in October was the testimony, or the lack of it, from a group later referred to as "the unfriendly ten," who either refused to answer the Committee's question about membership in the party or else tried to answer with long, involved harangues against the committee. The House of Representatives voted "the unfriendly ten" in contempt of Congress, and these writers and directors began surrendering to Federal marshals the week *The Senator Was Indiscreet* opened in Los Angeles.

Even before the picture opened, there were rumors about the government trying to suppress it or change it, but there was no such actual pressure. The sneak and press previews went well for the film, with people laughing in all the appropriate places. Yet there were rumors, again unfounded, that the previews had not gone well and that the picture was being cut. People seemed to change their minds about the picture. Johnson reported to Kaufman on Hedda Hopper:

> Judging from other reports, the local Joan of Arc, Miss Hopper, was somewhat taken aback by the picture but she has recovered her normal good sense and disapproves. She told Gene after the preview that it wasn't at all what she expected and that she found it very funny. But this morning, after a night of meditation and prayer, she had recovered her equilibrium and informed various publicity men that while the picture might have been all right a year ago and might still be all right a year from now, at the present moment she felt it was not all right. She feels that the world is so full of chaos that it is all one frail woman can do to keep this government from toppling. But she has no intention of weakening for one moment in her duty to America. She will speak forth frankly.[4]

Hopper was not the only one to change her mind. In their 14 December 1947 issue, *Harrison's Reports*, a trade paper, praised the picture heavily, and the following week came out with an editorial against the film, saying it should be withdrawn. The reviews in general were mixed, and columnists such as Erskine Johnson and Paul Gallico came out against the picture, while Robert C. Ruark defended it.[5]

In view of all the attacks on the film, Johnson fought back in the best, and perhaps the only way he knew how: with humor. In an article, "Confessions of a Confederate" for the *New York Times* (28 December 1947) Johnson, more in an effort to save the picture than to make a political statement, tried to put the whole matter in comic perspective:

> My Name is Nunnally Johnson. N-u-n-n-a-l-l-y, Nunnally. I was born December 5, 1897, in Columbus, Georgia, of white Methodist parents. I am married to another white Methodist and have, all told, four children, all of *them* white Methodists too.
>
> I am not a member of the Screen Writers' Guild.
>
> I am not a Communist.

I am not a Republican.

Yes.

The only organization of any kind that I belong to is the Limited Editions Club, which I am assured is as clean as a hound's tooth. I have not attended a meeting or gathering of any sort where anyone was scheduled to rise and speak on any subject whatever, political, educational, or just entertaining, for twenty-five years, or since I was a cub reporter and had to cover such enlightening exhibitions nightly. As for contributing money to causes, once in Dave Chasen's restaurant I slipped ten bucks to a girl in a low-cut blouse who turned out to be collecting for the Abraham Lincoln Brigade (and me a Confederate!) but the accepted view about town is that politically I am a tightwad from way back and would not give eighty-five cents to see Henry Wallace walk on water. I bat and throw right-handed.

The explanation for this unsolicited autobiographical information is that I am a Hollywood producer with a picture about to be released. . . .

In the whole history of our country nobody had ever before treated politics lightly. Nobody had ever used politics and politicians as material for comedy. Oh, well, a few perhaps, yes, if you want to count Reds like Mark Twain, Will Rogers, and Irving Cobb. But I mean real Americans, true blue and loyal to their country. Who today ever speaks lightly of politics and politicians with the sole exception of newspaper cartoonists, editorial writers, and radio comedians? It was an absolutely fresh subject that we had hit on, a virgin field for comedy, and we should have expected some totalitarian objection to its use in a picture.

As a matter of fact, we were not altogether negligent in our preparations for this courageous venture into the unknown. We took certain precautions. . . .

. . . Our most masterly stroke, really a matter of sheer inspiration, was in the selection of a writer. Since George S. Kaufman, the director, and I were not only Democrats but Roosevelt Democrats at that, the smartest move we figured we could possibly make would be to suck a Republican in on the deal. . . .

The Republican pillar of respectability we took in was named Charles MacArthur and while he didn't look the part and God knows didn't act it, he had the papers to prove himself a registered paid-up GOP card-toter and so we wasted no time in tying him up. When presently it turned out that he could also write and was in fact the possessor of a distinguished record of achievement both in the movies and on the stage, one can imagine our pleasure and satisfaction. Personally I hadn't even known there was such a thing as a witty Republican. Live and learn, though, live and learn.[6]

There was no official investigation of the picture, but one was scarcely needed. Exhibitors were either scared off or actively came out against the picture. In early January of 1948, for example, the board of directors of the Allied Independent Theatre Owners of Iowa and Nebraska requested the owners of 325 theatres in those states not to play the picture on the grounds that it was "a reflection on the integrity of every duly elected representative of the American people." It was not a financial success.

Johnson was more baffled than bitter about the experience with the "red scare." He looked back on the period years later with sadness and distaste:

> I was frank to say that I thought people were very foolish in those days. You couldn't believe that they'd start a Holmby Hills Nasturtium Club, and nasturtium lovers would become members of it, and one month later somebody proposed a resolution regarding the Civil War in Spain, and nine out of ten of these nasturtium lovers hadn't the faintest idea of who was fighting who. They certainly weren't as aware of it as the leftists were, and the next thing you know, on the list of subversive organizations was the Holmby Hills Nasturtium Club. This is hardly an exaggeration of what went on. . . . I don't like groups, and as it happened, I had no particular hobbies or any kind of special interests which made me join any organization like that. But I saw so many things happen, so many outrageous things that went on, that made me ashamed of the whole industry. You couldn't do anything about it. You couldn't even get an explanation from anybody. Suppose somebody wanted, oh, Lee J. Cobb. They found a reason why you should get, I don't know, some other bald-headed fellow. Among actors it's impossible. "You see, he wasn't right for the part. There were three others you could get who were better." Much too slippery. No way he could pin you down. Also there were so many incompetent actors who shouldn't have had jobs who were proud that they were turned down because they were Communists.
>
> Think of John Huston, having to go out and debase himself to an oaf like Ward Bond and promise never to be a bad boy again, and Ward Bond would say, "All right then, we clear you, but we've got our eye on you." This was just one of the most humiliating things. Some actors wouldn't do it. Some writers wouldn't do it. Harry Kurnitz, a very good writer, just left. He left because he would not go to this Ku Klux Klan and ask them for permission to write, even though Harry was about as apolitical as I was. I had a director, Irving Pichel, who'd been out of work, both as an actor and as a director, and you know what his crime was? There was a strike out here, one of those strikes around the studio, I forget what it was, but there was a fund being raised for the wives and children and Irving, who was almost Christ-like in his

sympathy for the unfortunate, made a contribution of more than he could afford. Boy, no more work for him. He finally went crawling out to Duke Wayne and Ward Bond and a number of them. Gary wasn't far from it, and Jimmie Stewart, a very good friend of mine, but neither Stewart nor Cooper were as loquacious as Wayne and Ward Bond. There were a number of them. Mostly Irish. Well, it never affected me at all. Nothing came up in the matter of selecting a story as to whether it might have any political consequences. I can't remember I ever thought about it after that any more than I'd thought about it before. I just hoped to make a good picture.

13
Son of Twentieth Century-Fox

"In Hollywood a personal difficulty is if you make two pictures in a row that are unsuccessful."[1]

Johnson was answering a question as to whether he had experienced any personal difficulties as a result of the furor over *The Senator Was Indiscreet*. It was the first of two financially unsuccessful pictures that resulted in Johnson's being told by the management at Universal-International that he was "available for employment elsewhere". He had been working on the second picture, *Mr. Peabody and the Mermaid*, when it was decided to rush production of *The Senator Was Indiscreet* to give the film as much playing time as possible before the 1948 Presidential elections.

The story of *Mr. Peabody and the Mermaid* was unusual for Johnson in that it was fantasy. The story deals with a proper Bostonian who is approaching his fiftieth birthday and who is happily married. Peabody, on vacation with his wife at an island in the Carribean, discovers on a fishing trip, a real, live mermaid. He takes her back to the vacation house and keeps her in the fish pond. His wife flies back to Boston without telling him, and the police begin to suspect he has killed her. As they come after him, he returns the mermaid to her island, giving up his dream of escaping with her from the real world.

Robert Emmett Dolan, who composed the music for the picture and had been a friend of Johnson's since their New York days, felt that the character of Peabody was something of a self-portrait of Johnson, who, at the time, was approaching fifty himself. The mermaid that Peabody finds is a romantic symbol for him not of love, but of escape. There is only the slightest hint of romance between them, but, at the end, when Peabody takes her back to the island where he found her, he tells her, in a touching speech, what she might have meant for him:

And then just think of it—away from the world completely! No radio, no newspapers, no silly news from Washington—no politics, no rent troubles, no food shortages—nothing but peace and quiet and sunshine! We'll loaf and fish and swim and sleep forever.

He is interrupted by the arrival of the police. The story has been told in flashback by Peabody to his doctor, who, in the final scene, reassures him that illusions such as the mermaid are quite common when a man hits the "air pocket" of age fifty.

Johnson's screenplay captures the fantasy spirit of the story, but, under Irving Pichel's direction, the opening scenes are played in such a matter-of-fact way that the introduction of the fantasy seems unbelievable. The film as a whole drags when it should float. The commercial prospects for the film were also severely hampered by a British film released at approximately the same time called *Miranda,* which had a similar plot.

In spite of Johnson's two flops at Universal, he did not find it hard to get a job after he left. He began negotiations with Fox to come back on exactly the same terms he had when he left in 1943, and he had just about agreed to return to Fox when he got a call from Louis B. Mayer at MGM. Since Mayer was still a power in the business, Johnson had lunch with him. Mayer tried to convince him to come to work at MGM, pointing out all the stars working at MGM. Given Johnson's hesitations about dealing with actors and actresses, this was perhaps not the best way to appeal to him. Still, Johnson was polite and allowed as how he thought he would probably go back to Fox.

Mayer asked, "Why do you want to go back there? What have they got?"

Johnson replied, "They've got Zanuck. I feel that when I'm working on a picture, he's a part of the picture."

Mayer said, "We're going to have somebody here soon." He was referring to Dore Schary, a former writer and producer at MGM who was at the time head of production at RKO. Mayer was going to bring him in in one of MGM's many attempts to find another Irving Thalberg.

Johnson was not impressed. He told Mayer, "I'm immensely flattered by your offer, but I'll feel more at home if I go back to Fox. I know where the water cooler is. I know where to go to sharpen the pencils. I won't have to learn forty-two different things. I know who to call if I want something."[2]

So Nunnally Johnson went back to Twentieth Century-Fox in the summer of 1948. It was, as Johnson said, "as if I'd never left." He continued to work with Zanuck in what he described as "a very close professional relationship." The center of that relationship was the films that Johnson worked on, and, as before, Zanuck was concerned with the details of their production.

Almost as a demonstration that things had not changed in five years, the first film he did was a remake of one he had done in 1939 under the title *Wife, Husband and Friend*. The original picture had not done as well as Zanuck and Johnson had hoped, so they decided to try again. Johnson's changes in the two scripts are minimal. In the earlier one, Leonard Borland is a contracter, and in the later one he is a wrecking contractor. In the earlier version, the opera at the end of the picture is a fictional one, while in the later one the opera is *Il Trovatore*. Johnson has also changed the phone numbers that people call, and one or two of the jokes. Otherwise, the later script is not so much a rewriting of the earlier script as a retyping of it. The early film is distinguished by an energy and drive replaced in the later one by a glossiness in the production, particularly in Joseph LaShelle's photography of the two leading ladies, Linda Darnell and Celeste Holm. *Everybody Does It*, as the new version was called, was not a hit either.

Because of the need to use up box office receipts that were frozen in foreign countries after the war, nearly all the studios tried to find stories to film abroad. Johnson did several scripts that were filmed overseas. *Three Came Home* was the true story of a woman who had been separated from her husband in the Philippines during the war, and, after several years in Japanese prison camps, was reunited with him. *The Mudlark*, from Theodore Bonnet's novel about the street urchin who convinced Queen Victoria to come out of seclusion after the death of Prince Albert, was filmed in England; almost the entire picture, however, consisted of interiors that could as easily have been built on the sound stages in Hollywood.

In between Johnson's two overseas excursions, he became, for the first time in several years, a producer of somebody else's screenplay. A screenwriter friend of Johnson's, William Bowers, worked out an idea he had in western form. Bowers had been having dinner one night at Jack Dempsey's restaurant in New York with Jack Dempsey himself, who had made a comment that had stuck in Bowers' mind. Dempsey said that the biggest problem he had when he was the heavyweight boxing champion was that everybody he met wanted to start a fight with him simply because he was the champion. He said he found that rather tiring after a while.[3] With the help of André deToth, a cameraman, director, and sometime writer, Bowers developed this comment into a story about a gunfighter who, because he was "top gun," was constantly being challenged. Bowers then went to work with still another writer, William Sellers, and developed the story into a ninety-four-page screenplay which they called *The Big Gun,* a title that was changed for the film to *The Gunfighter.*

Bowers had been unable to convince John Wayne to pay what Bowers wanted for the script so he brought the script around to Johnson and Johnson convinced Fox to buy it.[4] Johnson then set about expanding the script, since the 94 pages would not have been quite long enough for a feature-length film. Johnson did not change the structure of the story, but simply expanded the scenes to give them more detail. For example, the opening scene in the Bowers-Sellers script begins with Jimmy Ringo just having shot a young punk in a bar, a scene that Johnson expanded to include the punk first noticing Ringo and harassing him into a shootout. In the Bowers-Sellers script, there is a brief mention in the beginning that the three brothers of the man he has killed are chasing him. Johnson expanded their roles with scenes of them coming after Ringo throughout the picture. Johnson's revised final of the script ran 132 pages. Although several people suggested that Johnson ask for a writing credit on the picture, he refused to do so, since he felt he was just doing the work Bowers and the other writers would have done if they had had the time.[5]

The direction of the picture was assigned to Henry King, who paid his usual scrupulous attention to the accuracy of the physical details of the production, even though the picture was done on standing sets on the Fox lot. Johnson recalled, "The whole atmosphere was entirely Henry's. When it comes to designs for sets, he wants his period right and gets it right. He was responsible for that. He could be something of a tyrant about that. No matter what subject or what period you mention, Henry's an authority on it, and there's no arguing with him about it."

One of King's touches became as legendary as the film itself. This was the matter of Gregory Peck's mustache. King, to add to the authenticity of the picture, had Peck grow a mustache in the style of the period. Zanuck was in Europe while the picture was shot and did not see it until he returned. Henry King describes the first screening of the picture for Zanuck:

> We got into the projection room and Zanuck didn't say a word. He sat there. He said, "I would give $50,000 of my own money if I could get that mustache off that guy." I thought Nunnally Johnson was going to fall out of the chair. He didn't say a word. Nunnally, I think, probably wanted to defend me and yet he didn't know what he could do. Zanuck said, "This man has a young following. Young girls like this man. That mustache, I'm afraid, is going to kill it."
>
> I said, "What would you want me to do, Darryl, just change his clothes to change from the general (in *Twelve O'Clock High,* which King and Peck had just completed) to Jimmy Ringo?"

"Oh," he said, "God bless you, Henry. I'm not complaining about that at all. This is a Remington. Frederick Remington couldn't have done it better than this, but I'm only thinking of box office appeal."[6]

Zanuck did not reproach Johnson either, but Spyros Skouras, the president of Twentieth Century-Fox, introduced Johnson for years thereafter as the man who put the mustache on Gregory Peck and lost the studio a million dollars.

The Gunfighter did not "lose" a million dollars, but it did not make as much money as everyone at the studio had hoped. Perhaps Zanuck was at least partially right about the mustache, since the authenticity of the picture may have worked against it with audiences of the time. Henry King had consistently added such realistic physical details to all his pictures, but, in most of those pictures, such as *Jesse James*, the realistic details worked to reinforce popular myths. *The Gunfighter* is a reexamination of a myth, with the emphasis on the psychological stress on the Jimmy Ringo character. Audiences brought up on *Jesse James* were probably put off by the relatively realistic depiction of Ringo, especially since *The Gunfighter* was one of the first films to begin to dismantle the popular myths of the West. Because *The Gunfighter* was one of the first of its kind, it has been considered by Robert Warshaw and others a "classic". Unlike many classic films, it is still as good as its reputation suggests. The themes of the story, as well as various elements of its plot, have been used repeatedly since, but in the film they are told in a story line of classic simplicity that works itself out with what has been referred to as the inevitability of Greek tragedy. It was the power of the story that attracted Bowers, Johnson, and King, rather than the overtones and themes.

It is significant that Johnson and King would pick this story to work on at this time. Eleven years before, they had done *Jesse James* together, and the history of that film is an example of the kind of closeness that had existed in the late thirties and early forties between Zanuck's filmmakers and their audiences. It was a unity of shared values. But, by 1949, when *The Gunfighter* was made, this had begun to break up. The audiences had begun instead to watch television for cheaper entertainment or foreign films for greater realism. Zanuck himself, particularly in the years Johnson was away, had begun to involve himself in films that were more than just story films. He had done films about politics *(Wilson)*, anti-Semitism *(Gentleman's Agreement)*, mental hospitals *(The Snake Pit)*, and race relations *(Pinky)*.

In early 1950, Darryl Zanuck got a letter from a Jerry Pollinger suggesting that a new book about German Field Marshall Erwin Rommel might make a good film. Zanuck passed this information on to Johnson who read the book and was enthusiastic about the project.[7] He did foresee a problem in dealing sympathetically with one of the leading enemy generals of a war only five years past, so Johnson set out to make sure of his facts.[8] The bibliography of material he consulted ran nine pages single-spaced, and, in addition, he went to England to interview British officers and soldiers who had fought against Rommel. He met with Rommel's widow in Germany and Rommel's son Manfred in a restaurant in London.

The State Department agreed to support the picture if the American High Commissioner in Germany would give his approval of the production. Frank McCarthy, a Twentieth Century-Fox producer and an officer in the Army Reserve, particularly skilled in these kinds of negotiations, was in Germany at the time and used his considerable powers of political persuasion to convince the American High Commissioner to approve the project.

Johnson was writing the script of *The Desert Fox* while he was in London during the production of *The Mudlark,* and, across the alley from the soundstage where *The Mudlark* was shooting, James Mason was working in another picture. Mason had heard that Johnson was writing the story of Rommel and he very much wanted to do the part. Being a proper Englishman, he let his agent in Hollywood know of his interest in the part, rather than just going across the alley and talking to Johnson about it. Since the agent was part of the agency that handled Johnson, the word passed on easily to Johnson. Playing the game, Johnson sent word back to Hollywood that they should tell Mason to come across the alley and they could discuss the matter. When Johnson got back to Hollywood, he told Zanuck about his meeting, and Mason was eventually cast in the part.

The director signed to the project was Henry Hathaway, who helped Johnson out of a peculiar dilemma. Johnson had two possible openings for the film, and, since he was unable to decide which one to use, he wrote both of them into the script. The one that got the story going was a meeting between Rommel and the author, Desmond Young, then a British officer, after Young had been taken prisoner. The scene helped to show Rommel as a gentleman soldier, and, in addition, gave an introduction to Young, explaining how he got interested in doing the book. Johnson included the Young character because of a need to prove a certain documentary authenticity. The other possible opening was an exciting raid by British commandos attempting to assassinate Rommel in his North African headquarters. Hathaway turned the raid into a brilliant action set piece. The idea was conceived of putting the raid sequence before the main credits of the picture, something that had not often been done at that time. Johnson remembered watching the picture with the opening day audience in New York and hearing a spontaneous round of applause at the end of the raid sequence because the audience had been so caught up in the excitement of the scene.

The Desert Fox is one of the finest examples of the kind of narrative film that Zanuck and Johnson did so well, but the emphasis is on character, particularly the character of Rommel. Rommel is a subtle creation, rich with complexity. He is intelligent, vain, witty, decisive, and touched with a strong sense of irony (Rommel to the Gestapo investigating the attempt on Hitler's life: "You've been uncommonly successful in getting deathbed confessions"). The focus of the story is not on Rommel's activities in the desert as much as his involvement with the plot to assassinate Hitler. The dramatic center of the film is his confusion and hesitation about joining the plot against the government he has sworn to serve. The conflict is illustrated in brilliant scenes between Rommel and his wife (Rommel: "It's a great, dreadful, terrible thing he proposes . . . I didn't say he wasn't right"). The theme, as it is in many of Johnson films, is an examination of loyalty.

The picture opened to something of a mixed reaction. The reviews were generally favorable and the business was good, but there were some strong negative reactions. The first Saturday after the picture opened in New York, it was picketed by a group called The American Veterans for Peace Committee, and Johnson himself received some letters from Jewish moviegoers complaining of the sympathetic treatment of a Nazi general. What was most irritating was a negative review in *The New York Times* by Bosley Crowther that not only panned the picture but attacked Johnson for falsifying history. Johnson was particularly offended by this in view of the enormous amount of research he had done. Charles Einfeld of the Fox office in New York talked to Crowther about the review, and Crowther agreed to print a reply from Johnson, but Einfeld recommended that, since the picture was doing very well, it would be more trouble than it was worth to get into a fight with *The New York Times* over it. Johnson prepared a four page letter to Crowther dealing with the kinds of research he had done, but he decided in the end not to send it.

Johnson had another run-in with *The New York Times* about the picture two years later. In 1953, Twentieth Century-Fox produced a picture called *The Desert Rats*, which dealt with the British soldiers who fought Rommel in North Africa. The *Times* considered *The Desert Rats* an "apology for a blunder of two years ago called *The Desert Fox*." Johnson wrote a reply which the *Times* refused to print on grounds of "lack of space." Johnson's main point was that *The Desert Fox* had been so successful that he did not feel that Twentieth Century-Fox had any reason to apologize for it. Perhaps, but if Twentieth Century-Fox is not apologizing in *The Desert Rats*, it becomes rather difficult to explain the characterization of Rommel that James Mason, who was brilliant in *The Desert Fox*, has been given in the 1953 film, which is that of a crude, guttural, sadistic cliché Nazi villain. It is a long way from the brilliantly human characterization in *The Desert Fox*.

The founders of International Pictures: Leo Spitz, Johnson, and William Goetz.

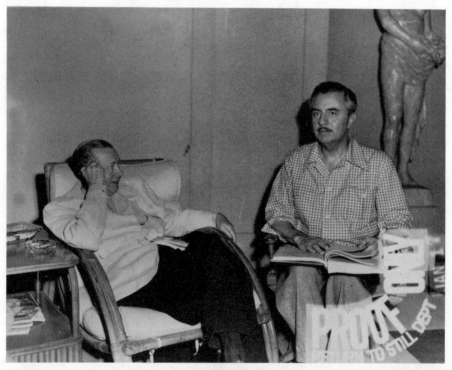

The reason Johnson is looking at William Powell with such admiration is that Powell took the trouble to ask Johnson for his interpretations of the lines in the script.

The things a producer finds in his living room. A publicity shot with an unknown starlet for *Mr. Peabody and the Mermaid.*

Lauren Bacall, Johnson, Marilyn Monroe at the premiere of *How to Marry A Millionaire.*

Johnson directing: first he checks the script . . .

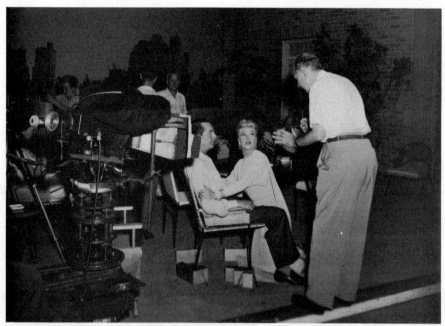

Johnson directing: . . . then he talks to the actors, in this case Reginald
Gardiner and Ginger Rogers in *Black Widow*.

Van Heflin, Johnson, Peggy Ann Garner, and Spyros Skouras on the set of
Black Widow. From the look on Johnson's face, Skouras has probably
mentioned Gregory Peck's mustache again.

Paul Newman, Joanne Woodward, and Johnson the night she won the Oscar for *The Three Faces of Eve.*

On location for *The Angel Wore Red:* Johnson, Ava Gardner, and Johnson's children: Scott, Roxie, and Christie

On the set of *The Angel Wore Red* with Dirk Bogarde. Johnson is about to give up directing.

14

Bette and Burton—and a Phone Call to Garbo

One day, Dusty Negulesco, the wife of director Jean Negulesco, was in a beauty parlor and was so taken with a novella in a *McCall's* magazine, *Phone Call from a Stranger*, that she told her husband about it. He, in turn, told Johnson, who decided it would make an interesting film.[1] The novella was about David Trask, who becomes acquainted with three people before the plane they are flying in takes off. After the plane crashes, Trask, the lone survivor, visits the families of each of the three victims. He helps straighten out the personal problems of the first two families, and, in turn, is helped by the wife of the third victim. In the novella, Trask is leaving his wife because she has written a book about the details of their family life which he feels is a betrayal of their marriage even though the details are not negative. When Trask meets Mrs. Hoke, the wife of the third victim, she convinces him that he should return to his wife.

The story as Johnson rewrote it continued his examination of the problems of loyalty, particularly within marriage, but in a very unfocused way. The emphasis is on the narrative line of the framing story at the beginning, but then the script bogs down in the details of the various plots. The best episode of the three is the middle episode, which still uses the basic idea from the novella of a man so dominated by his mother that he drives his wife away. The episodic structure was nevertheless appealing enough to win an award for best screenplay in the 1952 Venice Film Festival.

Johnson, as producer of the film, was the beneficiary of a gift he later wished he had declined. The role of David Trask was played by Gary Merrill, who was married at the time to Bette Davis, and Davis volunteered to do the part of Mrs. Hoke as a way of helping her husband.

Johnson was pleased to get her for a small part, but he became worried after the first two days' rushes. He spoke to Negulesco, "Is Bette doing something with her voice? It seems to me that it's not the way I think of it. Has she added some gimmick?" Negulesco had not noticed and did not particularly want to get into a fight with her about it. He said to Johnson, "Why don't you speak to her about it?"

Johnson, who never felt particularly comfortable with actors, turned pale at the thought but said, "Of course." He went out to her dressing room and began to explain that he felt her voice was not being used in the proper way. She became angry and said, "You certainly don't expect me to use the same voice or manner of Margo Channing, do you?"

Johnson said, "Oh no, of course not," being so upset himself at the time he could not think who Margo Channing was. She went on referring to her, and Johnson began to think, "Who the hell is Margo Channing? Is it somebody out of Shakespeare that I've forgotten?" He finally got out of the dressing room and went home. He told Dorris about the scene and Davis' reference to Margo Channing. Dorris immediately asked, "Wasn't that the name of the woman she played in *All About Eve?*"

Johnson said, "Oh, how can a man be so stupid. Of course she was talking about her last big hit part."

The next day Davis did not show up for work. Johnson explained what he had said to Gary Merrill, who had heard Davis' version and had unfortunately tried to explain that Johnson did not want to make her angry. She had then screamed so much that she had lost her voice and was not able to work for several days. When she did come back her voice was still hoarse, which Johnson felt fitted the part perfectly.

In the early fifties, Twentieth Century-Fox did a series of such episodic pictures. Johnson also got drafted for a collection of short stories that eventually carried the title *O. Henry's Full House.* Johnson's contribution was the screenplay for the episode based on *The Ransom of Red Chief,* a tale of two men who kidnap such a terror of a brat that they have to pay the family to take him back. He wrote it with the idea that the leading parts should be played by Clifton Webb and William Demarest. The roles were finally played by Fred Allen and Oscar Levant, and the episode was directed by Howard Hawks. So many changes were made in the screenplay during the shooting, and the tone became so extremely farcical, that Johnson requested his name be taken off the credits of the picture, even though a large portion of his original dialogue remained in the sequence.[2] Johnson did not feel the final form of the sequence represented his work.

In early 1951, Zanuck indicated to all the producers at Fox a need for more pictures each year, and he asked them to consider ways they could increase their output. Johnson responded by saying he could probably be responsible for at least two more pictures a year under the proper conditions. Since he had felt he had to write all the scripts himself when he had tried to be a producer in the thirties, he suggested to Zanuck that he have an assistant who would be on the lookout for stories.[3] The assistant could sit down with a writer and work out a treatment. The assistant, the writer, and Johnson could then meet and work out how the story could be handled. The writer would then do a first draft and bring it back to Johnson, who would at that point decide whether to rework the material himself. Johnson suggested David Hempstead be hired as his assistant. Hempstead had been Johnson's assistant at Fox and then a producer at RKO on his own, and was, by the early fifties, available. He was hired, and he provided the basic ideas for the Louis Calhern–Zsa Zsa Gabor and Eddie Bracken–Mitzi Gaynor stories in Johnson's next picture, another episodic film finally titled *We're Not Married*. The system lasted for less than a year. Johnson found he still felt he had to do it all himself to get the material written to his satisfaction.

Johnson began preparing *My Cousin Rachel* with George Cukor, the director of such hits as *Dinner at Eight, David Copperfield, The Philadelphia Story,* and *Camille.* One of the first possibilities Cukor suggested for the part of Rachel, the woman who may or may not have murdered her husband, was Greta Garbo. While Cukor went off to Italy to check on locations, Johnson, in spite of his opinions about performers, attempted to convince Garbo to come out of retirement for the part. He got as far as talking to her on the phone, as he reported to Cukor in a letter:

> She couldn't have been more charming or adamant. She repeated her several emotional reasons for not wishing to come back into pictures and did this so winningly that I was presently enthusiastically on her side, in fact provided her with several additional reasons which up to that moment she hadn't thought of. The passion was so evident in my voice and manner that she quite prudently avoided any suggestion of a meeting in person. This was no time for any of us to lose our heads.

The part went to Olivia de Havilland, and Cukor eventually left the picture because of differences with Johnson about their approaches to the story.

One of the problems in preparing *My Cousin Rachel* was casting the role of Philip Ashley, the young man who has an affair with Rachel. In early 1952, Johnson talked to Zanuck about the possibility of bringing over a young British actor whom Humphrey Bogart and Lauren Bacall had seen on the stage and recommended to Johnson. Johnson obtained a print of a low-budget film the actor had done and became convinced the actor would be right for the part. When Cukor was in Europe before he withdrew from the picture, he shot some footage of the actor, which was sent back to Hollywood. Zanuck and Johnson looked at the film, and Zanuck cabled Cukor to hire him for the part. And so Richard Burton was brought to this country.

Johnson remembered his first meeting with Burton:

> He came in my office with his agent. We sat there talking. He was a scruffy looking fellow, and after we'd got a little chummy, he said, "How do you get a dame in New York?"
> I said, "To tell you the truth, I don't know. That doesn't mean that the dames are not there. I know there are call girls, I think you can get them, but I've never had occasion to do that, so I would know. If somebody asked me in New York how to get a hold of a hooker tonight I wouldn't know what to say."
> He said, "Well, I nearly went crazy."
> I said, "How long were you there?"
> He said, "Three days."
> I thought, "Jesus Christ, what kind of man is this?"

Johnson was enormously impressed with Burton's passion as an actor, too. He came home one night and told Dorris, "This is the first time I've ever heard my lines read as though they were better than they were." Johnson was stunned by Burton's energy. Johnson was on the set one day when Burton had to climb a wall while saying a line. The wall had been prepared with little footholds, so he had no trouble climbing, but he did have trouble with the dialogue. Henry Koster, the director, told him that if it was too difficult to do the line while he was climbing he could say it when he got up, but as Johnson said later, "He felt that he ought to be able to do it. He felt: on foot, on horseback, or flat on my ass, I'm an actor and I ought to be able to say the line no matter what the hell I'm doing." He kept trying to get it right, and one time, after not getting it, he dropped to the ground and started to beat his hands against the wall. Johnson thought he had been bitten by a snake in the vines, but Burton was just upset with himself at missing the lines.

In the early fifties Hollywood was desperately coming up with gimmicks to try to lure audiences away from television. Twentieth Century-Fox threw its prestige behind CinemaScope, the anamorphic system which stretched the screen's proportions to 2½-to-1. Somebody naturally asked Nunnally Johnson if he would have to do anything different in writing pictures for CinemaScope. In view of the mail-slot shape of the screen, Johnson said drily, "I guess I'll have to put the paper in the typewriter sideways." It was not long before he was involved in stretching stories to fit the new screen shape.

It was, in a way, ironic that Fox introduced and pushed CinemaScope. Not only did the early CinemaScope lenses destroy the photographic gloss of the Fox films of the forties, but the emphasis at Fox under Zanuck had always been less on visual spectacle and more on story elements. The creative people at Fox, from Zanuck down, were simply not used to thinking of spectacle as the major ingredient in films. Zanuck began to pass up stories that he might otherwise have jumped at, such as *On the Waterfront,* in favor of what amounted to "B" picture material like *Beneath the Twelve Mile Reef* and *Untamed* simply because the latter kinds of stories were more suitable to CinemaScope.[4]

Perhaps the desirability of doing a project with "scope" led Johnson to one of several of his unproduced projects in the fifties. Shortly after the introduction of CinemaScope, Johnson began work on a script for a film dealing with the myth of the Wandering Jew. He found an old play dealing with the subject by E. Temple Thurston, which he began to adapt. The play was a sentimental religious melodrama of the worst sort, and Johnson borrowed almost none of the fustian dialogue. He used Thurston's four-part story of the character of the Jew at the time of the Cruxifixion, during the Crusades, in Palermo during the Thirteenth Century anti-Semitic persecutions, and in Spain during the Inquisition. Johnson straightened out Thurston's rather confused plot lines, but, in doing so, he makes each act so interesting in itself that the focus is shifted from the overall story line to each individual episode. The final screenplay, which was never produced, is similar in tone to Philip Dunne's screenplays for *The Robe* and *The Egyptian,* two early CinemaScope spectacles, but Dunne was much more skilled at this kind of expansive, relentlessly literate script than Johnson. Very little of Johnson's ability at capturing human feeling, one of his great strengths as a screenwriter, comes through. The script is competent but not impressive. Johnson simply had no great skill at writing the lavish spectacles seemingly required for CinemaScope.

15

"Put the Camera Here"

In 1953, Johnson directed a film for the first time, and his reason for doing so was to avoid being bored to death. In 1950, Johnson had gone to London with the production of *The Mudlark*. He found that, without the normal activity of the studio to keep him occupied, he had nothing to do. He said, "My position during those several months was uncomfortable to me. I can't lean over the director's shoulder and I didn't want to. I could generally occupy my time writing another script, which I was doing then with *The Desert Fox*. I don't know what a producer does if he only has one picture. When we decided to do *Night People* in Berlin, this experience suddenly occurred to me. So I became a director just so I wouldn't have to sit in my hotel room all day."[1]

Johnson's decision to direct can also be seen as part of the pattern of his career since 1943. He had left Fox for what he hoped would be the greater creative stimulation of independent production. When that change was not successful, he returned to Fox and Zanuck. At the same time, Johnson's scripts began to change. He was dealing more with themes and characterization than he had in the past. The move into directing in 1953 was another attempt at change.

Johnson brought up the possibility of his directing *Night People* on a visit to Zanuck's house in Palm Springs. Zanuck told him that it would be all right with him if Gregory Peck, who was to star in the picture, approved. Zanuck said, "Peck's a big star, and he's got a right to an O.K. on the director, and he certainly has the right to say he doesn't want a man who's never directed before." Johnson went over to London to talk to Peck about it and asked if he had any objections to his directing the picture. Johnson recalled that Peck looked a little surprised and said, "Well, you wouldn't be the first writer that turned director. It's all right with me."

Johnson was not totally without directorial experience. He had started

146

to co-direct *The Pied Piper*, but soon he was only too happy to leave the cast of child actors to Irving Pichel. He found it a bit easier to get along with adult actors. On *The Senator Was Indiscreet* and *Mr. Peabody and the Mermaid*, William Powell came in to see Johnson and asked him to read for him each of the lines in the script. Johnson recalled, "In the two pictures I made with him, we'd sit in the office for a whole afternoon, four or five hours. No line was too small or unimportant. He said, 'I've just got to know how you meant it because that's part of a mosaic.' You don't catch many of them doing that."[2]

Johnson continued this instruction with Powell on *How to Marry a Millionaire* and on that picture extended it, with the approval of the director, Jean Negulesco, to the entire cast. While Negulesco was composing the shots, Johnson would hold line rehearsals with the cast, giving them the emphasis and the tempo of the lines.[3]

When Johnson was in London on his way to Berlin, he ran into Henry Hathaway, who had directed *The Desert Fox*. Hathaway said, "What's this I hear about you going to direct a picture?"

Johnson said, "Yes, I'm going to have a go at it."

Hathaway said, "You'll be no good, you know."

"Maybe not. You may be quite right."

"You know why? Because you're not a bastard. Look at the big directors, all of them bastards, John Ford, George Stevens, Fritz Lang, Willie Wyler." Hathaway was obviously expecting Johnson to add, "And you," but Johnson found it a greater temptation not to. Hathaway continued, "You don't like a row. You won't make a fuss. You'll compromise."

Johnson replied, "I don't think I'll compromise on big things."

Hathaway said, "But suppose you make one compromise a day. The picture takes thirty-six days to shoot. You've made thirty-six compromises in an hour and a half's entertainment. You think that doesn't matter?"

Johnson said, "I don't think it matters enough and besides, I'm not that dedicated. I'm not going to spend my life arguing with people when I don't think it makes that much difference."[4]

The production of *Night People* began with a series of exterior locations in Berlin. Johnson remembered the first set-up vividly:

The first scene I was going to direct was on the roof of a building in Berlin. There were about six people in this scene, including Greg Peck. When we got it into shape where we thought we'd have a take, and I was just about to say, "Well, uh, let's go," I looked over at Greg. He was off camera, and he was looking at me and I thought to myself, "I know what this guy's thinking. He's saying to himself, 'Have I made a bloody, Goddamned fool of myself? This is it. This is the moment. Have I committed myself to a guy who may not know what the hell he's doing the next minute?' " When we looked at each other, we both realized what each other was thinking and busted out laughing. Then we were off, and it worked out all right, or well enough.

Back in Hollywood, people were not so sure it was working out that well. In early September 1953, they began to read front page reports in the *Hollywood Reporter* about difficulties between Peck and Johnson. The reports, appearing only in the *Reporter*, continued until it was announced that Zanuck was going to have to go to Europe to see what the difficulties were.

Johnson and Peck were baffled. They were getting along fine, as far as both of them knew, and were completely surprised when they heard from their friends back in Hollywood of difficulties between them. Both look forward to the impending visit of Zanuck in hopes that the matter might be explained to them. Zanuck never showed up. He called Johnson from Paris and asked, "How are things with you and Peck?"

"Fine."

"No fights?"

"No."

"Then I don't really need to come up there, do I?"

"No."

"O.K. Then I won't."[5]

When Johnson returned to Hollywood in late October, he found the supposed feud between Peck and himself was a prime subject of gossip, but nobody seemed to know the truth. He wrote to Peck that he felt Zanuck had

> seized on a rumor and had used it as an excuse for getting out of the country before *The Robe* opened. It seemed strange to me that he didn't want to attend that mighty affair but it seems quite evident that he didn't. But in fairness to him, I don't think for one moment that he had any idea that his little explanation would cause such a hubbub.[6]

It was not as simple as that. Zanuck apparently had a girl friend in Paris he wished to visit, and, rather than just making a trip to Paris to see her or bringing her to Hollywood, he himself invented the story of the Peck-Johnson feud and "leaked" it to Billy Wilkerson, the editor of the *Hollywood Reporter*, thus creating his own excuse for a trip.[7]

The experience of directing the film was a pleasurable one for Johnson, primarily because of the people he worked with. He loaded the cast with old friends like Buddy Ebsen, whom Johnson had known as a dancer in New York, and Peter Van Eyck, the German actor whom Dorris had stabbed with a pair of scissors in *The Moon Is Down*. Johnson and Peck had known each other since *The Gunfighter*, and, as Johnson said, "Peck's a genuinely nice man. He's stubborn. He's very opinionated, and sometimes I thought he was rather slow-witted, but he really isn't. He just has to be convinced of the necessity of doing something before he'll do it. It can become pretty exasperating because it takes up time, but he helped me on *Night People* in so many ways. He would make suggestions, but never try to impose his ideas."[8]

Working in Berlin in 1953 had its nerve-wracking aspects. They filmed one scene near the Brandenburg Gate, which was heavily guarded on the Russian side. The scene involved a girl in a telephone booth, and as with such sequences, the unit had its own portable telephone booth, which could be set up to get the best camera angle. As they tried out the booth in various locations, the top of the Brandenburg Gate began to fill up with Russian soldiers with binoculars, trying to figure out what sort of American trap this moveable phone booth was.[9]

The story of *Night People* deals with the attempts of the American military police in Berlin to get back an American soldier kidnapped by the Russians. The Americans—both the M.P.'s, led by Gregory Peck, and the officials of the State Department—are hampered in their efforts by the intervention of the boy's father, a wealthy industrialist, played by Broderick Crawford. The industrialist keeps wanting to buy off the Russians, but the Peck character works out a swap arrangement with the Russians, who want two elderly German citizens. In the end, the American colonel double-crosses the Russians and sends them not the Germans, but a woman who has been acting as a double agent and has betrayed and caused the death of Peck's Russian counterpart.

Johnson had no particular intention of doing a propaganda picture. He saw the film as just a thriller. In one of the sequences, he has the Peck character comment that he is "going up a dark alley, just like Mickey Spillane." Johnson, in what he described as a "probably thoughtless, facetious moment," described the picture to the local *Time* reporter as "Dick Tracy in Berlin."

The New York Daily Worker did not view the picture as a simple thriller. David Platt's review of the picture on 20 June 1954 began by stressing Johnson's connection with *The Desert Fox*, noting that

> This evil piece of Fascism ran the gauntlet of picket lines from coast to coast and overseas, then passed into history, but not before providing Nunnally Johnson with the necessary experience for coping with his filthy chore—a war-inciting anti-Soviet film.

Pauline Kael, on the other hand, in a *Film Quarterly* article entitled "Morality Plays Right and Left," attacked *Night People* for its simpleminded approach. She insisted the film's anti-Communism was merely window dressing to give the film a more modern look, whereas, in fact, the melodrama of the film is like that of the anti-Nazi films of the World War II era. Her view was that the Americans are seen strictly as heroes and the Russians as the bad guys, but she ignores the fact that, among other things, the character played by Peck respects his Russian counterpart. Replying to the question, "And he's still a friend of yours?" he says, "One of the best."

Both the critical and financial receptions of *Night People* were good, and, perhaps more importantly, Zanuck's reaction to the picture was good enough for Johnson to continue directing the scripts he wrote for the next seven years. His methods of directing were similar to those he recommended to George S. Kaufman. Johnson depended on his cameraman and his cutter. He would stage the sequence the way he thought best to convey what he had written in the script, and then he would ask the cameraman and cutter to look at the scene and figure out how many setups they would need to cover the scene. On *Night People* and three other of the eight films he directed, Johnson's cameraman was a Hollywood veteran, Charles G. Clarke, who was consistently assigned by Zanuck to work with writers such as George Seaton and Philip Dunne on the first pictures they directed. Clarke describes working with Johnson on *Night People:* "He was wonderful. He said, 'I'm a writer. I don't know anything about camera technique. I'd appreciate your help.' So you try to help them. You don't tell them what to do. You don't set up a camera and say, 'I'm going to do it here.' You don't take that attitude at all. You suggest. You help keep all the mechanics in film making straight. You can suggest when we should move in for a closer shot, and the techniques of having to put a film together with the necessary cuts."[10]

The editor on three of the eight films Johnson directed was his daughter, Marjorie Fowler. She had completed the editing of *Woman in the Window,* was the sole editor on *Mr. Peabody and the Mermaid,* and, by the middle of the fifties, was working regularly as a cutter. She ran into a problem with studio protocol at Twentieth Century-Fox when she returned there after having worked at other studios. She had been an apprentice at Fox in the early forties and was still considered an apprentice by many of the people there. She suggested to Johnson the possibility of her coming down to the set and checking each scene for possible additional angles that she as the cutter might require. Johnson thought it was a good idea, but editors had not been on the set before, and she met resistance from some of the old studio hands. Johnson insisted. He was, in fact, surprised that an editor could or would come down to the set to help out, and wished he had thought of the possibility before. He was helped by what he called the "movie magic" she was able to work. At one point in the cutting of *Three Faces of Eve,* he expressed unhappiness over a scene between Lee J. Cobb and David Wayne. Marjorie offered to recut it the way he wanted, but he said the problem was in the writing; what needed to be done was to change the order of the lines. Marjorie had him rewrite the scene the way he wanted it, and then she was able to recut the completed scene to fit the changed order of the lines.

What is characteristic of Johnson's work as a director is not any sort of noticeable, dazzling directorial brilliance, but simply a professional competence. Even in *Night People,* there is, in the staging of the action and the performance of the actors, a sense of ease with the procedures of film making that almost works against the attempts to create suspense. In the opening scenes involving Peck and his counterparts in the State Department, there is a feeling of easy camaraderie between the people that establishes a sense of professionalism about both them and the film. The sequence where the elderly German couple is arrested in a restaurant is done in one take, beautifully composed with Peck and Broderick Crawford at both sides of the frame in the foreground and Buddy Ebsen and the couple in the background between them. This may well have been the kind of suggestion that Clarke, the cinematographer, made but Johnson as the director had the option of staging the scene in that way or not, and Johnson is certainly the one responsible for the naturalness of the action.

On the other hand, in the direction of *Night People* there is not as much drive and tension as there might be, given the story, and the ending does not seem as forceful as it does in the screenplay. One is left with the feeling that there ought to be some sort of action sequence at the climax of the picture, either a fight or a chase. Again, when the industrialist changes his mind, deciding to let his son take his chances, the change seems to be played too abruptly by Broderick Crawford and is not as believable in the film as it is in the script.

There are many of the same kinds of virtues and faults in the other seven films he directed. In the thriller he did after *Night People, Black Widow,* there are several strikingly staged bits of business, such as Van Heflin entering and quickly leaving a cocktail party, and a witty visual introduction to a cocktail party by means of a waiter with a tray of cocktails which seem to disappear whenever the waiter brings the tray down to get through the crowd. At the same time, there is not, in *Black Widow,* anywhere near the tension that Fritz Lang gets in *Woman in the Window,* nor are there the kind of powerful performances Lang gets. Part of this is undoubtedly because Johnson had to settle for an actress he did not particularly want for the leading part, a compromise in the casting that nearly destroys the film. The actress who played the part, Peggy Ann Garner, has neither the star quality nor the acting ability to bring off the part, especially in a cast that includes Ginger Rogers, Van Heflin, Gene Tierney, and George Raft.

While Johnson was good at staging scenes, he was not a visually oriented director. There are no striking compositions or tricky camera setups in his films. His emphasis was on the story as told through the characters. He was interested in the temporal organization of the film, not its visual organization.

Johnson was the first to admit that he was not a great director. He said, "I was what you might call a run-of-the-mill director. I got the stuff, but nobody was going to say, 'This is Lubitsch doing it,' and I never cared very much really. To be a director you have to be more dedicated than I am. I never spent all night thinking of how to do this or that. I generally came on the set without knowing what was going to happen and went at it. I don't know that I, or the picture, suffered in any way by that, but nobody ever gave me an Oscar for it either."

16
The Changing of the Guard

Zanuck was tired, and with good reason. To add to other postwar problems, the motion picture industry had been hit with anti-trust action by the United States Government. As early as the thirties, several independent theatre owners had suggested it was a violation of the Sherman Anti-Trust Act for the motion picture companies to have holdings in all three sides of the business: production, distribution, and exhibition. In 1944, the Justice Department began proceedings against the movie industry. The case was concluded in 1948 with a Supreme Court opinion which led to consent decrees in which the industry agreed to separate the production and distribution sides of the business from the exhibition side. On the simplest level, it meant the movie companies were not going to own their own theatres any more. On a deeper level, it meant the beginning of the end of the major studio system of producing motion pictures.

Without effective control of their own theatres, the studios had no guarantees of playing time for a program of films, which, in turn, meant that it became more difficult to plan a production schedule for a year. It then became less possible for a major studio to keep under contract a large group of actors, writers, directors, producers, and technicians. There was no longer any guarantee of work for a full year as there had been in the past, and the overhead caused by paying weekly salaries was too large for the companies to afford. The studios began to let their creative personnel go. But when the studios found themselves hiring back many of the people they had fired—for one picture rather than on a lengthy contract—the writers, directors, producers, and particularly the stars insisted not only on more money, but on more control.

Zanuck found himself less and less in control of a major studio. In former days, he had been able to cast the writer, director, and stars for a picture from a card index file on his desk. Now, he had to negotiate with each actor, each writer, each director, and, worse, each agent. In 1956, he told Abel Green of *Variety*, "It's now a new game between studios and agents on how to outsmart these smart cookies with their terms, percentages, 'must have script approval,' and all the rest of their demands which reflect the present law of supply and demand. Result is that if I'm being employed for my talents, only 10% roughly nowadays goes into actual production and 90% into administrative and executive chores."[1]

Those who had been working for Zanuck for many years had noticed the difference in Zanuck. He did not have the energy or drive he had had previously, particularly in story conferences. More and more, he wanted to devote himself to independent production, and, in 1952, he had his contract amended to permit independent production of films, although in fact he continued to produce films for Fox. By 1956, he had decided to leave Fox and Hollywood altogether, a move prompted not only by his feelings about his job, but also by the disintegration of his marriage of thirty-two years. Zanuck told his biographer, "My mood was to escape, to get away from the scene, the social scene, the studio scene, and everything connected with it."[2]

The Man in the Gray Flannel Suit did not begin as one of Darryl Zanuck's personal productions. It was originally assigned to Robert Jacks, Zanuck's son-in-law and a successful producer of low- and medium-budget pictures. As Johnson began to develop the material, it became apparent that his approach was closer to Zanuck's and Gregory Peck's, and Zanuck took over as producer. He indicated to Johnson that they would work as they had done since *The Grapes of Wrath*, with Johnson writing a first draft, and then Zanuck making suggestions on it. But there was a difference. Nearly all Zanuck's notes on the first draft of *The Grapes of Wrath* dealt with ways to make the story move more effectively. His notes on the first draft of *The Man in the Gray Flannel Suit* emphasize the importance of themes.[3]

The story deals with Tom Rath and his family. Rath has gone to work temporarily as a public relations man for Hopkins, an important broadcasting executive. Rath feels the pressure of working for a man like Hopkins and eventually turns down a permanent job with him. Johnson's first draft deals almost entirely with Rath and the problems with his family, and Hopkins appears in only three small scenes. The point Zanuck makes most strongly in his notes is that Hopkins should be a major character. Hopkins is in the long line of Zanuck-like characters who appear in Zanuck's films, which perhaps gives some indication of Zanuck's personal interest in the material. Like Zanuck, Hopkins is having problems with his marriage. It was Zanuck who suggested using Hopkins' speech to Rath when he turns down the permanent job:

Big successful businesses just aren't BUILT by men like you!—
nine to five and home and family! You LIVE on 'em—but you never
BUILD one! Big successful businesses are built by men like me—who
give up everything they've got—who live it—body and soul!—who lift
it up regardless of anybody or anything else! And without men like
me, there wouldn't BE any big successful businesses . . . My mistake
was in BEING one of those men.

Johnson expanded the character of Hopkins, including his wife and
daughter as characters, and, as a result, the script is less focused in
terms of the story lines, but what becomes its main theme is particularly
appropriate to the fifties. The story now centers on Rath being torn
between working for the interests of society, as represented by Hopkins's
work for mental health, or his personal interests, especially his family.
In the thirties and forties there had been an interest in social questions
which made possible the success of such Zanuck films as *The Grapes of
Wrath, Gentleman's Agreement,* and *Pinky*. In the fifties, there seemed to
be more of a turning inward, a greater concern with personal rather than
social values. At the end of *The Grapes of Wrath,* Tom Joad leaves his
family to try to learn how to help all the poor people. At the end of *The
Man in the Gray Flannel Suit,* Tom Rath passes up an important job
because of his family.

If *The Man in the Gray Flannel Suit* is representative of the fifties in
its themes, it is perhaps even more so in its production. The story line, or
lines, is diffuse, and the film is overlong. The elaborate physical
production Zanuck provided makes the film seem glossy and overstuffed;
color and CinemaScope emphasize the looseness of the storytelling. The
story, under Johnson's direction, does have its compelling moments, and
the acting is good, with one exception. Jennifer Jones plays Betsy Rath,
Tom's wife, in a rather neurotic fashion, and the character is not as
interesting on the screen as she is in the script.

The picture was filmed in late 1955 and early 1956 and edited after
Zanuck left in February 1956 to set up his independent production unit,
with Zanuck sending detailed notes back to Dorothy Spencer, the cutter,
on what was to be done.

Zanuck's position as head of production was now taken over by Buddy
Adler, a producer Zanuck had brought to the studio. The power, in fact,
had shifted to Spyros Skouras, president of Twentieth Century-Fox.
While Zanuck had been head of production, he had been strong enough
to fight off the efforts of Skouras to involve himself in the production of
films, but Adler simply did not have that kind of personality or authority.

Johnson had never been particularly fond of Skouras. It was Skouras
who taunted Johnson, every time they met, about Gregory Peck's

mustache in *The Gunfighter* and how much money it had cost the company. When Johnson was in London researching *The Desert Fox*, he arranged a meeting with retired British General Auchinleck Johnson made the mistake of mentioning this to Skouras, who promptly invited himself to the meeting. He literally drove Auchinleck away by monopolizing the conversation with lengthy stories of how the Skouras family had won the war singlehandedly by sending Greek ships full of food.

If Johnson did not care for Skouras before the premiere of *The Man in the Gray Flannel Suit*, he cared even less after it. Johnson described the screening in a letter to Zanuck:

> I sat directly in front of Spyros and I can tell you that this is not the best way to look at a picture. When he was not nervously kicking the back of my seat, he was heaving and groaning and yawning, for he had been on the plane the night before and hadn't gotten any sleep, and in addition to that, whenever a point came up on the screen that he liked, he hit me on the back. I didn't mind this so much. It was the constant kicking of the seat that made me unhappy. But what could I do? Tell the president of the company to keep his Goddamn foot still?[4]

Johnson had good reason to be apprehensive about the growing interference by Skouras in the production side of the company. Skouras fancied himself as having the ability to think up titles for pictures, as he had with *Everybody Does It*. This made him rather difficult about titles, as in the case of a script Johnson wrote in the late fifties which was variously titled *Flaming Lance, The Brothers of Flaming Lance, Flaming Arrow, The Brothers of Flaming Arrow*, and which was finally called *Flaming Star* when it was produced in 1960. At one point in the discussion about the title, Johnson wrote to Adler, "Skouras doesn't like *Flaming Arrow* and he doesn't like *The Brothers*. This leaves us with *Of*. So apparently we'll just have to build a new title around *Of*."[5]

Skouras was also responsible for the final decision not to film *The Wandering Jew*. Johnson had been working on the screenplay since 1953 with Zanuck's approval, and, after Zanuck left, with the apparent approval of the studio heads. He and his research associate, Joseph Gaer, spent considerable time not only insuring that the story was historically and theologically accurate, but that it would not be offensive. Johnson checked out the script with four different rabbis and a man from the Jewish Community Relations Council, as well as with a professor of literature at the Catholic Loyola University in Los Angeles. Skouras finally turned the picture down, not on the legitimate grounds of the lack of quality of the script, but on the grounds that it was in some way anti-Semitic. Johnson said, "The only way I can figure it is that he was anti-Semitic, because he found so much anti-Semitism that nobody else found. George Stevens told me that Skouras did not want to make *The Diary of Anne Frank* because it was anti-Semitic. George asked him, 'Whoever said a thing like that?' and Skouras said, 'Bernie Gimbel told me.' I thought, 'My God, who's making pictures now, department store owners?' I sent the script to Sam Goldwyn. He read it and said, 'Skouras is yellow. Skouras is a coward. There's nothing to take exception to in this story.' "[6]

Johnson had, at least in the beginning, hopes that if he could get no assistance from Skouras, he might get help from Buddy Adler. Shortly after Adler took over as head of production, Johnson made a curious admission in a memo to him:

> It is an odd fact that the projects assigned to me by Darryl almost invariably turn out better than those I pick for myself, which leads me to believe that I leave something to be desired as a picker of stories. Accordingly, I would like to look to you for suggestions for my next one. . . . All I ask of it is that it provide something that I will make some money out of . . .

and then, in a curious, almost plaintive last line, Johnson added, "Please answer this. I have no file for 'Adler, Buddy—Interoffice Memos' and I would like very much to have one."[7]

Adler proved to be a disappointment. They were personally friendly, and Adler could be quite charming, but Johnson recalled, "Adler looked like a very fine, intelligent man, but it was a real facade. I'm afraid that was like working with a nobody. I don't know how Zanuck decided to put him in there, if he did. Adler wasn't very bright and he did us all harm while he was there."[8]

Johnson's primary objection to Adler seemed to be that he wasn't Zanuck. He was not a story man. He had an assistant who read scripts and made notes on them for the writers. He would keep telling Johnson, "I'll be dictating my notes shortly." When Johnson would try to discuss the scripts or particular story points with Adler, it would become apparent that Adler had not read the scripts himself. Johnson found it more and more difficult to get an answer from Adler, not only about scripts, but about details of production, since Johnson was concerned about the decline in the quality of the physical production being provided for Fox films in the late fifties.

Perhaps the change from Johnson's relationship with Zanuck to his relationship with Adler can best be seen in the tone of his memos. In the

correspondence with Zanuck, there is an almost relaxed feeling, a sense
of two professionals going about their business. Johnson is making
suggestions knowing that even if they are not accepted, they will be
listened to and respected. There is a confident tone about them. There is
no such sense of ease in Johnson's memos to Adler. The nearest thing to
an exception to this is his memo on *The Three Faces of Eve:*

> Dear Buddy:
>   I did everything I could possibly think of to make this picture long
> enough to justify an intermission. I know how important length is
> these days and how proud it would have made all of us to be able to
> say that we too have an intermission to save our audiences from
> paralysis. But it's no use lying to you. You have a watch. The truth is
> that the picture still runs well under two hours. I'm terribly sorry. All
> we can do now, I suppose, is aim our campaign at restless people,
> with tender behinds, and make an all-out effort next time at that big
> saddle-sore audience. Repent![9]

To Johnson's astonishment, at one point Adler suggested this picture be
introduced by a title song. Johnson replied in a memo, "Frankly, I don't
want to have anything to do with it. And if it cost more than a dollar and a
quarter, my vote is no."[10]

Johnson's first picture for Adler was a play he had turned down once
before, *Oh Men! Oh Women!* The script shows the lack of a good story
editor. The dialogue scenes become very repetitive, along with the whole
one-joke premise of the piece: a psychoanalyst who thinks he is above
ordinary emotions discovers he is not. The play was by Edward
Chodorov, a blacklisted writer, who, in order to sell his script to the
movies, had to agree his name would not appear in the credits of the film.
Johnson discovered this after filming of the picture had been completed,
and he complained to Adler. Johnson's position was that leaving
Chodorov's name off the credits was not only objectionable on moral
grounds, but it would leave them wide open for an attack on the picture
by the New York press when the picture opened. The credits remained
without Chodorov's name, and Johnson was so incensed by this decision
he voluntarily took his name off the credits of the picture as the
screenwriter, so that the picture has no writing credits at all. The
absence of Chodorov's name was merely commented on by the review-
ers.[11]

In 1956, Johnson had become interested in a book he had seen in
galley proofs prior to its publication. The book was originally called *A
Case of Multiple Personality,* and was a case history written by two
Georgia doctors, Corbett H. Thigpen and Hervey M. Cleckley. Johnson

suggested to Adler that the story would make a good film, and, since the book was not published yet, it might be worthwhile to get together with the two doctors and the publisher and come up with a more appealing title. It was Johnson who suggested *The Three Faces of Eve*.

The single biggest problem in the production of the film was the casting of the leading role, that of the young Georgia housewife with a triple personality.[12] A number of top stars were discussed, including Lana Turner, Olivia de Havilland, Jean Simmons, Doris Day, and Jennifer Jones, who told Johnson that "she would be terrified to do the part." Johnson thought of Judy Garland and, in an effort to convince her, he went up to Las Vegas, where she was performing at the time. Johnson took with him films that Dr. Thigpen had provided of the real Eve going through her personality changes. Garland had read the script and was baffled by it, thinking it was some sort of comedy. She simply did not believe that such a thing could happen, so Johnson took along the films to convince her. After the last show, about three in the morning, they set up a projector and a screen and Johnson showed the films. Johnson recalled that, as soon as she saw the films, she understood the part immediately and told Johnson, "You've got to swear that I play this part. We've got to cut our wrists and mingle our blood."

Johnson replied, "That's what I'm up here for. Wrist cutting." Johnson returned to Hollywood and soon thereafter got a note from Garland saying she could not do the role. The studio had by now given up on the idea of getting a star, and Johnson was willing to listen to anybody with a suggestion. Somebody mentioned a young actress under contract to Fox who had done two pictures and some television and stage work—Joanne Woodward. Johnson looked at a television show she had done and she was hired without even a screen test. Woodward, who was in New York at the time, was scheduled to appear in another film for the studio, but was told by her agent she was to do the roles of Eve instead. The agent gave her a copy of the script to read on the train. She recalls, "I read it and almost got off the train in Chicago." She, too, was afraid of the part.

In Hollywood for her first meeting with Johnson, she asked him, "Do you want me to do it with a Southern accent?"

"Over my dead body," Johnson replied. "If there's anything I loathe, it's a phony Southern accent, and I can detect it."

She said, "It's not phony. I'm from Thomasville, Georgia."

Johnson replied, "That'll be useful then." It turned out to more useful than Johnson perhaps realized at the time. Woodward looked at the films of the real Eve, and the only thing she consciously borrowed from them was Eve's accents. When the real Eve changed personalities, she also changed accents. Since this was taken directly from the real Eve,

Woodward was upset when at least one reviewer criticized her for "losing" her accent in the personality of the third face, Jane.

The biggest change from the real Eve was in the speed of the transformations from one personality to another. In the doctors' films, these were instantaneous, but Johnson felt audiences would not accept such abrupt shifts, so he had Woodward slow them down. Johnson also aided the illusion by shooting the first changes so that they occur in the film offscreen, while the camera is on Lee J. Cobb, who played the doctor. This increases the impact of the later shifts, particularly in the sequence where Woodward goes through all three personalities in a single take.

Johnson recalled that she was easy to direct in the part: "She could have almost directed herself. She's very, very knowledgeable. You can't teach an actor anything on the stage once they get started anyway. You have to use what you've got. And she had it." As for Johnson's modesty about his contribution as a director, Woodward says, "Don't be fooled for a minute. He's got the greatest thing a director can have: taste. And he trusted the actors and he let them know he trusted them. It was a very difficult part, but it was one of the happiest experiences I've had." She won an Academy Award in 1958 for her performance.

17

Let Somebody Else Say, "Put the Camera Here"

The Man Who Understood Women could be considered—in spite of, or perhaps because of, its failure—the quintessential Nunnally Johnson film of the fifties. It was the last film he wrote and directed at 20th Century-Fox.

Johnson's script was based on a 1953 novel by Romain Gary, *Colors of the Day,* which was brought to Johnson's attention in 1957. The Gary book is primarily about Marco Rainier, a professional soldier who is in Nice at the time of the carnival, thinking philosophical thoughts about his life as a soldier. He meets Ann Garantier, a film star married to Willie Bauché, an actor-writer-producer-director. Ann has told Willie that their partnership will be only an artistic one. He intends to try to make love to her on their wedding night but falls asleep while talking about his next film. Ann has been constantly looking for love, which she finds with Rainier. Willie, in desperation, hires two men to kill Ann, but one of the killers shoots the other and leaves. Willie has, meanwhile, decided that he does not want Ann to die, and, in chasing after the two killers, falls over a cliff and is killed.

Johnson reworked the material considerably. The focus is shifted to Willie Bauché and his marriage to Ann. In the book, the similarities between Willie and Orson Welles are obvious: his reputation for genius, particularly with those who "identify art with failure," his marriage to a movie star, and his escape to Europe after the failure of his pictures. Johnson wanted Orson Welles for the part, but Buddy Adler told him in effect to "forget it." Eventually, the role was played by Henry Fonda. In Johnson's script the correlation of Willie with a real-life figure becomes blurred. There are still the Wellesian traits, but there is also the emphasis on Willie's having won Oscars for writing and directing two years in a row in the late forties, which suggests Joseph Mankiewicz. There is even more correlation with Johnson himself, which produces some strange effects, as when Willie tells Ann:

> I've got a confession to make to you, darling. All reports to the contrary notwithstanding—I am a very old-fashioned fellow. This is strictly confidential, you understand. You have read that I was born in Shanghai, the love child of a Chinese mandarin and a beautiful but tubercular White Russian Grand Duchess—how these stories get started is beyond me!—but the truth is—I was born and brought up in the State of Louisiana—in a flea-bitten little town near New Orleans—and beneath this gaudy haberdashery beats the simple heart of a Methodist. You won't repeat this, will you?

Perhaps the final line has a touch of Herman Mankiewicz in it too. Willie is also given lines that are almost pure Nunnally Johnson:

> Scarcely a man is still alive whose hair doesn't stand on end at the very thought of marriage. Marriage is the last frontier of life—a dark and unexplored continent—steaming with impenetrable jungles, bottomless rivers, and mysterious horrors beyond the human imagination—and few men face it without remembering what happened to Dr. Livingstone.

In the movie, Ann marries Willie because she loves him. On their wedding night, he is on the phone getting her out of her contract with the studio, since his gift of love will be to make her immortal through his independent productions. In the end, she comes back to Willie, who has only been hurt in the fall, and not killed as in the book. She is beside Willie's bed in the hospital, and, as the script says, "The look that they exchange is one of grave acknowledgement and forgiveness, of understanding and acceptance." Willie admits that he has been a "dreamer . . . with astigmatism" and he asks Ann to marry him again. As she accepts, he begins to describe the house they will have some day. Ann begins to laugh at the idea of them living in a house, and Willie speaks the curtain line, "There you have the history of my life. Here I lie in the valley of the shadow of death, and what do I get—yoks!"

The script brings together the themes of Johnson's films of the fifties. It is primarily a re-examination of married love. Johnson is once again suggesting the complexities of marriage, as he does in *Phone Call from a Stranger, We're Not Married, Black Widow, The Man in the Gray Flannel Suit, Oh Men! Oh Women!,* and *The Three Faces of Eve,* all of which deal in either the main plot or a major subplot with the problems within marriage. Johnson is approaching marriage as a subject as Ann and Willie approach it at the end of *The Man Who Understood Women*, with "acknowledgement and forgiveness, understanding and acceptance." He is more aware of the possibilities within marriage both for problems and for individual growth.

This is not to suggest that Johnson set out consciously to do a series of films about marriage or about women in marriage. He was not that self-conscious a writer, and was not even aware of any particular trend in his writing. He said, "I can only say that every picture, or every story, was isolated. I couldn't say that I followed any trend, or any change in my viewpoint. It just depended on what story caught my attention and convinced me that I could make it into an entertaining picture. My taste may have altered. I would hope that it broadened. When I was beginning, I would never have attempted anything like *The Man Who Understood Women*, that complex a story about love. Let's say a certain maturity, or growth, or aging, whatever you want to call it, made me feel an interest in such situations that I never would have found when I was younger."[1]

What is notable about Johnson's women characters in the fifties is that, for the first time, he was consistently going against the trends of the films of the time. He had gotten into his personal feelings so much in his writing that he was getting away from the elements the audiences of the time were accepting, which is perhaps one reason why several of his fifties films did not do as well at the box office as his films of the thirties and forties. In the late thirties, Johnson's women were the loyal wives, who lived exclusively in relation to their husbands. Such portraits represented one of the major trends of that period, but not the only one, as can be seen in more independent women portrayed by Katharine Hepburn and Rosalind Russell. By the fifties, however, the movies' view of women had narrowed considerably into two kinds of basic roles: the virgin princesses played by Audrey Hepburn, Grace Kelly, and Doris Day, and the sex goddesses played by Marilyn Monroe, Jayne Mansfield, and others.[2]

Johnson was aware that, in *The Man Who Understood Women*, he was dealing with a situation that was at the time rather unique in American films, the wife who has an affair and is not destroyed because of it. Johnson was attempting as well to combine farce and drama. The total combination never quite works in the script, and seems even more awkward in the film itself. Johnson, as both writer and director, is unable to bring off the same kind of mix Francois Truffaut achieved later in *Jules and Jim* and *Shoot the Piano Player*, and that Robert Benton, David Newman, and Arthur Penn were to bring to the American film in *Bonnie and Clyde*. Johnson was once again looking for a change. He was simply too well-trained in the Zanuck method of film making to bring it off.

There are other problems in the script. Observations of the movie business are not exceptionally witty. One character describes the audience at a premiere: "Among those present at the opening of Willie's first independent production—remember?—was the entire board of directors of the bank that financed it—each accompanied by a heart specialist." The dialogue between Ann and her lover seems less like dialogue than a collection of song cues end to end. Johnson admitted to a problem in writing scenes between lovers: "I think that there's a certain grace of mind for romantic scenes that I lack. I can't think of what to have them say. It's just something that I can't handle very well, and I'd just as soon avoid them if possible."

Henry Fonda's performance as Willie is brilliant, particularly in his ability to suggest an actor playing an actor playing an actor *ad infinitum*, or his ability to suggest the "simple heart of a Methodist" under the "gaudy haberdashery." But Fonda brings to the part all the accumulated imagery of his career, which is totally opposed to the flamboyant, emotionally shifty kind of character Willie is. Johnson was the beneficiary of Gary Cooper's star image in *Casanova Brown;* he is defeated here by Fonda's image, which makes it impossible to believe Fonda as this character.

Just when Johnson was in the same kind of "mood to escape" that Zanuck had been in three years before, he had an opportunity to make a picture in Italy. Johnson said, "That was the story of nothing but misfortune. I was offered a lot of money with all expenses for my family and myself to go to Rome and do this picture. Lord, it's something I never talk about, the whole thing is so distressing to me."

The story was based on a book called *The Fair Bride*, and dealt with a priest who, in the middle of the Spanish Civil War, leaves the church temporarily, has an affair with a prostitute (played by Ava Gardner), and then returns to the church. It is not the most perfect material for a Methodist from Georgia to deal with, and Johnson, used to the relatively organized procedures of a Hollywood major studio, found himself completely baffled by the way the Italians worked. Even in the beginning, the notes from the producer, Goffredo Lombardo, on the script were of very little use, since Lombardo seemed primarily concerned about the censorship problem, which led him to suggest in one note that the priest's act in leaving the church and going to the woman resulted not from passion, but from an "exuberance of conscience." When the production was actually begun, Lombardo seemed primarily concerned about how many Communists and how many Catholics were being employed by the production, and kept asking Johnson for a count of each. Johnson had no knowledge or interest in such a thing, beyond noticing that "Every day, the balance of Communists and Catholics in Italy varies, like the Stock Exchange."

The picture had a sequence to be filmed in a cathedral. Johnson recalled,

> The Italian in charge of arrangements with the Vatican got the O.K. from the Vatican to use this cathedral, except that, about every other day for two weeks leading up to this time, there was another cablegram saying that there had been a reconsideration and it would be impossible to let us use this cathedral. I said, "My God, what do we do?"
>
> The Italian said, "Send them more money. They deal with you just exactly like everybody else." So they'd send some more lira and get more permission. Even to the last day before shooting. They did that three times, and three times we raised the ante and the Vatican found reasons why it was in the best interests of the Church for us to use the thing.

On another occasion, the assistant came to Johnson and said, "Have you ever heard of the Mafia? Well, they have let us know that they will be in charge of the extras."

Johnson replied, "Extras are extras to me. This is your problem. I don't want to get in with these fellows."

The extras were divided into groups of one hundred, each with an assistant in charge. One day, one of the assistants came into the dressing room and found a crude sketch of himself with a great slash drawn on the throat with stitches on it. Johnson recalled, "He didn't stop to ask for explanations. He figured they didn't want him around, so he suddenly flew back to Rome." The Mafia-led extras at least helped make one of the scenes vividly realistic: they were supposed to charge inside the cathedral and ransack it.

Johnson not only had trouble with the Mafia, but also with his own production unit. He kept complaining that he could not see the dailies printed up in color, and he was constantly given excuses as to why he could not have them in color. No one ever told him the film was being photographed in black-and-white. Johnson was used to working in the Hollywood system where the assistant director would constantly keep him informed of how much more time until quitting time, but one night they were out on location for some night shooting, and finally, at about three in the morning, Johnson asked the assistant director, "When do we stop?"

The man replied, "Well, when you say stop."

"Well stop," Johnson said quickly. "I was waiting for somebody from the union."

The assistant director replied, "They wouldn't do anything like that. They all get extra money." The company had worked some four hours overtime. Johnson also found himself appalled by the fact that the Italian assistant directors would get the extras to cry by hitting them.

It was during the production of this picture that Johnson finally decided to give up directing. He remembered the night vividly. The company was filming on location in Sicily, and Johnson was setting up a night scene in which Joseph Cotten was crawling along a field near a rock. Johnson told the cameraman, "Put the camera here," and then immediately said to himself, "What am I doing here? Two o'clock in the morning. In Sicily. At the age of sixty. On a slippery rock. On a cold night. Saying, 'Put the camera here.' Look, this is the end of it. From now on, let somebody else say, 'Put the camera here.' I'm going to be at home in bed. To hell with the night." Johnson recalled, "The day I finished the photography, I was given a ticket to leave town. I never saw the final cut. I've never seen the picture. I don't know what happened to it."

The picture was put together and eventually released in this country as *The Angel Wore Red,* but not before it had been severely edited and dubbed. One of the more curious aspects of the American version of the film is particularly bad dubbing of the character played by Vittorio DeSica, a communist general. Johnson was pleased to have the opportunity to work with DeSica: "He's a wonderful actor, a charming man, very intelligent, and he collects a thousand dollars at noon every day before going on the stage. He doesn't trust anybody. In Italy, you shoot from twelve o'clock to eight. That's in theory. But at noon they break for lunch, so you really start at one, if you can get them back. It's a very loose organization. But at twelve noon DeSica appears at the cashier's office and he wants the money, in lira. He doesn't want one of these pieces of paper that says he can get it down at the office. He wants the money right there and gets it. Then he's available for work."

The picture was a disaster both financially and as a personal experience for Johnson, and he was more than willing to "get out of town" when it was over. The family moved from Rome to London, where they found it much more enjoyable to live, and Johnson returned to writing scripts for others to direct. It was still not the best of times for him. He had been shaken by his experiences both with Fox after Zanuck left and in Rome, as well as by the complete failures of his last two pictures. He was drinking heavily again in the late fifties in Hollywood, and then in Rome and London.

Johnson's daughter Roxie, remembers that it was in London she first saw her father very drunk. The Johnsons invited James Thurber and his wife for dinner and, even before the meal, Johnson started drinking. After dinner, while Thurber was making several drawings for Roxie, Johnson started asking everybody to go home. Finally, he was demanding it, shouting it: "Everybody go home."

18
Marilyn

The major studio system was only beginning to disintegrate when Nunnally Johnson first met Marilyn Monroe. In the late forties, Johnson's agent, Johnny Hyde, brought her around to see him one day. Hyde also represented performers, and he was trying to get somebody to hire Marilyn. She had been under contract to Fox for a year in 1947 and then to Columbia in 1948, but she was now out of work. Johnson might have hired her, but he did not have any part small enough for a girl with her lack of experience. Johnson was not particularly impressed with Marilyn the first few times he met her. He remembered, "I'd see her sometimes at lunch with Johnny. She never said anything. I can't remember her saying a word. And I wasn't bowled over by her beauty, either. I thought, 'She's another one of Johnny's little girl friends.' But I must say, he died like a brave hero. Johnny had a heart attack, and the doctor told him that by leading a quiet life he could live a good many more years. Leading a quiet life meant giving up Marilyn Monroe. He wouldn't give that up. Johnny died like a man."[1]

In 1951, Marilyn went back under contract to Twentieth Century-Fox. One of the first pictures she did under the new contract was *We're Not Married*. In Marilyn's episode, she begins as the winner of a Mrs. Mississippi beauty contest and, upon discovering she is not married, enters the Miss Mississippi contest and wins that. The idea for this episode, Johnson said, "came to me out of her figure." He had seen the pin-up pictures of her that the studio was sending out and thought that, with a figure like hers, it would be easy for anyone to believe that, having won one contest, she could turn around and win the other. To add authenticity to the swimsuit competition sequences, a number of "professional bathing-beauty contestants" were hired. One day, Johnson asked one of them how she thought Marilyn would have done in a real contest. The girl said, "She'd win them all."

Johnson found Marilyn difficult to talk to. He said, "I just couldn't get to her, or feel that I had established any kind of communication with her at all. Sometimes I didn't know whether she understood what I said. When I tried to talk to her, I felt as if I was trying to talk to somebody under water."

He also felt she was obtuse. In a scene in her episode, she was remarrying her husband. By that time, they had a baby, which she held during the ceremony, and Johnson went down to the set when this sequence was being filmed. He remembered:

There she was with this baby in her arms. It was crying like hell, and Marilyn didn't even look down at it. I said to Eddie Goulding, the director, "Now look, don't you think that that's a little unbelievable? Unless she's a complete idiot, a mother would look at her crying baby and show some consideration for it."

Eddie, who agreed with everything said, "Quite true. Stop. Wait a minute." He went over and reminded her that this was her baby, and that the baby was crying, and perhaps it would be just as good to try to comfort the baby during the scene.

"My God," I said, "What kind of woman is this that wouldn't just naturally see that the baby needed some attention?" Little things like that, I must say, made me dislike her.

Johnson was quoted in the press as calling Marilyn "a phenomenon of nature, like Niagara Falls or the Grand Canyon. You can't talk to it. It can't talk to you. All you can do is stand back and be awed by it."[2] Johnson was not awed by Marilyn Monroe. He simply saw her as he saw everybody else: complete with both virtues and defects. Years later, he recalled, "She was never promiscuous, as far as I heard. From the time she fell in love with Joe DiMaggio, I'm sure she was faithful to him. My conviction is that she just bored the hell out of everybody. She just didn't have the intelligence, and she was aware she didn't have it. That's why she'd buy Dr. Eliot's Five Foot Shelf of Books and why she was busy reading this writer and that. When she married Arthur Miller, my guess is that she wasn't smart enough for him."

Under Darryl Zanuck, the emphasis at Twentieth Century-Fox was on stories, not stars. At MGM and Warner Brothers, the stories were fitted to the stars, but at Fox the opposite was true. The Fox organization had little idea how to build up Marilyn Monroe. She became a star almost accidentally, and she did so at Fox only after the emphasis on stories, which was so strong in the thirties and forties, had begun to fade in the fifties, and it was possible to do scripts with parts specifically written for her. In spite of his feelings about her, Johnson continued to write screenplays with Marilyn in mind. Her episode in *We're Not Married* was written to take advantage of her body, and the part he wrote for her in *How to Marry a Millionaire* was to present her personality in the most appealing way possible.

Johnson started off with an old play by Zoe Akins, *The Greeks Had a Word for It*, which had been filmed before in the early thirties. The play deals with three gold diggers. Schatze is good-natured, Polaire is witty and intelligent. He then added material for Betty Grable from another play, *Loco*.

How could Monroe's seeming insensitivity be played in a funny way? Johnson's solution was to make her character astigmatic and too vain to wear glasses when men were around. She keeps bumping into things and people, and she only ends up with the right man because she gets on the wrong plane when she is supposedly going off for a weekend with the wrong man. The man she sits next to on the plane also wears glasses and, in one of Johnson's most delightful scenes, he convinces her she looks better with glasses.

This is the most recognizably human of the roles Monroe played in the early part of her career. She is not just the standard dumb blonde, but a girl whose "dumbness" comes from her vulnerability and her inability to cope with her one physical defect.

Johnson was not particularly aware it was going to be done in CinemaScope when he was working on the script. He said, "They may have told me, but I didn't pay any attention to it, because my business was to get the story down on paper. It wouldn't have altered anything in the writing." *How to Marry a Millionaire* was the second film released in CinemaScope, and the dazzle of the physical production in the new process helped make the film a tremendous box office success. It is still a charming movie, if not quite as funny as *Roxie Hart*.

Because of the success of *How to Marry a Millionaire*, Johnson looked around for another vehicle for Marilyn. He again found himself combining two plays. The first play was *She Loves Me Not*, in which a chorus girl who witnessed a murder in a night club hides out from the murderer in a dormitory at Princeton. The second, *Sleep It Off*, is also set in a college, and the plot concerns a wealthy alumnus who is supposed to give money to the school. A bubble dancer is imported to impress him. She is inadvertently hypnotized by one of the students, and she pretty much goes through the story just being vacant, which is rather uninteresting to watch.

Johnson wrote the part of Curly for Monroe, but she turned it down. She wanted out of her contract with Fox, and she simply left the studio. She announced that she wanted to do more serious parts. Fox assigned the part to a young dancer recently put under contract, Sheree North, who did not have the star quality of Monroe and who, at that time, was completely unskilled as an actress. (She has since given excellent performances in films, on television, and on the stage). Johnson said, "I don't much like to think of it because it brought fame and fortune to nobody."

Johnson did not see or work with Marilyn Monroe for seven years after that, although, in 1956, he suggested her to Adler for *The Three Faces of Eve*. In early 1962, Johnson was back at Fox discussing another project. He recalled,

Somebody at the studio told me they had bought *My Favorite Wife*, the Leo McCarey picture, and they wanted me to write the script for a remake.

They had three scripts there, either whole scripts or half scripts that George Cukor, the director, gave me to read. I read them, but they were far from what I remembered the picture to be, so I said, "Let me look at the picture." They ran it for me, and I said, "I think the mistake you're making is in trying to change this. I think Leo has utilized every situation beautifully. I don't think the dialogue is the best I've ever heard, but it served its purpose. It was a successful comedy. What I would do if I were you is take a stenographer in there and just let her take down in shorthand what went on on the screen."

They said, "Why don't you do it then?"

I said, "I don't think you need what I cost for this, but that's your business. I don't except it to be very hard at all, because I don't expect to change it." So they turned it over to me and I made alterations only where the change in the period called for something. The rest of it I made just about as it was, and they were very pleased with it.

That's when I had nearly all of my experience with Marilyn. The script was for her, and as I started to work on it I heard what the situation was. Marilyn owed Fox a picture at a price that had been established some years before. Now she was getting more money on her own and resented having to do this picture. There was another side of it, though. She was slipping a bit. The last picture she'd done there, *Let's Make Love*, had not done well, and she was scared.

She sent word, "Nunnally won't write a script for me. He won't want me." Henry Weinstein, the producer, asked her why. She said, "Because I once turned down a script he wrote."

I told Henry, "You go back and tell Miss Monroe that if everybody who turned down a script I wrote was no longer a friend of mine, I wouldn't have any friends. Plenty of people have done that." But she was very wary, so I went over and had a meeting with her in the Polo Lounge at the Beverly Hills Hotel. I must say it was one of the most enchanting three hours I'd ever spent. We drank three bottles of champagne. Well, I thought I owed it to the company.

She said, "Have you been trapped into this thing like me?"

I said, "No, I haven't been trapped in the least. I think it's a good story. It was a good story when it was made before. I was offered half a dozen different things to do and I selected this." She was so wary. She was trying to figure out whether I was in on the plot or not. I think that by the time we'd finished that third bottle we were very close friends, and she believed everything I said, and I believed everything she said.

I wrote it in London. I came back here, and they wanted some revisions, so I went down to Ensenada. I couldn't write in this country because I was a resident abroad and it would mess up my income tax status. I could consult about a job, but I couldn't do actual work. After consulting, I went down to Ensenada and stayed there for about a month, doing the revisions. Marilyn came down there and so did Cukor, and we finally got something that everybody seemed quite pleased about, especially Marilyn. They called it *Something's Got to Give*.

Marilyn was like many actresses: she had no confidence in her own judgment. Helen Hayes says the same thing, "I just have to go by my first reaction. If you ask me to try to figure out whether it's right for me or not, I can't do it." I know Marilyn liked it. She thought it was very funny, and a very funny part for her, but she didn't have the courage to say so until after she talked to Dean Martin, whom they wanted to get for the man. He was the old pro as far as she was concerned. Martin told her, "It's a first-rate script. I only read fifty pages and I signed. That was enough for me." She was so relieved. It had confirmed her own opinion, which she couldn't accept by herself. When Dean Martin said so, she was ready to go along with it. She was very enthusiastic by then. When I'd first come there, she'd been so wary and so suspicious of everybody. When I left there, she was really soaring, she was so happy.

When I was getting ready to leave Marilyn offered to get up at 8:30 to drive me from the hotel to the airport. Of course, I didn't expect her to show up at that hour, but at 8:30 I got a call from Marilyn. She was down in the lobby, and she said the clerk wouldn't let her come up. I told her to go tell the clerk she was a hooker and had been "sent for." She went away and then returned to the phone a few seconds later. She was giggling and she said, "It worked, I'll be right up."

Before I had left the studio, I had a last talk with Weinstein, Cukor, and Ted Strauss, who was the story editor and who had the best analytical mind of any of them. They all expressed themselves as very well satisfied. We all shook hands and I was going to go back to London feeling, "My God, it's been a very satisfying trip." Henry and I were walking back to my office, and Henry said, "George wants a writer on the set for just little things."

I said, "What does he want a writer for? He's OK'd the script."

He said, "You know, sometimes a line doesn't carry a fellow out, or . . ."

I said, "That's what George told you, isn't it?"

He said, "Yes, oh yes."

I said, "You can do what you want, but let me tell you something. You've only done one picture here, I believe. You give a director a writer on the set, and no matter what he tells you, you've lost your picture. It won't be yours anymore, because he will tell the writer what to write. He can change it any way he wants and it will no longer be your picture or mine. I object to it, but I know there's a limit to what I can control." Henry was a bright fellow and a nice guy, but George Cukor is really an overwhelming man. He's very articulate. You have to be quite strong. I don't think I'd have been strong enough to go up against him, and I don't think Henry was.

The minute the wheels of my plane got off the ground, George had another writer changing my stuff.[3] Henry just simply didn't have the strength. When the blue pages began coming in, it was just like hitting Marilyn with a hammer. Not that these pages were worse. They may even have been better, but they were different. Her opinion turned out again not to be worth anything. Even if Dean Martin had agreed with her, there was Cukor. Most of those young actresses always think the director is God, and he was changing all these things. It shot her right down to the bottom, to the point where she wouldn't get out of bed. She was terrified. She dreaded Cukor. He terrified her and he loathed her. He told me so.

I was back in London, and I kept hearing about all the trouble that was going on. First, she tried to get me back. She went in a very devious way to her agent, to my agent, wanting me to come back and take over as the director of the picture. That would have been impossible. As a director, I didn't have the standing or the talent of Cukor. For another thing, I couldn't do anything in this country except consult. Dorris said, "Why don't you do it?"

I said, "I don't want to do it." She was absolutely infatuated with me. Not romantically. Not in the least. Nothing like that. It was just that I had become somebody she relied on and could believe in and thought could handle everything. I told Dorris, "I couldn't possibly do it. This girl is neurotic beyond description. I might go back there and they might be nutty enough to let me take George's place, which I don't think they would for one second. Two weeks later something would happen and she would come to hate me as much as she hated George. There's no relying on her. I couldn't do a thing like that. I wouldn't try it. Much too dangerous."

Marilyn kept retreating farther and farther from reality. Then they tried to slip the pages in on white paper, but she was too smart. She saw that they were alterations. Every time there was an alteration, it was just slapping her face again for having had an opinion. Finally, I read in the paper that Peter Levathes, who was head of the studio by then, said he was going to take Marilyn out of the picture. I sent him a cable, "If you're going to take anybody off of this picture, hadn't you better first decide who brings people in, George Cukor or Marilyn Monroe? You should remove George because he and Marilyn are so antipathetic." But Levathes took Marilyn out and called off the picture. They sold the thing to Doris Day's company and she made it. It was called *Move Over, Darling*.

The thing is, if you have such a neurotic girl, and you've got her with a script which she likes, which she's completely happy about, you do not do anything to disturb her, especially since everybody else had OK'd the script. You do not shake the whole boat. That's just what they did, and, just through this foolishness, she got worse and worse.

Dorris sent her a cable and asked her to fly over to London and stay with us a week or so. Maybe she could have gotten another point of view. She'd have gotten away from the studio and perhaps it would have helped her. The cable she sent back was something like this: "Thank you so much, Dorris and Nunnally, and please believe me, Nunnally, it wasn't my fault," which meant nothing to me until I read the next day that she'd been taken out of the picture, and the picture called off.

She never recovered. I had thought she really had been saved. The whole thing was quite sad for me. I had come to know this girl, and I found out how vulnerable she was, how helpless and how lonely. She had nobody. She just didn't know how to cope with life at all.

19

Reenter the Family, Exit Zanuck

Since *The Man in the Gray Flannel Suit*, Johnson's films had dealt with material that was rather unconventional, especially for him. There was psychoanalysis in *Oh Men! Oh Women!*, a split personality in *The Three Faces of Eve*, an egotistical and artistic movie director in *The Man Who Understood Women*, and a Spanish priest who leaves the church in *The Angel Wore Red*. In the early sixties, he was working on scripts with other subjects that were equally alien to his experience. *Stranger in Gallah*, a novel whose original location was Australia, was reset by Johnson in South Africa to give the story a racial conflict, and, because of this, the script consistently ran into hesitations on the part of both the studio and the stars who were approached to do it.

Johnson even took a turn on the screenplay of *Cleopatra*, working about a month on the script with director Rouben Mamoulian, who was shooting tests. Johnson went around one night to view what Mamoulian was shooting. After looking at the tests, Johnson told the producer, Walter Wanger, that he was convinced Mamoulian would never get the project going. Wanger asked why. Johnson replied, "He's testing fabrics. A man is really desperate when he begins testing fabrics. He's afraid to come to bat."[1] Wanger was skeptical of Johnson's assessment and bet him a pound that Mamoulian would start the film. About a month later, Johnson received an envelope from Wanger with just a pound note in it. With Mamoulian off the film, Johnson was off the job. Johnson's friend Joseph Mankiewicz took over as writer and director.

If Johnson was dealing with exotic material in his scripts of the later fifties and early sixties, he was also using his best efforts to make them intelligible to ordinary people. Johnson's most interesting attempt to adapt the alien to the commonplace was in his effort to turn Friederich Durrenmatt's play *The Visit*, set in central Europe, into a western.

Surprisingly, Johnson's version works rather well, particularly in the
beginning, which seems to have something of the relentless feel of Sergio
Leone's Italian westerns of the later sixties, but with the Clint Eastwood
character a woman. Johnson's screenplay is not faithful either to the
letter or the spirit of Durrenmatt's play, but it is an interesting reworking
of the material. Johnson had been encouraged to go ahead with his
version, both by Zanuck and by Ingrid Bergman, who wanted to play the
lead. As Johnson wrote about the project later, "She told me she very
much wanted to play a bitch, but, when she read my script, she felt that I
had misunderstood. This was a real bitch, and what she wanted was a
lovable bitch." Johnson's ideas for the project were eventually dis-
carded, and, when *The Visit* was filmed in 1963, it was returned to the
original setting of the play.

The details of his life as well as his scripts had become more worldly.
The family had lived in Rome for several months and then moved to
London, and Johnson did what he could to adapt to the English way of
life. In 1960, he wrote to a friend:

> I am now very English. Dorris and I have a house that Bob
> Goldstein refers to as Dragonwyck. We have a butler so stately that it
> took him some time to identify me as the occupant. Something like a
> week after I moved in, I found a notation from him by the telephone. It
> simply said, "Mr. Nunnally Johnson called." Later that evening I
> introduced myself to him.[2]

There were also activities in Switzerland, as befitted American expa-
triates. Johnson had his own Swiss company, Spectator, S.A., that
loaned his services to the studios he worked for.

The move to Europe also had the virtue of bringing the family closer
together. Their house in Rome was much smaller than the Beverly Hills
home with its separate wing for the children, and they got the feeling
they were seeing each other more often. Dorris later described the first
few years in London as "a continual toothache": she was without servants
for the first time and had to do all the housework herself. But the social
life in London was stimulating. They now found themselves getting
together with interesting people who were not in the motion picture
business.

Johnson's increased awareness of his family became part of the writing
projects he became involved with. He was turning away from the more
unconventional stories of the late fifties and returning to the middle-class
values of his previous work. The first of four films about families that he
wrote was based on *Mr. Hobbs' Vacation*. In some ways, it is a return to
the kind of scripts he had been doing in the forties, since he is dealing in

a comic way with married life. There is, for example, an innocent flirtation between Hobbs's wife and a member of the yacht club that, in tone, is exactly like Mrs. Peabody's innocent flirtation with a friend in *Mr. Peabody and the Mermaid*, and Hobbs's and his son-in-law's meetings on the beach with Marika, a local bikini-clad gold digger, are similar to Peabody's meetings with the mermaid. Mrs. Hobbs's care and feeding of her husband has its roots in Alice's treatment of Farll in *Holy Matrimony*. At the same time, the script shows signs of the changes in Johnson's work throughout the fifties. The subplots with Hobbs's two eldest daughters show an awareness of the tensions possible within family relationships, but the greatest change from earlier scripts is Johnson's getting away from a straight narrative line. The story has a more episodic form, which gives it a loose charm. Unfortunately, the charm and humor of the script are lost in the movie, which merely seems sprawling. The script is played by director Henry Koster for more slapstick humor than it can support.

If Koster gets the blame for the imperfections of *Mr. Hobbs*, then blame for *Take Her, She's Mine* can be shared by Johnson and Darryl Zanuck. Originally a charming play by two of Johnson's screenwriter friends, Phoebe and Henry Ephron, it deals with the experiences of a father and daughter when the daughter goes away to college.

Johnson may have been too close to the daughter-going-off-to-college situation to have the kind of distance the Ephrons had managed in the play; he was also writing it from overseas. One of the comic highlights of the first act of the play is the daughter's Mollie's, return home from college for Christmas vacation, during which she puts on a show of sophistication. In the Ephrons' writing, there is a very sharp sense of the phoniness of Mollie's sophistication, but, in Johnson's version, the texture is smoothed out and the scene becomes conventional. Another difference: in the play, the father was concerned with the whole process of his child growing up and away from the family, but, in the screenplay, his interest seems to have narrowed to sexual activities. The result of this, completely unintended by Johnson and everybody else connected with the film, is to make the film's theme appear to be sublimated incest. This does tend to spoil the fun.

Just as Johnson was completing the script to the satisfaction of Peter Levathes, the head of production, the whole situation at Fox abruptly changed. The studio had been pouring money into *Cleopatra*, and Spyros Skouras had hoped to show the film to the stockholders at the May 1962 stockholders' meeting, but it was still not completed. In June, Skouras was forced to resign as president of Fox and Darryl Zanuck issued a statement blasting the board of directors and the management committee which was trying to run the company. Zanuck was at that time living in Paris and putting the final touches on his film *The Longest Day*. Zanuck was afraid the people running the company would push his film into mass release too quickly instead of playing it in roadshow engagements. In July, Zanuck returned to New York and held discussions with Skouras and others on the board of directors. On 25 July, a meeting of the board of directors of Fox was held. Skouras moved upstairs to chairman of the board and Zanuck was elected president.

One of Zanuck's first activities was to look at Johnson's script for *Take Her, She's Mine* and decide that, because it dealt with an American girl going to an American college, it was not likely to appeal to the foreign market.[3] He was undoubtedly remembering the almost total disaster overseas in the early fifties of another Fox picture, *Take Care of My Little Girl*, which was also set in an American college.[4] Zanuck requested that Johnson try to figure out a way in which at least part of the story could be set in Paris, and Johnson, totally displeased with the idea but unwilling to let anybody else rewrite his material, eventually came up with the idea of sending Mollie off on an art scholarship to Paris in the last half of the script. Johnson also took a suggestion of Zanuck's for a running gag that was incorporated into the entire picture. Since the father was to be played by James Stewart, Zanuck was reminded of a man he had read about whose name was James Stewart and who was constantly being mistaken for the movie star. The gag in the film is that everybody the Stewart character runs into thinks he is Stewart. It is a weak gag at best, although Johnson seemed fond enough of it to reuse it in a later script, *Dear Brigitte*, in which the character played by Fabian is taking singing lessons so that he can sing like Fabian.

Johnson's troubles with Zanuck on *Take Her, She's Mine* were not only with the story line. Johnson had made an agreement with Peter Levathes to write two pictures in 1962 for $150,000 per script, and *Take Her, She's Mine* was to be the first of the two. Johnson considered that, when he completed the script in the summer of 1962 and it was approved by Levathes, it had fulfilled his obligations for the first script. When Zanuck returned, he insisted that, since he had not approved the script, Johnson would not be paid until after the revisions.[5] This meant that Johnson would not have the time to write a second script in that year, and, in addition, would not get paid for several more months. Johnson suggested he be paid in September 1962 as though *Take Her, She's Mine* were completed, thus giving him an opportunity to do a second script, in return for which he would come back and rewrite *Take Her, She's Mine* according to Zanuck's specifications the following year.[6] This was turned down by Zanuck, who was acutely aware of the lack of money available at Fox to settle contracts because of the massive investment in *Cleopatra*. Fox was willing to gamble on losing a lawsuit the following year, when there would be some cash flow from *Cleopatra*, to avoid paying out money in 1962. Johnson agreed to do the revisions, although he did get his own form of revenge within the script of *Take Her, She's Mine*. In the climactic ball in Paris, at least half the girls, including Mollie, are dressed as Cleopatra.

Zanuck and Johnson came to a final break on Johnson's next script.

In 1958, Johnson's daughter Nora had written a novel about her childhood in New York. It was called *The World of Henry Orient*, and Johnson, while admiring the book, had not thought it could be turned into a movie, since the two leading parts were young girls in their early teens. He saw no way to cast the two roles. In 1962, he saw Hayley Mills and Patty Duke in different pictures and thought that they could play the two girls, so he prepared a screenplay from the book and gave it to his agent, who began negotiations with United Artists. While United Artists considered the property over a period of several weeks, Johnson let his friend Henry Koster read the script, pointing out to Koster that it was "bespoke," since United Artists had expressed an interest. Koster liked the script and took it to Richard Zanuck, Darryl Zanuck's son, whom the elder Zanuck had installed as head of production at Fox. The younger Zanuck was also impressed with the script and called Johnson in. Johnson explained that, since United Artists had taken such a long time to decide on the material, and, in fact, had still not made a definite offer, it would be permissible for Richard Zanuck to call Johnson's agent and make a specific bid. Richard Zanuck felt it was necessary to have his father read the script before they could do that. It was sent to Darryl Zanuck, who delayed reading it. At the same time, negotiations with United Artists continued, for, as Johnson said, "The day had passed when you heard that 'Darryl's interested in it' and everything stopped." Eleven days after the script had been given to Fox with the understanding, at least on Johnson's part, that it was not being officially submitted to them, Johnson's agent called him with the news that United Artists had agreed to a deal. Darryl Zanuck was furious when he heard this, and, on 14 March 1963, he fired off a five-page cablegram to Johnson recalling the years they had worked together and denouncing him for betraying the studio. Johnson sent Zanuck a one-page cable restating the fact that the script had never actually been submitted to Fox, and he followed the cable up with a letter detailing the situation.[7] There was no further response. Johnson met with Zanuck professionally one more time, in July of that year, to discuss a script he had been working on for *High Wind in Jamaica*.[8] Johnson's script was considered too costly, and eventually the project was turned over to another producer and another writer. The long and successful professional relationship between the two men was over.

Johnson's script for *The World of Henry Orient* is an interesting reconstruction of his daughter's novel. According to the credits, they coauthored the screenplay, but this is not altogether true. Nora Johnson had written a screenplay which Johnson found unusable, and he started from scratch. Nora says, "The truth is that script was really written by him, so anything that isn't in the book is Pop's. I had very little to do with it. It was awfully nice of him to call it a collaboration, but it wasn't, and I imagine if we'd really tried to collaborate there never would have been a film at all." Johnson simplified some of the density of psychological detail of the novel, particularly near the end of it, but in return gave more comic detail to the story line itself. He also expanded the role of Henry Orient, who appears only at a distance in the book, partly by creating a woman whom Orient is constantly trying to seduce. This gives the two young girls a variety of activities as they succeed, inadvertently, in breaking up his liaisons. Johnson also added a very subtle and comic seduction scene between Val's mother and Henry Orient in a restaurant, and another even subtler scene near the end of the picture when Val's mother returns from her assignation with Henry Orient. It becomes apparent through the dialogue between the mother and father that he knows where she's been and she knows that he knows, and, further, that she knows that he knows that Val knows, all done on the level of suggestion without anything definite being said.

The script for *The World of Henry Orient* is a family affair in a variety of ways. Nora Johnson's book is autobiographical, and the character of Gil is a self-portrait of sorts. Gil's mother, nicknamed "Wimpole" in the book, is, as Nora says, "The way my mother seemed when I was a child, which she really isn't, if you know what I mean," and Johnson's character in the script is faithful to Nora's portrait and perhaps even gentler, certainly the nicest characterization a man ever gave of his ex-wife. A speech Johnson added for Gil, about the possibility of her mother and father getting reunited, is not from Nora, but from his first daughter, Marjorie, who admits that for years she hoped Johnson and Alice would get back together again. The final sequence includes a line from his daughters by his third marriage: when Val and Gil are trying out make-up, Gil indicates that she is going to use bright red lipstick, saying that she wants "a mouth like a crimson gash."

The script was turned over to producer Jerome Hellman and director George Roy Hill, a fortunate choice. Hill was a stage director who had only directed two movies prior to this assignment, but he was able to add a number of inventive touches to the film. In one of the early scenes, the two girls decide to go adventuring around New York City. None of their activities before they stumble across Henry Orient and his would-be mistress are indicated in the script. Hill shot a lot of improvised activity, including a number of striking shots of the girls jumping up and down in slow motion. He had them bouncing on trampolines just out of camera range so that, in the film, they seem to be floating in the park. Hill also added several sprightly sight gags to the first Henry Orient concert the girls attend, such as the conductor silently mouthing the chord Orient has repeatedly failed to play correctly.

Johnson was delighted with the picture, even more so when it proceeded to get what Johnson feels were the best reviews of any picture he had done. Unfortunately, outside of New York, the picture did not do well at the box office and failed to break even, perhaps because it is so "New York" in tone and style—and perhaps, as Johnson thought, because of the title, which he felt did not suggest to anyone what the film was about. Johnson also felt that Peter Sellers was wrong for the part of Orient, giving a vaudeville-skit kind of performance. Johnson's original choice had been Rex Harrison.

Johnson's fourth and last family film does not have his name on the credits. He was asked to do the screenplay of a book called *Erasmus with Freckles*, and, while he felt that there was hardly enough material in it for a feature film, he went ahead and did the script (retitled to his relief *Dear Brigitte*) since he knew it was to be directed by Henry Koster and would star James Stewart. He had faith that Koster and, particularly, Stewart could make it work. But Koster brought in Hal Kanter to do revisions and, although the changes were in fact relatively minor, Johnson requested his name be taken off the credits for the picture. He wrote to Koster, "Not in something like twenty-five years have I shared a screen credit except with a member of my own family. For better or worse I would like to preserve this record, so I withdrew my name from the screenplay."[9] Hal Kanter received the sole credit.

Johnson had worked on four scripts in a row that dealt with family situations. His work was reflecting what was happening in his life. At the beginning of his script of *Dear Brigitte*, the family is seen together playing a collection of musical instruments. The young son, Erasmus, is playing off-key. At the end of the script, after all the troubles have been taken care of, the family is once again playing and Erasmus is still playing off-key. The mother complains, but the father says adamantly, "I want EVERYTHING the way it was." For Johnson, everything was not "the way it was," because he had had to work his way to a more profound acceptance of his original values. Perhaps the more operative line should be one from *The Man Who Understood Women:* "It may be, you know, that there are people on this earth who can never really know each other until they've been through the roof together."

20
Stage Frightened

The film rights to *The Dirty Dozen*, a novel by E. M. Nathanson, were originally sold to the production unit at MGM run by William Perlberg and George Seaton. Two scripts were done for them, the second one by Nathanson himself, before the book was turned over to Kenneth Hyman to produce for MGM. Hyman hired Nunnally Johnson to write a screenplay, and Johnson went to work trying to compress the 540-page novel into normal feature length.[1]

The central story deals with an assignment given to World War II Army Captain John Reisman to take twelve men, convicted by Army court-martial of the worst possible offenses, and retrain them as a special fighting unit. At the end of training, the unit is dropped behind enemy lines to blow up a chateau where the German generals worked and relaxed. The emotional climax of the book is the training exercise in which the men in the unit prove they can work together. The final attack on the chateau is almost an afterthought, taking up only the last fifteen pages of the book, ten of them done in the style of an official Army report.

Johnson recognized the attack would have to be a big sequence, but, in both the book and the script, the war game exercise comes immediately before the attack, which bunches up the two big action sequences at the end. Johnson attempted to overcome this problem by making the prisoner Franko's attempts to kill Reisman into a subplot, with Franko's final attempt at the chateau, only suggested in the book, a complete scene in the screenplay. This subplot returns to Johnson's old theme of loyalty, since Reisman feels that, in order to make the mission work, he must make the men act as a unit. Therefore, in the beginning, their combined hatred is directed toward their training officer—a negative form of loyalty. Johnson's theme of loyalty is also carried over in his

183

handling of what in the novel is an ordinary love interest between
Reisman and Tessie, a barmaid at a local pub. When Reisman leaves to
go on the mission in the book, he simply bids good-bye to Tessie, but, in
the script, Johnson has him note that Tessie has already begun to take up
with someone else.

Johnson's screenplay, apart from the structural problem mentioned
above, moves quickly and entertainingly and holds together on an
intellectual level as well as a narrative one. What is more surprising is
the vigor of the writing, not only because Johnson was 66 when he wrote
it, but also because Johnson's scripts usually have a smoothness that at
times seems almost genteel. There is an abrupt vitality about the
characters which is unusual.

Hyman hired for *The Dirty Dozen* Robert Aldrich, who had directed
such films as *The Big Knife, Attack!*, and *Whatever Happened to Baby
Jane?* Johnson described him thus: "Just as a generality, Aldrich is, let's
say, a he-man director. He thinks he's going to be another John Ford and
feels he must be harsh and cruel and tough and all that kind of stuff."[2]
Aldrich's first reaction to the script was so enthusiastic that Johnson
asked Hyman rather uncertainly, "Is that *our* script he's talking about?"
Aldrich later said: "This would have made a very good, very acceptable
1945 war picture. But I don't think that a 1945 war picture is necessarily
a good 1967 war picture."[3] Johnson left London to return to New York,
and Aldrich immediately brought in a writer he had worked with before,
Lukas Heller. Aldrich told an interviewer:

> The next problem was to try to get a new script. I wanted a whole
> new concept. Well, despite considerable resistance, we *got* a whole
> new concept, and with the exception of Bosley Crowther, I think you
> will discover that most people adored—that's a pretty rich word—
> were fascinated by the anarchy of the picture's first two-thirds, and
> tolerated and were excited and/or stimulated and/or entertained by
> the last third. The first two-thirds were Mr. Heller's contribution
> towards making it a 1967 picture and not a 1947 picture, and the last
> third was a pretty high-class, well-done war adventure.[4]

Heller's changes were for the worse, and, furthermore, a comparison
of Johnson's script to the final picture reveals that Heller's contribution
is to make the film more of a 1947 war picture rather than less. Heller's
major contribution was in cutting from the script several story elements.
The entire Reisman–Tessie relationship has been cut, as has been the
motivation for the conflict between Reisman and Dasher-Breed. As a
result of the latter cut, an understandable personal conflict between the
two men becomes, in the film, psychopathic on the personal level on one

hand, and, on the other, simply a cliché conflict between a non-regulation officer (Reisman) and a very regulation type (Dasher-Breed). Heller has also cut most of the ironies from the story, particularly those involving Franko. A scene in which Franko tries to get a group of men to kill Reisman on the firing range has been cut, as well as the scene of Franko trying to kill Reisman during the attack on the chateau. The loss of the latter scene (and the irony of the unit being hit by an American Army unit as they try to escape, which has also been cut by Heller) leaves the final attack a standard action scene. In the book, the attack is given as proof these kinds of men could become their own kind of heroes. In Johnson's script, the attack shows that the men are not really different from what they were before—some heroes, some villains. In the film, all the members of the unit have become traditional war picture heroes, and the ironies of both the book and Johnson's screenplay have been dropped in favor of a more conventional ending. No wonder Stephen Farber called the film "the most importantly confused movie of 1967."[5]

Heller and Aldrich were also responsible for getting the German officers and their women trapped in a bomb shelter so that the "heroes" can pour gasoline and hand grenades down the air shafts of the shelter. Johnson said later, "I won't say I wouldn't have used it. I just never thought of it."[6]

The question of screenplay credit went to the Writer's Guild of America for arbitration. Since the rules of the guild say that a writer is entitled to co-credit if 33⅓ percent of the work is his, Heller got the co-credit. The rules do not say the 33⅓ percent has to be an improvement.

When Johnson returned to New York in 1965, he was going back to work on a stage musical adaptation of Truman Capote's novella, *Breakfast at Tiffany's*, for producer David Merrick. Capote liked the first draft, but Merrick did not. He told Johnson what he had in mind was a "valentine to New York."[7] Johnson was taken aback and asked Merrick if he had bothered to read Capote's book. Johnson did a second draft, but later another writer was brought in by Merrick and the musical adaptation of *Breakfast at Tiffany's* went on to become one of Broadway's most famous flops. Johnson watched the debacle from a distance.

He was now involved in a stage musical version of *The World of Henry Orient*, working with composer-lyricist Robert Merrill, his partner in the abortive *Breakfast at Tiffany's*. The producer was to be Jerome Hellman, producer of the film, and the director was also to be the same, George Roy Hill, which pleased Johnson. The show was eventually produced by Edward Specter and Norman Twain. It opened to mixed notices in Detroit, then moved to Philadelphia, where it got good notices. In New

York, however, the all-powerful Clive Barnes of *The New York Times*
said he knew the show was going to be a bore as soon as he heard the
overture. The show closed in ten weeks for a loss of $400,000. An
analysis of the musical (which was finally called *Henry, Sweet Henry*) and
the reasons for its commercial failure are given in William Goldman's
book, *The Season*.[8]

Johnson was involved with another musical that opened on Broadway
in the 1967-68 season. As early as 1960 there had been discussion of a
musical version of Arnold Bennett's *Buried Alive*, which Johnson had
turned into the movie *Holy Matrimony*. In the summer of 1966, Johnson
returned to the idea, doing a first draft of the libretto. The show opened
for its Toronto try-out under the title *Married Alive*, with music by Jule
Styne, the composer of *Funny Girl*, and lyrics by E. Y. Harburg, the
lyricist of *Finian's Rainbow*. The stars were Patricia Routledge in the
Gracie Fields part and Vincent Price in the Monty Woolley role.

The problem was Vincent Price, Johnson recalled: "Ninety-nine out of
one hundred actors want to be loved. They've just killed their mothers,
their fathers, three children, but they want to be loved. I talked to him
about it beforehand. He looked so good for the part, and I said, 'Have
you heard of Beecham, the conductor?' He said, 'Oh, yes, yes, yes.' I
said, 'Try to think of yourself as Beecham, very cultivated, very
aristocratic, egotistical, acrid, a little nasty. Play it that way.' 'Wonderful,' he said, and then he went out and played it like Zasu Pitts."[9]

Johnson also had difficulties with the director, Steven Vinaver, who
was rewriting scenes as well as failing to control the actors. Johnson
suggested in a letter that the actors were reaching for laughs and "any
actor caught reaching for laughs should be automatically fined $100."
Finally, the changes in the material by others were just too much for
him, and he removed his name from the show before it opened in New
York under the title *Darling of the Day*. The show received good notices
from the four main newspaper critics, but it closed after thirty-three
performances for an estimated loss of between $700,000 and $750,000.

There is no simple explanation for Johnson's failure as a writer for the
stage. He said jokingly, "It was all other people's fault." At least a major
portion of his lack of success appears to have been typical show business
bad luck. Part of the problem, particularly in the middle sixties, may
have been that he had become used to working in a way not suited to the
theatre. When Johnson was assigned to a screenplay, he would go off and
write it pretty much on his own, then discuss possible changes with the
producer and/or director, then do revisions on his own. In the theatre,
the writer is much more of an on-the-spot collaborator, rewriting in the
midst of tryouts and helping to get the production on the road.

Johnson's writing itself may also be more suited to the essay, short story, and the film than to the stage. Johnson is a very life-sized writer, which suits the realistic tradition of the film. His writing is not, even in the vigor of *The Dirty Dozen,* larger than life-sized. The scenes in Johnson's screenplays are well-written and well-constructed, but almost never theatrical. The emphasis is on character and narrative rather than the obviously dramatic. Consider the final speeches of the young hero from the South in Johnson's musical *Park Avenue,* which he wrote with George S. Kaufman:

> But—sooner or later I think the country's got to face some of these problems in the North—in the backward districts, I mean. Not the whole North, of course. Because there are some really WONDERFUL people up here—people you wouldn't mind asking into your own home—but some of them, gosh! You certainly wouldn't want your SISTER to get mixed up with them. . . . Please understand, I don't mean anything personal about this. It's really none of our business HOW people carry on up here, but if there's any way we can be of help—like sending social workers and magazine writers to tell you what's wrong with you—I just want you to know you can really count on the South's friendship, 100 percent.

It was a funny speech, in a quiet, subtle way, but hardly a perfect finale for a musical.

Johnson, extremely discouraged with his lack of success in the Broadway theatre, returned in 1968 to writing screenplays. His first assignment was a script entitled *The Frontiersman* for producer Jack Warner. Johnson recalled, "I never saw Jack Warner after we first talked it over and he gave me very explicit directions. He said, 'I want a big two-a-day western.' Next time I saw him was about eight months later when I handed in the script. Then we did some revisions."[10] Warner at the time had stepped down as head of the Warner Brothers studio and was, in theory, just another producer on the lot. He eventually left the studio he had given his name to and produced films for release through Columbia Pictures, but *The Frontiersman* was not one of them and the script remained on the shelf. Later, Johnson was assigned the screenplay for Bruce Jay Friedman's bizarre stage comedy *Scuba Duba,* which is mostly about a white liberal whose wife has run off with a black scuba diver. Its production has suffered a series of indefinite postponements.

Johnson was never completely at home at Warner Brothers. He had his long-time secretary, Betty Baldwin Stewart, working for him, and he was trying to work in the same old way. But there was no longer the family feeling of the old studios. He was working not so much for the studio as for individual producers, and some of them could be a problem:

> This time I have a producer who wants to work closely with me, and I
> don't want to work closely with him. It really slows me down. It
> impedes me. He's a nice fellow, but I can't get away from him. He
> calls me nearly every day and says, "What about lunch?" There's only
> one place to lunch there, and I don't want to sit and talk to him every
> day. He's not very entertaining. And I don't want to talk about the
> script because I don't know what I'm going to do. So I think maybe I'll
> have to go away. Maybe to Hawaii or something like that for a couple
> of weeks, or else talk to the studio about sending *him* away."[11]

Johnson was suffering from emphysema, and, although he had been
told by his doctors to stop smoking, he felt giving up cigarettes "would be
like giving up old friends." In early 1970, he announced that he was
formally retiring. When Helen Hayes heard this, she asked him how he
"formally" retired. He said, "Very easily. I simply put on my white tie
and tails—and I retired."

After he retired, he watched sports on television and, sometimes, an
old movie, sometimes even his own. He and Dorris went to parties
occasionally, and he saw some of the newer movies. Johnson also gave
interviews to graduate students from UCLA and USC, entertaining them
with comments about his contemporaries, such as Leo McCarey, a
director whose "camera technique," Johnson said, "was to tell the
actors, 'If you want to be in the movie, get in front of it.' " He wrote a
little: a book review, a letter to the *Los Angeles Times* when its
entertainment editor mistakenly identified John Ford as the director of
Jesse James instead of Henry King.

On 25 March 1977, at the age of 79, Nunnally Johnson died.

21
Museum/Set/Piece

In late 1972, a month after the second Los Angeles International Film Exposition (FILMEX), the Los Angeles County Museum of Art held a series of events honoring screen writers. The screenings were in connection with FILMEX, which had included as part of its program a series of seminars with screenwriters from around the world. Among the writers honored were Frances Marion, Dalton Trumbo, John Lee Mahin, and, one evening in December, Nunnally Johnson.

The museum was only about half full that night. Writers were not yet as big a draw as directors. There were a number of local film buffs there, but no stars or even star directors. Dorris was there, of course, and Roxie, and Marjorie and Gene Fowler. Christie was there with her eight-year-old son, Alex. Johnson, who normally avoided speaking in public, had agreed to talk about his films, "as long as I don't have to make a speech." The program began shortly after eight when Ron Haver, the head of the Museum's film department, announced that unfortunately Norman Corwin, a well-known writer who had been scheduled to be the moderator for the evening, was ill. They did have a replacement, the fellow who had been helping them select the film clips, and at least he had the good sense to introduce Johnson right away and get him talking about his days as a New York reporter, when, as Johnson said, "a murder was fun."[1]

Johnson was his charming, witty, storytelling self. He told about how he came from New York to Hollywood, and he put in the story of Herman Mankiewicz asking him how he discovered there was no ribbon in the typewriter. He described how he started out doing the same kind of light comedies he had done for *The Saturday Evening Post*, enjoying the money and not worrying too much about the craft of writing. Then he told about going to work for Zanuck, who asked him to do a drama, and not being sure he could do it. The first sequence from *The House of*

189

Rothschild was shown. It begins harshly, with the chain being pulled across the entrance to the ghetto. Then there is the family of Mayer Rothschild, with the children mimicking Mayer's activities as a money changer. The scene turns serious again as the tax collectors come and Mayer and his family outsmart them by hiding the real ledgers.

This sequence from *The House of Rothschild* was serious in two ways. First of all, this was a drama, not a light comedy—and not only a drama, but one dealing with anti-Semitism. Johnson was also dealing with what were to become major themes in his work, marriage and family life, seen here in a slightly idealized way. Second, the sequence shows Johnson's attitude toward his craft. Screenwriting was and is a craft with its own skills and rules, and Johnson was beginning to develop the skills and learn the rules.

Johnson was by now enjoying himself, in spite of his professed reluctance to speak before large groups. He was recalling his boyhood days in Georgia, particularly the time spent watching the Jewel Kelly version of *Jesse James,* and how that came to convince him, and ultimately Zanuck, that they ought to make a movie about Jesse. The sequence shown was the train robbery, rich in color, action, excitement, and humor.

The train robbery sequence is a perfect example of the kind of narrative film making Zanuck, King, and Johnson did so well. There is not a shot, not a line, not a bit of action that does not at once entertain and also push the story forward.

There had to be a sequence from *The Grapes of Wrath,* and it was Johnson's favorite, the roadside diner scene. The Joads, transposed from the anonymous family in the book, go in and ask to buy a loaf of bread. The waitress at first refuses, then, at the urging of the cook, sells them the bread and also lets the kids buy two pieces of nickel candy for a penny. Two truck drivers, watching the waitress, leave her an extra tip.

Perhaps the charge most often leveled at Hollywood films in general, at this film on occasion, and at this scene in particular, is sentimentality. If the whole movie were made up of scenes with this tone and attitude, such a charge might hold up, but Johnson constructed scenes to be fitted into the context of the film as a whole. In the film, this scene, showing how unexpectedly good people can be, immediately follows the death of Grandpa and the most harrowing scene in the film, in which a man returning from California describes how his children starved to death.

The effect of the diner scene in its context is to give a richer view of humanity in all its variety.

Then there was Alec Guinness's long speech from *The Mudlark*, during which, as Disraeli, he attempts to show how the only sin of the small boy who tried to get to see Queen Victoria was that he believed in everything England was supposed to stand for.

Nunnally Johnson writes screenplays actors can act. This is not as simple as it seems. Many writers, particularly those who work primarily in prose rather than in some dramatic form, have great difficulty writing lines that can not only be spoken, but acted. Johnson's lines move the story forward, but they also provide the actors with some emotion or attitude to put across while saying the line. It is true that Johnson did not believe the Disraeli speech would hold up without cuts away from the actor to reactions, but it is still a measure of his skill that the speech was played successfully in one take entirely on the actor and remains in the film that way.

The commandos sneak onto the beach in North Africa. They climb the wall of the villa. The shooting begins. The radio room is blown up. The German soldiers cut down the commandos. A dying commando asks, "Did we get him?" The German replies scornfully, "Are you serious, Englishman?" The credits for *The Desert Fox* begin.

Nunnally Johnson writes screenplays that can be filmed. Even though the primary responsibility of the screenwriter is to define the temporal structure of the film, he must also provide elements that can be presented visually, just as the director, in visualizing the film, must have some sense of its temporal structure. Johnson's scripts permit visualization in the separate directorial styles of Ford, King, Lang, and, in the case of *The Desert Fox*, Henry Hathaway. The story line of the opening sequence is told exclusively, with the exception of the punch lines, through exciting visuals.

Johnson talked about Marilyn. He mentioned the early days, but mostly he talked about working with her the last time. There was no sensationalism, no exploitation, no speculation, just his warm, funny, and sad account. The "glasses scene" from *How to Marry a Millionaire* was shown.

What ultimately kept Johnson so successful a writer for so long was his middle-class sense of humanity. It came through in his affection and his understanding both of the people he worked with and the characters he wrote. The mass audience responded to that.

There was an intermission. Roxie came up to the front and said she always knew Dad was a terrific sit-down comedian, and Dorris sent word up that Nunnally should speak more into the microphone. The second half of the program began with Johnson telling how Nora came to write *The World of Henry Orient*, how it was a semi-autobiographical novel, and how Henry Orient was really Oscar Levant. Then all of *The World of Henry Orient* was shown, and the audience—not New Yorkers—loved it. Johnson, taking material from Marion, Nora, Marjorie, Dorris, Christie, and Roxie, had, with the film, communicated with and entertained the audience.

If Nunnally Johnson had not existed, it would have been necessary for Hollywood to invent him. He performed a crucial function in the making of feature motion pictures: the writing of the screenplay. The screenplay is not only the beginning for a film. It is the center of it, establishing the coherence that direction alone cannot provide.

After the movie, everybody began to move out slowly, and a few more of Johnson's friends came to him to say hello. In the lobby, a few young free-lance photographers mistook Dorris for Debbie Reynolds, who is at least ten years younger, which proved Louella had been wrong years before—Dorris was just as beautiful as ever. She posed for a few pictures and signed an autograph or two, and then she joined Johnson and his friends and his family out in front of the Museum, and they all talked a bit in the cool night air.

And, after a while, finally, everybody went home.

Notes

Direct quotations from Nunnally Johnson are primarily from the interviews I did as part of the Oral History of the Motion Pictures Project at UCLA, herein abbreviated NJOH, with page numbers from the final transcript. To keep these notes reasonably short, I have listed for each chapter the NJOH section that the material in the chapter is primarily from. Items from other sections of the transcript are listed in individual notes. For access to that transcript, see acknowledgments.

Further material from Johnson was obtained in additional interviews, abbreviated NJAI. Since these interviews were not recorded or transcribed, no page numbers are given.

Much written material was found in the collection of Nunnally Johnson's papers at the Mugar Memorial Library at Boston University. Items in that collection are noted with the abbreviation NJCBU. Because many of the items are in clipping files (as are items from the Margaret Herrick Library of the Academy of Motion Picture Arts and Sciences in Beverly Hills), page numbers often cannot be listed. One of the most useful items in the Boston University collection is "My Best to You All," the first draft of Pete Martin's article on Johnson that appeared under the title "Hollywood's Number One Wit" in *The Saturday Evening Post* in two parts, 2 and 9 November 1946. The first draft ran 239 pages and included a great deal of interesting material that had to be cut to fit the length requirements of the *Post*. Much of Martin's research material is also in this file. I have used material from that draft and the research material and have indicated this in the notes.

The material from Johnson's screenplays is from his personal copies of the shooting scripts, and the material from earlier drafts, treatments, and story conference notes is from the files at Twentieth Century-Fox in Los Angeles.

In the interest of brevity, I have not listed the sources that seemed obvious from the material in the text, such as interviews with friends and co-workers, or books mentioned in the text.

Introduction:

1. Griffith's "reported" working method is from the conventional sources: Lillian Gish's *The Movies, Mr. Griffith, and Me* (Prentice-Hall Inc., 1969); Kevin Brownlow's interview with Joseph Henabery in *The Parade's Gone By* (Alfred Knopf, 1968); Benjamin Hampton's *History of the American Film Industry* (Dover Publications, Inc., 1970—although this is a republication of Hampton's original *A History of the Movies*, which was published in 1931 by Covici, Friede); Lewis Jacobs' *The Rise of the American Film* (Teachers College Press, 1967—although this is a new edition of a work published in 1939 by Harcourt, Brace and Company); and Karl Brown's *Adventures with D. W. Griffith* (Farrar, Straus and Giroux, 1973).

Chapter 1: Georgia

1. Nunnally Johnson, "New York-My Mammy," *There Ought to Be a Law*, (Doubleday, Doran, 1931), pp. 166–167.
2. The descriptions of Nunnally Johnson's boyhood throughout this chapter are from interviews with Johnson, Dorris Johnson, and Marjorie Fowler; a letter from Patrick Johnson, and clippings in Johnson's scrapbooks.
3. Letter from Julius Harris to Pete Martin dated 13 November 1945, in NJCBU.
4. Nunnally Johnson, untitled article for *The Columbus Enquirer-Sun*, manuscript dated "5–11–48," in NJCBU.
5. Pete Martin's first draft, NJCBU, p. 20.

Chapter 2: New York Columnist

1. William Leuchtenberg, *Perils of Prosperity 1914–1932* (University of Chicago Press, 1958). This specific reference to the Scopes Trial also sums up the theme of the book.
2. The short stories mentioned and quoted are all from *There Ought to Be a Law*. See note one on chapter one.
3. Pete Martin's first draft, NJCBU, pp. 27–28.
4. Interviews with members of the family.
5. See note four above.
6. Walter Winchell's column: undated clipping in Nunnally Johnson's scrapbook.
7. Letter from Mrs. Rogers Flynn (formerly Marion Byrnes Johnson) to the author, 1 February 1973.

Chapter 3: First Films

1. Material on his first films from NJOH, pp. 11–37.
2. Frank Capra, *The Name Above the Title*, (Macmillan, 1971), pp. 72–76.
3. NJAI.
4. NJOH, p. 14.

5. *Mama Loves Papa* file, NJCBU.

6. Eileen Creelman, "Picture Plays and Players," *New York Sun*, 9 November 1934, clipping in NJCBU.

7. Interview with Dorris Johnson.

8. NJAI.

9. Letter from Mrs. Rogers Flynn, 1 February 1973.

10. Harold Ross quoted in William Froug, *The Screenwriter Looks at the Screenwriter*, (Macmillan, 1972), p. 242.

11. Aaron Latham, *Crazy Sundays*, (Viking, 1971), pp. 172–173.

Chapter 4: Enter Zanuck

1. The background of the various moguls is taken from Mel Gussow, *Don't Say Yes Until I Finish Talking* (Doubleday, 1971), and Philip French, *The Movie Moguls* (Weidenfeld and Nicolson, 1969).

2. Quotations from Nunnally Johnson throughout this chapter are from NJOH, pp. 20–38.

3. Ben Hecht, *A Child of the Century* (Signet, 1954), p. 450.

4. See note six for chapter three.

Chapter 5: Rewriting Faulkner

1. Upton Sinclair, *Upton Sinclair Presents William Fox* (Sinclair, 1933); Glendon Allvine, *The Greatest Fox of Them All* (Lyle Stuart, 1969); Gussow, *Don't Say Yes*; French, *The Movie Moguls*; Mae Huettig, *Economic Control of the Motion Picture Industry* (University of Pennsylvania, 1944); Tom Stempel, unpublished oral history interviews with Henry King and Robert D. Webb (American Film Institute, 1970–1971).

2. Quotations from Nunnally Johnson throughout are from NJOH, pp. 48–86.

3. NJOH, pp. 140–142.

4. Stempel, King oral history, p. 34.

5. Stempel, Webb oral history, p. 38.

6. NJOH, pp. 116–117.

7. NJOH, p. 422.

8. Johnson interview with Eileen Creelman, n.d., clipping in NJCBU.

9. Joseph Blotner, *Faulkner, A Biography* (Random House, 1974), p. 923. There are some interesting variations on this in Tom Dardis, *Some Time in the Sun* (Scribners, 1976).

10. NJOH, pp. 80–82. In a phone interview, Joel Sayre confirmed that Johnson wrote the final script of *The Road to Glory*. The story is also told in more detail in Blotner, *Faulkner*, pp. 1028–29.

Chapter 6: Jesse James

1. Material on *Jesse James* is from NJOH, pp. 91–113. It has been enriched by the files at Twentieth Century-Fox, which include not only all the treatments and the scripts,

but all the research material, a lot of the correspondence the studio received about the film, and the Telex messages between the location unit in Missouri and the home office in Los Angeles. Further material is from Stempel, King and Webb oral histories.

2. Zanuck, in his 29 March 1938 notes on the treatment, wrote: "Page 46: Mr. Zanuck was agreeable to permitting Mr. Johnson to retain his pet gag—scattering *l'argent*—and we are all hoping it works out as funny as the esteemed writer feels it will."

3. *Jesse James* clipping file, Margaret Herrick Library of the Academy of Motion Picture Arts and Sciences.

Chapter 7: *The Grapes of Wrath*

1. Darryl F. Zanuck, "Zanuck Finds Odds Longer Than Roulette's," *The Los Angeles Times*, 21 November 1954, p. 8. Curiously enough, this story does not appear in Mel Gussow's semi-authorized biography of Zanuck. While the story may be self-promotion on Zanuck's part, it appeared in print fifteen years after the release of the picture, so it was hardly promotion for the film. My own guess is that there is at least a germ of truth in the story, although it is also my guess that the meeting probably took place before Zanuck bought the film rights. At least in film making, Zanuck seemed careful to hedge his bets (e.g., all-star casts to help the box office when he did controversial material).

2. *The Grapes of Wrath* material is from NJOH, pp. 119–139. The material in the Fox story files includes a photostatic copy of Johnson's first-draft screenplay dated 13 July 1939 (this copy has Zanuck's handwritten notes in the margin), the story conference notes on that draft dated 19 July 1939, a typed second draft dated 29 July 1939, and the revised, temporary shooting script dated 5 August 1939 (which appears to be just the mimeographed form of the July 29th script).

3. Nunnally Johnson, "Should *The Grapes of Warth* Be Shelved?" *Photoplay*, November 1939, pp. 22, 23, and 88.

4. Pauline Kael, *Kiss Kiss Bang Bang* (Atlantic-Little, Brown, 1968), p. 276, says, "*The Grapes of Wrath* is full of the 'they can't keep us down, we're the people' sort of thing, and one's outrage at the terrible social injustices the film reveals is blurred by its gross sentimentality."

5. In the story files at Fox, Johnson's ending appears in the 13 July first draft as well as all subsequent drafts. Gregg Toland's copy is in the Graduate Research Library at UCLA.

6. Frank Condon, "The Grapes of Raps," *Colliers*, 27 January 1940, p. 64.

7. Condon, p. 67.

8. Johnson alludes to this in his *Photoplay* article; Philip Dunne also comments on this in Tom Stempel, unpublished oral history interview with Philip Dunne (American Film Institute, 1970–1971), p. 70.

9. John Springer, "Henry Fonda," *Films in Review*, November 1960, p. 526.

10. Ernest Havemann, "Darryl Zanuck: The Last of the Movie Moguls," *McCalls*, October 1963, p. 224; also NJOH, pp. 213–214.

Chapter 8: About Directors

1. The *Tobacco Road* material is from NJOH, pp. 153–160.

2. NJOH, pp. 231–232.

3. Ibid., p. 238.

4. John Cromwell's letter to Nunnally Johnson, dated 22 September 1944, and Johnson's letter to Cromwell, dated 27 September 1944, are both in NJCBU.

5. NJOH, p. 39.

6. Ibid., p. 268.

7. Ibid., p. 57.

8. Ibid., p. 63.

9. Ibid., pp. 171, 232–233.

10. Charles Higham and Joel Greenberg, *The Celluloid Muse* (Angus and Robertson, 1969), p. 113. See also Philip Scheuer, untitled article, *The Los Angeles Times*, 27 January 1945, in the Nunnally Johnson clipping file at the Margaret Herrick Library of the Academy of Motion Picture Arts and Sciences.

11. Pete Martin first draft, in NJCBU, p. 63.

Chapter 9: Middle Class

1. Pete Martin, "Hollywood's Number One Wit," *The Saturday Evening Post*, 2 November 1946.

2. Leo Rosten, *Hollywood: The Movie Colony, The Movie Makers* (Harcourt Brace, 1941), pp. 273–274.

Chapter 10: A Family of His Own

1. The information in this chapter comes from interviews with Nunnally Johnson, Dorris Bowdon Johnson, Dorothy McBrayer Stahl, Christie Johnson, Roxie Johnson, Scott Johnson, and Marjorie Fowler.

2. *Stag at Bay* was finally produced in February 1975 at the Charles MacArthur Center for the Development of American Theatre at Florida State University. The note is in the *Stag at Bay* file, NJCBU.

3. NJOH, pp. 155–156.

4. NJCBU includes Wood's original manuscript, Johnson's rewrite, and the correspondence between Stout and Johnson. The letter in which Stout told Johnson he was buying the manuscript with the understanding it would be rewritten is dated 10 March 1939.

5. George Eells, *Hedda and Louella* (Warner Paperback, 1973), p. 205. Wood, because he did not have Johnson's position in the industry, was effectively blacklisted as a publicist by Parsons until he was hired by Joseph Schenck to work on *Oklahoma* (1955).

6. Martin first draft, NJCBU, p. 98.

7. Louella's comment about Dorris has been quoted so often by so many members of the family it has taken on the aura of a family legend. Nobody remembers exactly when she said it.

Chapter 11: A Twentieth Century-Fox Dropout

1. Details of the proposed Nunnally Johnson contract are deduced from a memo from Lew Schreiber to George Wasson dated 16 August 1948 in the Johnson folder in the

writers' file at Fox. The memo seems to suggest Johnson was coming back to Fox in 1948 on the same terms he was offered earlier. These terms vary a bit from the figures Johnson mentioned in the NJOH (p. 207), but in the NJOH, he was talking without notes and, given his lack of a head for figures, I feel the figures in the memo are probably more accurate.

2. NJOH, pp. 207–244.

3. Ibid., p. 366.

4. Johnson letter to George S. Kaufman, dated 23 January 1947, in NJCBU.

5. NJOH, pp. 227–230. Lang's feelings are also apparent in the interview with him in Higham and Greenberg, *The Celluloid Muse*, pp. 113–114.

6. Material throughout about Marjorie Fowler is from interview with Marjorie Fowler.

7. NJOH, p. 239.

Chapter 12: Mr. Johnson Was Indiscreet

1. The material on Nunnally Johnson throughout is from NJOH, pp. 248–266.

2. *The Senator Was Indiscreet* file, NJCBU.

3. Ibid.

4. Ibid.

5. Ibid.

6. Ibid.

Chapter 13: Son of Twentieth Century-Fox

1. Quotations throughout from Nunnally Johnson are from NJOH, pp. 255–305.

2. NJOH, pp. 208–209.

3. William Bowers, in discussion with a screenwriting class, UCLA, Spring 1968.

4. Froug, *The Screenwriter Looks at the Screenwriter*, p. 42.

5. Nunnally Johnson specifically declined to take screenplay credit for *The Gunfighter* in a letter from his secretary, Betty Baldwin, to Johnny Hyde dated 24 June 1949, and in a memo from Johnson to Frank McCarthy dated 17 November 1949, in NJCBU.

6. Stempel, King oral history interview, p. 152.

7. The Pollinger letter about the book on Rommel is with an unsent memo from Johnson to Zanuck dated 14 February 1950, in NJCBU.

8. Material on *The Desert Fox* is from correspondence, particularly between Johnson and Desmond Young, in NJCBU.

Chapter 14: Bette and Burton—and a Phone Call to Garbo

1. Material throughout from NJOH, pp. 306–329.

2. Memos in NJCBU.

3. Ibid.

4. Gussow, *Don't Say Yes*, p. 179.

Chapter 15: "Put the Camera Here"

1. Nunnally Johnson on directing, NJOH, pp. 51–56.
2. NJOH, pp. 259–260.
3. Ibid., pp. 61–62; also, Johnson memo to Negulesco dated 22 November 1952, in NJCBU.
4. NJOH, pp. 102–103.
5. NJAI.
6. Johnson letter to Gregory Peck dated 2 November 1953, in NJCBU.
7. A private, very reliable source close to the production of *Night People*.
8. NJOH, pp. 333–335.
9. Ibid., pp. 333–335.
10. Tom Stempel, unpublished oral history interview with Charles G. Clarke (American Film Institute, 1970–1971), pp. 66–67.

Chapter 16: The Changing of the Guard

1. Abel Green, "Darryl Zanuck Might Resume Despite Man Breaker Situation in Agent-Bossed Hollywood," *Variety* (weekly), 13 June 1956, clipping in Zanuck clipping file, Margaret Herrick Library, Academy of Motion Picture Arts and Sciences.
2. Gussow, *Don't Say Yes*, pp. 182–185; also, Stempel, Dunne oral history, pp. 28, 169–170.
3. Memos in NJCBU, including Zanuck's memos to Johnson as well as Johnson's memos to Zanuck.
4. Johnson letter to Zanuck dated 13 April 1956, in NJCBU.
5. Johnson memo dated 9 May 1958, in NJCBU.
6. NJOH, pp. 426–427.
7. Johnson memo to Adler dated 20 March 1956, in NJCBU.
8. NJOH, pp. 430, 432.
9. Johnson undated memo to Adler, in NJCBU.
10. Johnson memo to Adler dated 8 January 1957, in NJCBU.
11. Johnson letter to Charles Einfeld dated 28 January 1957, in NJCBU, mentions that the condition that Chodorov's name not appear on the screen was part of the deal selling the play to producer Charles K. Feldman before it was sold to Fox; Johnson took his own name off the credits in a letter to the Writers Guild dated 14 December 1956, in NJCBU; for an example of the critical reaction, or lack of it, to the absence of a writing credit, see the review in *The New York Times* dated 22 February 1957.
12. Material on *The Three Faces of Eve* from memos in NJCBU, NJOH pp. 388–400, and an interview with Joanne Woodward. The part of the psychiatrist, played in the film by Lee J. Cobb, was offered to Orson Welles, who could not do the part, but told Johnson that the part of Eve was sure to get an Academy Award nomination.

Chapter 17: Let Somebody Else Say "Put the Camera Here"

1. Material and quotations from Nunnally Johnson throughout are from NJOH, pp. 402–422.

2. Molly Haskell, *From Reverence to Rape* (Holt, Rinehart and Winston, 1974), pp. 231–276.

Chapter 18: Marilyn

1. Johnson's comments on Marilyn Monroe throughout are from NJOH, pp. 199, 314–315, 330, 439–447.
2. James Robert Parrish, *The Fox Girls* (Arlington House, 1971), p. 621.
3. For a view of the last days by the writer who took over for Johnson, see Walter Bernstein, "Marilyn Monroe's Last Picture Show," *Esquire*, July 1973.

Chapter 19: Reenter the Family, Exit Zanuck

1. Material throughout from NJOH, pp. 367–371, 424–437, 449–456.
2. Johnson letter to Lew Screiber dated 20 May 1960, in Johnson's private files.
3. Darryl Zanuck letter to Johnson dated 21 August 1962, in NJCBU.
4. Memo from Zanuck to Fox producers dated 1 December 1952, in the Philip Dunne collection at the University of Southern California.
5. Johnson letter to Norman Tyre dated 29 August 1962, in NJCBU. The details of the Johnson-Levathes agreement are derived from several items of correspondence in the *Take Her She's Mine* file in NJCBU and NJOH, pp. 367–368.
6. Johnson letter to Zanuck dated 1 September 1962, in NJCBU.
7. The Johnson and Zanuck cablegrams and letters are in NJCBU.
8. Memo from Frank Ferguson to Richard Zanuck dated 23 July 1963, in the writers' file at Fox.
9. Johnson letter to Henry Koster dated 17 June 1964, in the writers' file at Fox. Johnson had, in fact, shared a credit with Claire Huffaker in 1960 when *Flaming Star* was finally filmed. Huffaker, the author of the novel the script was based on, did minor rewrites and, with Johnson's permission, received co-screenplay credit with him. Johnson had, by then, been off the project two years, so he was probably not as emotionally involved with it.

Chapter 20: Stage Frightened

1. Correspondence between Johnson and E. M. Nathanson is in NJCBU.
2. NJOH, p. 463; also NJAI.
3. Higham and Greenberg, *The Celluloid Muse*, p. 38.
4. See note three above.
5. Stephen Farber, "The Outlaws," *Sight and Sound*, Autumn 1968, p. 174.
6. NJOH, p. 462.
7. Johnson letter to Truman Capote dated 25 January 1965, in NJCBU.
8. As luck would have it, William Goldman was covering the 1967–1968 Broadway theatre season when Johnson was involved with two shows, *Henry, Sweet Henry* and *Darling of the Day*. Both shows are discussed in Goldman's book, *The Season* (Harcourt,

Brace and World, 1969). Much of the information about those two shows in this chapter is from that source.

9. NJOH, pp. 179–180.
10. Ibid., pp. 76–77.
11. Ibid., p. 473.

Chapter 21: **Museum/Set/Piece**

1. The material here is all from personal observation, since I was the "fellow who had been helping them select the film clips."

Filmography

**Rough House Rosie   Release date: May 1927

Cast:

Clara Bow, Reed Howes, Arthur Houseman, Doris Hill, Douglas Gilmore, John Miljan, Henry Kolker.

Credits:

Written by:	Nunnally Johnson
Titles by:	George Marion, Jr.
Director:	Frank Streyer

Story:

Fighter Joe Hennessy's manager complains that Joe cannot fight because he is paying too much attention to Rosie O'Reilly. She becomes a hit in a cabaret act called "Rough House Rosie and Her Smooth Little Roughnecks". The manager advises Joe to act like a caveman, which he does in a dream sequence.

Distribution:

Paramount

Notes:

Although the film is based (very loosely) on a Johnson story, he had nothing to do with the writing of the film.

**For the Love of Mike   Release date: August 1927

Cast:

Ben Lyon, George Sidney, Ford Sterling, Claudette Colbert, Rudolph Cameron, Hugh Cameron, Mabel Swor, Richard Skeets Gallagher.

Credits:

Written by:	John Moroso
Director:	Frank Capra

Story:

Mike, an orphan left on a doorstep, grows up to go to Yale, where he wins the big crew race.

Distribution:
First National

Notes:
Although uncredited, Johnson worked on the script for this film.

**A Bedtime Story   Release date: April 1933

Cast:
Rene: Maurice Chevalier; *Sally:* Helen Twelvetrees; *Victor:* Edwart Everett Horton; *Paulette:* Adrienne Ames; *"Monsieur":* Baby Leroy; *Max:* Earle Foxe; also, Gertrude Michael, Ernest Wood, Reginald Mason, Henry Kolker, George MacQuarrie, Paul Panzer.

Credits:

Screenplay:	Waldemar Young, Nunnally Johnson
Adaptation:	Benjamin Glazer, Waldemar Young, Nunnally Johnson.
From the novel by:	Roy Horniman
Director:	Norman Taurog
Cinematography:	Charles Lang
Music:	Ralph Rainger, Lee Robin

Story:
A Frenchman returns from Africa and finds a baby in the back seat of his car. He decides to bring it up by himself. He hires a nurse and finds himself growing to love her as well as the baby.

Distribution:
Paramount

Running Time:
87 minutes

**Mama Loves Papa   Release date: July 1933

Cast:
Wilbur Todd: Charles Ruggles, *Jessie Todd:* Mary Boland, *Mrs. McIntosh:* Lilyan Tashman, *Mr. Kirkwood:* George Barbier, *Tom Walker:* Morgan Wallace, *Sara Walker:* Ruth Warren, *Basil Pew:* Andre Beranger, *Mr. Pierrepont:* Tom Ricketts, *"The Radical":* Warner Richmond, *The Mayor:* Frank Sheridan, *O'Leary:* Tom McGuire.

Credits:

Screenplay:	Nunnally Johnson, Arthur Kober
Story:	Douglas MacLean, Keene Thompson
Additional Dialogue:	Eddie Welch
Director:	Norman McLeod
Cinematography:	Gilbert Warrenton
Film Editor:	Richard Currier
Recording Engineer:	John A. Goodrich

Story:

Jessie Todd tries to convince her husband Wilbur to behave like a successful man. He wears a Prince Albert to work, and everyone thinks he is going to a funeral. His boss gives him the afternoon off, and, as he is sitting in the park, he is mistaken for the parks commissioner. Through a series of adventures he actually becomes the parks commissioner.

Distribution:
Paramount

Running Time:
70 minutes

**Moulin Rouge   Release date: January 1934

Cast:

Helen Hall: Constance Bennett, *Douglas Hall:* Franchot Tone, *Victor LeMaire:* Tullio Carminati, *Mrs. Morris:* Helen Westley, *McBride:* Andrew Tombes, *Joe:* Russ Brown, *Frenchman:* Georges Renevant, *Eddie:* Fuzzy Knight, *Ramon:* Ivan Lebedeff, *Drunk:* Hobart Cavanaugh.

Credits:

Screenplay:	Nunnally Johnson, Henry Lehrman
Director:	Sidney Lanfield
Cinematography:	Charles Rosher
Film Editor:	Floyd Nesler

Story:

Helen, to convince her composer husband, Doug, that she still has talent, pretends to be her old partner in a sister-act, Raquel. Helen goes into Raquel's new show and is a hit. As Raquel, she tries to seduce Doug. He is tempted to run away with "Raquel," but eventually decides against it and pretends that he knew all along that it was Helen.

Distribution:
Twentieth Century Pictures
United Artists

Running Time:
70 minutes

**The House of Rothschild   Release date: March 1934

Cast:

Mayer Rothschild and *Nathan Rothschild:* George Arliss, *Ledrantz:* Boris Karloff, *Julie Rothschild:* Loretta Young, *Captain Fitzroy:* Robert Young, *Duke of Wellington:* C. Aubrey Smith, *Hannah Rothschild:* Mrs George Arliss, *Baring:* Arthur Byron, *Gudula:* Helen Westley, *Herries:* Reginald Owen, *Metternich:* Alan Mowbray, *Rowerth:* Holmes Herbert, *Solomon:* Paul Harvey, *Amschel:* Ivan Simpson, *Carl:* Noel Madison, *James:* Murray

Kinnell, *Talleyrand:* Georges Renevant, *Prussian Officer:* Oscar Apfel, *Prince Regent:* Lumsden Hare.

Credits:

Screenplay:	Nunnally Johnson
From an unproduced play by:	George Hembert Westley
Director:	Alfred Werker
Cinematography:	Peverell Marley
Associate Director:	Maude Howell
Musical Score:	Alfred Newman

Story:

The children of Mayer Rothschild grow up to run the biggest group of banking houses in Europe. When Ledrantz convinces the countries of Europe not to let the Rothschilds get the loan that will re-establish Franch, Nathan Rothschild forbids his daughter Julie to marry a Gentile. The opponents of Napoleon are later forced to come to the Rothschilds to finance the war.

Distribution:

Twentieth Century Pictures
United Artists

Running Time:

88 minutes

Bulldog Drummond Strikes Back   Release date: May 1934

Cast:

Hugh Drummond: Ronald Coleman, *Lola Field:* Loretta Young, *Prince Achmed:* Warner Oland, *Algy:* Charles Butterworth, *Gwen:* Una Merkel, *Inspector Nielson:* C. Aubrey Smith, *Dr. Owen Sothern:* Arthur Hoke, *Singh:* George Regas, *Lola's Aunt:* Ethel Griffies, *Hassan:* Mischa Auer, *Parker:* Douglas Gerrard.

Credits:

Screenplay:	Nunnally Johnson
From a novel by:	H. C. McNeile
Director:	Roy Del Ruth
Producer:	Darryl F. Zanuck
Associate Producers:	William Goetz, Raymond Griffith
Cinematography:	Peverell Marley
Art Director:	Richard Day
Film Editor:	Allen McNeil
Music:	Alfred Newman
Costumes:	Gwen Wakeling

Story:

Drummond, back in London for the marriage of Algy and Gwen, discovers a dead body in a house. When he returns with the police, the body has vanished. Drummond traces the body to a ship owned by Prince Achmed.

Distribution:
Twentieth Century Pictures
United Artists

Running Time:
80 minutes

**Kid Millions   Release date: October 1934

Cast:
Eddie Wilson Jr.: Eddie Cantor, *Dot:* Ethel Merman, *Joan:* Ann Sothern, *Louie:* Warren Hymer, *Gerald Lane:* George Murphy, *Colonel Larrabee:* Berton Churchill, *Mulhulla:* Paul Harvey, *Ben Ali:* Jesse Block, *Tanya:* Eve Sully, *Khoot:* Otto Hoffman, *Toots:* Doris Davenport, *Pop:* Jack Kennedy, *Herman:* Edgar Kennedy, *Oscar:* Stanley Fields, *Adolph:* John Kelly.

Credits:

Screenplay:	Arthur Sheekman, Nat Perrin, Nunnally Johnson
Director:	Roy Del Ruth
Producer:	Samuel Goldwyn
Cinematography:	Ray Rennahan
Color Direction:	Willy Pogany
Choreography:	Seymour Felix
Songs:	Walter Donaldson, Gus Kahn, Burton Lane, Harold Adamson, Irving Berlin

Story:
Eddie, the son of an Egyptologist, is left $77 million by his father, but he must get to Egypt to get it. He is threatened with death by Shiek Mulhulla, who has promised to kill the late Egyptologist's heirs.

Distribution:
United Artists

Running Time:
90 minutes

**Cardinal Richelieu   Release date: March 1935

Cast:
Cardinal Richelieu: George Arliss, *King Louis:* Edward Arnold, *Father Joseph:* Halliwell Hobbes, *Lenore:* Maureen O'Sullivan, *Andre de Pons:* Cesar Romero, *Baradas:* Douglas Dumbrille, *Queen Marie:* Violet Kimble-Cooper, *Queen Anne:* Katherine Alexander, *Gaston:* Francis Lister, *Fontrailles:* Robert Harrigan, *Duke of Brittany:* Herbert Bunston, *Duke*

of Lorraine: Murray Kinnell, *Duke of Normandy:* Gilbert Emery, *D'Esperron:* Keith Kenneth, *DeBussey:* Joseph R. Tozer, *Le Moyne:* Russell Hicks.

Credits:

Screenplay:	Maude Howell, Cameron Rogers, W. P. Lipscomb
Adapted from the play by:	Edward Bulwer-Lytton
Director:	Rowland V. Lee
Producers:	William Goetz, Raymond Griffith
Cinematography:	Peverell Marley
Film Editor:	Sherman Todd

Story:
Richelieu discovers a plot to turn France over to Spain, but, through his brilliant political maneuvering, exposes the plotters and saves the country.

Distribution:
Twentieth Century Pictures
United Artists

Running Time:
83 minutes

Notes:
Johnson wrote the screenplay with Cameron Rogers, but requested his name be removed when George Arliss made changes in the script.

Baby Face Harrington Release date: June 1935

Cast:
Willie: Charles Butterworth, *Millicent:* Una Merkel, *Ronald:* Harvey Stephens, *Uncle Henry:* Eugene Pallette, *Rocky:* Nat Pendleton, *Dorothy:* Ruth Selwyn, *Skinner:* Donald Mack, *Edith:* Dorothy Libaire, *Albert:* Edward Nugent, *Judge Forbes:* Richard Carle, *Hank:* G. Pat Collins, *Colton:* Claude Gillingwater.

Credits:

Screenplay:	Harry Segall, Barry Ravers
Dialogue:	Charles Lederer
Adaptation:	Nunnally Johnson, Edwin Knopf
From the play:	*Something to Brag About* by Edgar Selwyn, William LeBaron
Director:	Raoul Walsh
Producer:	Edgar Selwyn
Cinematography:	Oliver T. Marsh
Film Editor:	William S. Gray

Story:
When mild-mannered Willie is mistakenly arrested, he is thought to be a member of the notorious Rocky Bannister gang. He eventually captures the real Rocky Bannister.

Distribution:
Metro-Goldwyn-Mayer

Running Time:
65 minutes

**Thanks a Million   Release date: October 1935

Cast:

Eric Land: Dick Powell, *Ned Allen:* Fred Allen, *Sally Mason:* Ann Dvorak, *Phoebe Mason:* Patsy Kelly, *Orchestra Leader:* David Rubinoff, *Band:* Paul Whiteman and his Orchestra, *Yacht Club Boys:* Charles Adler, James V. Kern, Billy Mann, George Kelly, *Tammany:* Benny Baker, *Governor:* Charles Richman, *Mrs. Kruger:* Margaret Irving, *Mr. Kruger:* Alan Dinehart, *Mr. Grass:* Andrew Rombes, *Judge Culliman:* Raymond Walburn, *Maxwell:* Paul Harvey, *Casey:* Edwin Maxwell, *Mr. Bradley:* Russell Hicks.

Credits:

Screenplay:	Nunnally Johnson
Story:	Melville Crossman (Darryl F. Zanuck)
Director:	Roy Del Ruth
Producer:	Darryl F. Zanuck
Music and Lyrics:	Gus Kahn, Arthur Johnston, Bert Kalmar, Harry Ruby

Story:

Eric, a band singer, takes over as a candidate for governor when the regular candidate keeps getting drunk. Eric just wants to use the campaign to boost his chances of getting on the radio. He ends up telling voters about the crooked politicians in his own party, but he gets elected anyway.

Distribution:
Twentieth Century-Fox

Running Time:
87 minutes

Notes:

"Melville Crossman" was one of the three pseudonyms used by Darryl F. Zanuck when he was a screenwriter at Warner Brothers.

**The Man Who Broke the Bank at Monte Carlo Release date: October 1935

Cast:

M. Gallard: Ronald Colman, *Helen Berkeley:* Joan Bennett, *Ivan:* Nigel Bruce, *Bertrand:* Colin Clive, *Director:* Montagu Love, *Office Man:* Ferdinand Gottschalk, *Second Assistant Director:* Frank Reicher, *Third Assistant Director:* Lionel Pape, *Croupier:* Charles Fallon, *Chief:* Leonid

Inegoff, *Check Room Girl:* Georgette Rhodes, *Taxi Driver:* Alphonse Du Bois.

Credits:

Screenplay:	Nunnally Johnson, Howard Ellis Smith
From the play by:	Ilia Surgutchoff, Frederick Swann
Director:	Stephen Roberts
Producer:	Darryl F. Zanuck
Associate Producer:	Nunnally Johnson
Cinematography:	Ernest Palmer
Musical Direction:	Oscar Bradley

Story:

Gallard breaks the bank at Monte Carlo, and the Casino sends Helen to seduce him and to get him to return to the Casino to lose the money back. He does return and loses the money. He ends up as a taxi driver in Paris, while she goes on to become a singing star.

Distribution:
Twentieth Century-Fox

Running Time:
70 minutes

The Prisoner of Shark Island   Release date: February 1936

Cast:
Dr. Samuel Mudd: Warner Baxter, *Mrs. Peggy Mudd:* Gloria Stuart, *Martha Mudd:* Joyce Kay, *Colonel Dyer:* Claude Gillingwater, *General Ewing:* Douglas Wood, *Sergeant Cooper:* Fred Kohler Jr., *Commandant:* Harry Carey, *David Herold:* Paul Fix, *Sergeant Rankin:* John Carradine, *John Wilkes Booth:* Francis McDonald, *Erickson:* Arthur Byron, *Dr. McIntire:* O. P. Heggie, *Lovett:* John McGuire, *Hunter:* Paul McVey, *O'Toole:* Francis Ford, *Buck:* Ernest Whitman, *Abraham Lincoln:* Frank McGlynn Sr.

Credits:

Screenplay:	Nunnally Johnson
Director:	John Ford
Executive Producer:	Darryl F. Zanuck
Associate Producer:	Nunnally Johnson
Cinematography:	Bery Glennon
Film Editor:	Jack Murray

Story:

The true story of Dr. Samuel Mudd, who, unaware of the assassination of Lincoln, treats John Wilkes Booth's broken leg. As a result, he is tried as a co-conspirator in the assassination and is sent to Fort Jefferson. His heroic actions during a yellow fever epidemic result in his case being reconsidered.

Distribution:
Twentieth Century-Fox

Running Time:
95 minutes

**The Country Doctor

Release date: March 1936

Cast:

Quintuplets: The Dionne Quintuplets, *Dr. Roy Luke:* Jean Hersholt, *Nurse Andrews:* Dorothy Peterson, *Mary:* June Lang, *Odgen:* Slim Summerville, *Tony:* Michael Whalen, *MacKenzie:* Robert Barrat, *Mike:* J. Anthony Hughes, *Asa Wyatt:* John Qualen, *Greasy:* George Chandler, *Sir Basil:* Montagu Love, *Dr. Paul Luke:* Frank Reicher, *Dr. Wilson:* George Meeker, *Nurse:* Jane Darwell, *Governor General:* David Torrence.

Credits:

Screenplay:	Sonya Levien
Based on newspaper	
stories by:	Charles E. Blake
Director:	Henry King
Executive Producer:	Darryl F. Zanuck
Producer:	Nunnally Johnson
Cinematography:	John Seitz, Daniel B. Clark
Film Editor:	Barbara McLean
Technical Supervisor:	Dr. Allan Defoe

Story:

Dr. Roy Luke is a typical country doctor in the backwoods of Canada. His practice is threatened by the arrival of a new doctor hired by the major industry in the area. Dr. Luke eventually delivers quintuplets to a local family, and his practice is saved.

Distribution:
Twentieth Century-Fox

Running Time:
110 minutes

**The Road to Glory

Release date: June 1936

Cast:

Michel Denet: Frederic March, *Paul LaRoche:* Warner Baxter, *Papa LaRoche:* Lionel Barrymore, *Monique:* June Lang, *Bouffion:* Gregory Ratoff, *Regnier:* Victor Kilian, *Relief Captain:* Paul Stanton, *Duflous:* John Qualen, *Lieutenant Tannen:* Julius Tannen, *Major:* Theodore von Eltz, *Rigaud:* Paul Fix, *Ledoux:* Leonid Kinskey, *Courier:* Jacques Lory, *Doctor:* Jacques Vanaire, *Nurse:* Edythe Raynore, *Old Soldier:* George Warrington.

Credits:

Screenplay:	Joel Sayre, William Faulkner
Director:	Howard Hawks
Executive Producer:	Darryl F. Zanuck
Associate Producer:	Nunnally Johnson
Cinematography:	Gregg Toland
Film Editor:	Edward Curtis
Art Direction:	Hans Peters
Set Decoration:	Thomas Little
Music:	Louis Silvers

Story:

During World War I, both Denet and LaRoche find themselves in love with Monique, a nurse at a nearby hospital. LaRoche is killed in battle, and Denet takes command of the Regiment.

Distribution:

Twentieth Century-Fox

Running Time:

95 minutes

Notes:

The story was adapted from a French film, *Croix de Bois*, and several of the battle scenes from that picture were used in *The Road to Glory*.

**Dimples   Release date: September 1936

Cast:

Dimples: Shirley Temple, *Professor:* Frank Morgan, *Mrs. Drew:* Helen Westley, *Colonel Loring:* Berton Churchill, *Allen Drew:* Robert Kent, *Betty Loring:* Delma Byron, *Cleo March:* Astrid Allwyn, *Hawkins:* Julius Tannen, *Mr. St. Clair:* Paul Stanton, *Cicero:* Stepin Fechit, *Rufus:* Billy McClain, *Policeman:* Robert Murphy, *Uncle Tom:* Jack Clifford, *Topsy:* Betty Jean Hainey.

Credits:

Screenplay:	Arthur Sheekman, Nat Perrin
From an idea by:	Nunnally Johnson
Director:	William Seiter
Executive Producer:	Darryl F. Zanuck
Associate Producer:	Nunnally Johnson
Cinematography:	Bert Glennon
Film Editor:	Herbert Levy
Sound:	Gene Grossman
Art Direction:	William Darling
Set Decoration:	Thomas Little
Music and Lyrics:	Jimmy McHugh, Ted Koehler

| Dances staged by: | Bill Robinson |
| Musical direction: | Louis Silvers |

Story:

Dimples, an orphan, is adopted for a trial period by Mrs. Drew. Dimples returns to the Professor and his shows, and the Professor and Mrs. Drew end up together.

Distribution:
Twentieth Century-Fox

Running Time:
78 minutes

Banjo on My Knee Release date: December 1936

Cast:

Pearl: Barbara Stanwyck, *Ernie:* Joel McCrea, *Grandma:* Helen Westley, *Buddy:* Buddy Ebsen, *Newt:* Walter Brennan, *Leota:* Katherine DeMille, *Chick Bean:* Anthony Martin, *Ruby:* Minnie Gombell, *Jules:* George Humbert, *Warfield Scott:* Walter Catlett, *Lope:* Spencer Charters, *Hattie:* Cecil Weston, *Eph:* Louis Mason, *Gertha:* Hilda Vaugh, *Slade:* Victor Kilian.

Credits:

Screenplay:	Nunnally Johnson
From the novel by:	Harry Hamilton
Director:	John Cromwell
Executive Producer:	Darryl F. Zanuck
Associate Producer:	Nunnally Johnson
Cinematography:	Ernest Palmer
Film Editor:	Hanson Fritch
Songs:	Jimmy McHugh, Harold Adamson

Story:

Pearl and Ernie are newlyweds, but Ernie must escape when he thinks he has killed a man. He returns, but Pearl goes off to New Orleans. Both become involved with others, but come back to each other.

Distribution:
Twentieth Century-Fox

Running Time:
80 minutes

Nancy Steele Is Missing Release date: March 1937

Cast:

Dannie O'Neill: Victor McLaglen, *Michael Steele:* Walter Connolly, *Sheila O'Neill:* June Lang, *Jimmy Wilson:* Robert Kent, *Professor Sturm:* Peter

Lorre, *Dan Mallon:* Frank Conroy, *Wilkins:* John Carradine, *Doctor on Farm:* DeWitt Jennings, *Nancy:* Shirley Deane, *Crowder:* George Taylor, *Miss Hunt:* Margaret Fielding, *Mrs. Flaherty:* Jane Darwell, *Mr. Flaherty:* Granville Bates, *Guiseppi:* George Humbert

Credits:

Screenplay:	Hal Long, Gene Fowler
From the short story "Ransom" by:	Charles Francis Coe
Director:	George Marshall
Executive Producer:	Darryl F. Zanuck
Associate Producer:	Nunnally Johnson
Cinematography:	Edward Cronjager
Film Editor:	Jack Murray

Story:

Dannie kidnaps baby Nancy Steele in 1917 as a protest against industrialist Michael Steele leading the country into war. Dannie is put in prison for his pro-German sentiments. When he is released, he is about to tell Steele that Dannie's supposed daughter is Nancy Steele when Steele offers him a job. A former cellmate of Dannie's tries to pass off another girl as Nancy Steele, but Dannie exposes him and tells Steele who the real Nancy is.

Distribution:

Twentieth Century-Fox

Running Time:

85 minutes

**Cafe Metropole　　　　　　　　　　Release date: April 1937

Cast:

Laura Ridgeway: Loretta Young, *Alexis:* Tyrone Power, *Victor:* Adolphe Menjou, *Paul:* Gregory Ratoff, *Ridgeway:* Charles Winninger, *Margaret:* Helen Westley, *Leroy:* Christian Rub, *Monnett:* Ferdinand Gottschalf, *Maitre d'Hotel:* Georges Renevant, *Artist:* Leonid Kinskey, *Thorndyke:* Hal K. Dawson

Credits:

Screenplay:	Jacques Deval
Original screen story:	Gregory Ratoff
Director:	Edward Griffith
Producer:	Nunnally Johnson
Executive Producer:	Darryl F. Zanuck
Cinematography:	Lucien Andriot
Film Editor:	Irene Morra
Musical Direction:	Louis Silvers

Story:

Victor, to pay back money he has "borrowed" from the Cafe he runs, persuades Alexis to pretend to be a Russian prince and to try to get the money from a rich American girl. Alex falls in love with Laura and refuses to go through with the plan, but Victor manages to get the money from Laura's father, indicating the money is to pay off the Russian prince to leave Laura alone.

Distribution:

Twentieth Century-Fox

Running Time:

84 minutes

**Slave Ship   Release date: August 1937

Cast:

Jim Lovett: Warner Baxter, *Jack Thompson:* Wallace Berry, *Nancy Marlowe:* Elizabeth Allen, *Swifty:* Mickey Rooney, *Lefty:* George Sanders, *Mrs. Marlowe:* Jane Darwell, *Danilo:* Joseph Schildkraut, *Grimes:* Arthur Hohl, *Mabel:* Minna Gombell, *Atkins:* Billy Bevan, *Scraps:* Francis Ford, *Proprietor:* J. Farrell MacDonald.

Credits:

Screenplay:	Sam Hellman, Lamar Trotti, Gladys Lehman, William Faulkner
Screen Story:	William Faulkner
From the novel	
The Last Slaver by:	Dr. George S. King
Director:	Tay Garnett
Executive Producer:	Darryl F. Zanuck
Associate Producer:	Nunnally Johnson
Cinematography:	Ernest Palmer
Film Editor:	Lloyd Nosler
Music:	Alfred Newman
Sound:	Al Bruzlin
Art Direction:	Hans Peters

Story:

Jim Lovett is the captain of a slave ship. He meets and marries Nancy Marlowe, for whom he promises to give up running the ship. When he tells his first mate, Jack Thompson, to pay off the crew, Thompson mutinies and takes over the ship. Lovett regains control of the ship and blows it up.

Distribution:

Twentieth Century-Fox

Running Time:

92 minutes

**Love under Fire Release date: August 1937

Cast:
Tracy Egan: Don Ameche, *Myra Cooper:* Loretta Young, *Pamela Beau-
mont:* Frances Drake, *Tip Conway:* Walter Catlett, *Delmar:* John Carradine,
Borrah Minevitch and Gang: Themselves, *General Montero:* Sig Rumann,
Lieutenant Chaves: Harold Huber, *Rosa:* Katherine DeMille, *Captain
Bowden:* E. E. Clive, *Cabana:* Don Alvarado, *Bert:* Clyde Cook, *DeVega:*
George Regas, *Porter:* George Humbert.

Credits:

Screenplay:	Gene Fowler, Allen Rivkin, Ernest Pascal
From the play *The Fugitives* by:	Walter Hackett
Director:	George Marshall
Producer:	Nunnally Johnson
Executive Producer:	Darryl F. Zanuck
Cinematography:	Ernest Palmer
Film Editor:	Barbara McLean
Musical Direction:	Arthur Lange

Story:
Tracy Egan, an investigator from Scotland Yard, is on vacation in Spain
where he meets Myra. He suspects she has stolen some jewels, but Pamela
is the thief. They all escape from Spain just as the Spanish Civil War
begins.

Distribution:
Twentieth Century-Fox

Running Time:
75 minutes

**Jesse James Release date: January 1939

Cast:
Jesse James: Tyrone Power, *Frank James:* Henry Fonda, *Zee:* Nancy Kelly,
Will Wright: Randolph Scott, *Major Cobb:* Henry Hull, *Jailer:* Slim
Summerville, *Runyon:* J. Edward Bronberg, *Barshee:* Brian Donlevy, *Bob
Ford:* John Carradine, *McCoy:* Donald Meek, *Jesse James, Jr.:* John
Russell, *Mrs. Samuels:* Jane Darwell, *Charles Ford:* Charles Tannen, *Mrs.
Ford:* Claire DuBrey, *Clark:* Willard Robertson, *Lynch:* Paul Sutton,
Pinky: Ernest Whitman, *Bill:* Paul Burns, *Preacher:* Spencer Charters,
Tom: Arthur Aylsworth, *Heywood:* Charles Halton, *Roy:* George Chandler,
Old Marshall: Erville Alderson.

Credits:

Screenplay:	Nunnally Johnson
Director:	Henry King

Executive Producer:	Darryl F. Zanuck
Associate Producer:	Nunnally Johnson
Cinematography:	George Barnes
Technicolor Cameraman:	W. H. Green
Film Editor:	Barbara McLean
Music:	Louis Silvers

Story:

In the Post Civil War period, the St. Louis Midlands Railroad is using unscrupulous practices to obtain land. One of their agents accidently kills the mother of Jesse James, and Jesse begins robbing their trains. When the railroad appears to offer him a deal, he gives himself up, but the railroad goes back on its word and he escapes from jail. He is killed by one of his gang.

Distribution:

Twentieth Century-Fox

Running Time:

105 minutes

**Wife, Husband and Friend   Release date: March 1939

Cast:

Doris: Loretta Young, *Leonard:* Warner Baxter, *Cecil Carver:* Binnie Barnes, *Hugo:* Cesar Romero, *Major Blair:* George Barbier, *Rossi:* J. Edward Bromberg, *Mike Craig:* Eugene Pallette, *Mrs. Blair: Carol:* Ruth Terry, *Wilkins:* Harry Rosenthal, *Mrs. Craig:* Renie Riano, *Hertz:* Lawrence Grant, *Jaffee:* Charles Williams.

Credits:

Screenplay:	Nunnally Johnson
From the novel	
Career in C Major by:	James M. Cain
Director:	Gregory Ratoff
Executive Producer:	Darryl F. Zanuck
Associate Producer:	Nunnally Johnson
Cinematography:	Ernest Palmer
Film Editor:	Walter Thompson
Art Direction:	Richard Day, Mark Lee Kirk
Set Decoration:	Thomas Little
Musical Direction:	David Buttolph
Music and Lyrics:	Samuel Pokrass, Walter Bullock, Armando Hauser

Story:

Doris Borland wants to be an opera singer, but her husband, Leonard, is discovered to have the talent. He goes on tour with singer Cecil Carver, but his first appearance in an opera is a disaster.

Distribution:
Twentieth Century-Fox

Running Time:
80 minutes

Notes:
Johnson remade the same story ten years later as *Everybody Does It*.

**Rose of Washington Square   Release date: May 1939

Cast:
Bart Clinton: Tyrone Power, *Rose:* Alice Faye, *Ted Cotter:* Al Jolson, *Harry Long:* William Frawley, *Peggy:* Joyce Compton, *Whitey Brown:* Hobart Cavanaugh, *Russell:* Moroni Olson, *Barouche Driver:* E. E. Clive, *Louis Prima:* Himself, *Cavanaugh:* Charles Wilson, *Chumps:* Hal K. Dawson, Paul Burns, *Toby:* Ben Weldon, *Irving:* Horace MacMahon, *District Attorney:* Paul Stanton, *Dexter:* Harry Hayden, *Kress:* Charles Lane, *Specialty Act:* Igor and Tanya.

Credits:

Screenplay:	Nunnally Johnson
From an unpublished story by:	John Larkin and Jerry Horwin
Director:	Gregory Ratoff
Executive Producer:	Darryl F. Zanuck
Associate Producer:	Nunnally Johnson
Cinematography:	Karl Freund
Film Editor:	Louis Loeffler
Music:	Louis Silvers

Story:
Rose, an aspiring singer, falls in love with Bart, an attractive crook. He is arrested, and she is left alone to sing "My Man."

Distribution:
Twentieth Century-Fox

Running Time:
80 minutes

**The Grapes of Wrath   Release date: January 1940

Cast:
Tom Joad: Henry Fonda, *Ma Joad:* Jane Darwell, *Casy:* John Carradine, *Grandpa:* Charley Grapewin, *Rosasharon:* Dorris Bowdon, *Pa Joad:* Russell Simpson, *Al:* O. Z. Whitehead, *Muley:* John Qualen, *Connie:* Eddie Quillan, *Grandma:* Zeffie Tilbury, *Noah:* Frank Sully, *Uncle John:* Frank Darien, *Winfield:* Darryl Hickman, *Ruth Joad:* Shirley Mills, *Thomas:*

Roger Imhof, *Caretaker:* Grant Mitchell, *Wilkie:* Charles D. Brown, *Davis:* John Arlidge, *Policeman:* Ward Bond, *Bert:* Harry Tyler, *Mae:* Kitty McHugh, *Bill:* William Pawley, *Joe:* Charles Tannen, *Lloyd:* Paul Guilfoyle, *Frank:* David Hughes, *City Man:* Cliff Clark, *Bookkeeper:* Joseph Sawyer, *Tim:* Frank Faylen, *Truck Driver:* Irving Bacon, *Muley's Wife:* Mae Marsh.

Credits:

Screenplay:	Nunnally Johnson
From the novel by:	John Steinbeck
Director:	John Ford
Executive Producer:	Darryl F. Zanuck
Associate Producer:	Nunnally Johnson
Cinematography:	Gregg Toland
Film Editor:	Robert Simpson
Sound:	George Leverett, Roger Heman
Music:	Alfred Newman
Art Direction:	Richard Day, Mark Lee Kirk
Set Decoration:	Thomas Little

Story:

The Joad family is driven off their Oklahoma farm. They make the journey to California, only to find that it is not the promised land they had thought.

Distribution:
Twentieth Century-Fox

Running Time:
129 minutes

**I Was an Adventuress   Release date: May 1940

Cast:

Countess Tanya Vronsky: Zorina, *Paul Vernay:* Richard Greene, *Andre Desormeany:* Erich Von Stroheim, *Polo:* Peter Lorre, *Herr Protz:* Henri Gautier:* Fritz Feld, *Aunt Cecile:* Cora Witherspoon, *Cousin Emil:* Anthony Kemble Cooper, *Fisherman:* Paul Procasi, *Fisherman's Wife:* Inez Palange, *Jacques Dubois:* Egon Brecher, *Henrich Von Kongen:* Roger Imhof, *Orchestra Leader:* Fortunio Bonanova.

Credits:

Screenplay:	Karl Tunberg, Don Ettlinger, John O'Hara
Based on an original production by:	Gregor Rabinovitsch
Written by:	Jacques Companeeg, Herbert Juttle, Hans Jacoby, Michael Duran
Director:	Gregory Ratoff
Associate Producer:	Nunnally Johnson
Cinematography:	Leon Shamroy, Edward Cronjager

Film Editor:	Francis D. Lyon
Sound:	W. D. Flick, Roger Heman
Art Direction:	Richard Day, Joseph C. Wright
Set Decorations:	Thomas Little
Music Direction:	David Buttolph
Dances staged by:	George Balanchine

Story:
Groups of jewel thieves try to outsteal each other in the lavish hotels of Europe.

Distribution:
Twentieth Century-Fox

Running Time:
81 minutes

**Chad Hanna   Release date: December 1940

Cast:
Chad Hanna: Henry Fonda, *Albany Yates:* Dorothy Lamour, *Caroline:* Linda Darnell, *Huguenine:* Guy Kibee, *Mrs. Huguenine:* Jane Darwell, *Bisbee:* John Carradine, *Fred Sheptey:* Ted North, *Ike Wayfish:* Roscoe Ates, *Bell Boy:* Ben Carter, *Burke:* Frank Thomas, *Ciscoe Tridd:* Olin Howard, *Mr. Proudfoot:* Frank Conlan, *Fiero:* Edward Conrad, *Elias:* Edward McWade, *Pete Bastock:* George Davis, *Budlong:* Paul Burns, *Mrs. Tridd:* Sarah Padden, *Mr. Mott:* Tully Marshall, *Joe Duddy:* Edward Mundy, *Mr. Pamplon:* Leonard St. Leo, *Mrs. Pamplon:* Elizabeth Abbott, *Mrs. Mott:* Almira Sessions.

Credits:
Screenplay:	Nunnally Johnson
From the novel by:	Walter D. Edmonds
Director:	Henry King
Producer:	Nunnally Johnson
Executive Producer:	Darryl F. Zanuck
Cinematography:	Ernest Palmer, Ray Rennahan
Film Editor:	Barbara McLean
Art Direction:	Richard Day
Sound:	Arthur Von Kirbach, Roger Heman
Music:	David Buttolph

Story:
In the early 1800's in upstate New York, Chad, a young farm boy, runs away to join the circus. He falls in love and marries a girl from his home town who has also run away to join the circus. Chad saves the circus by finding an elephant for it.

Distribution:
Twentieth Century-Fox

Running Time:
  86 minutes

Notes:
  The novel this film was based on was called "Red Wheels Rolling" when
  serialized in *The Saturday Evening Post*, but was published as a book
  under the name *Chad Hanna*.

**Tobacco Road   Release date: February 1941

Cast:
  Jeeter Lester: Charley Grapewin, *Sister Bessie:* Marjorie Rambeau, *Ellie
  May:* Gene Tierney, *Dude Lester:* William Tracy, *Ada Lester:* Elizabeth
  Patterson, *Captain Tim:* Dana Andrews, *Peabody:* Slim Summerville, *Lov:*
  Ward Bond, *George Payne:* Grant Mitchell, *Grandma:* Zeffie Tilbury, *Chief
  of Police:* Russell Simpson, *County Clerk:* Spencer Charters, *Teller:* Irving
  Bacon, *Auto Dealer:* Harry Tyler, *Major:* Charles Halton, *Clerk:* George
  Chandler.

Credits:

Screenplay:	Nunnally Johnson
From the play *Tobacco Road* by:	Jack Kirkland
Based on the novel by:	Erskine Caldwell
Director:	John Ford
Producer:	Darryl F. Zanuck
Cinematography:	Arthur Miller
Film Editor:	Barbara McLean
Art Direction:	Richard Day, James Basevi
Set Decorations:	Thomas Little
Sound:	Eugene Grossman, Roger Heman
Musical Direction:	David Buttolph

Story:
  Jeeter Lester keeps trying to find the money to pay off the mortgage to keep
  his land, but he is ultimately unsuccessful.

Distribution:
  Twentieth Century-Fox

Running Time:
  84 minutes

**Roxie Hart   Release date: February 1942

Cast:
  Roxie Hart: Ginger Rogers, *Billy Flynn:* Adolphe Menjou, *Homer Howard:*
  George Montgomery, *Jake Callahan:* Lynn Overman, *E. Clay Benham:*
  Nigel Bruce, *Babe:* Phil Silvers, *Mrs. Morton:* Sarah Allgood, *O'Malley:*

William Frawley, *Mary Sunshine:* Spring Byington, *Stuart Chapman:* Ted
North, *Velma Wall:* Helen Reynolds, *Amos Hart:* George Chandler,
Charles E. Murdock: Charles D. Brown, *Martin S. Harrison:* Morris
Ankrum, *Judge:* George Lessey, *Gertie:* Iris Adrian, *Announcer:* Milton
Parsons.

Credits:

Screenplay:	Nunnally Johnson
Based on the play	
Chicago by:	Maurine Watkins
Director:	William Wellman
Producer:	Nunnally Johnson
Cinematography:	Leon Shamroy
Film Editor:	James B. Clark
Art Direction:	Richard Day, Wiard B. Ihnen
Set Decoration:	Thomas Little
Music:	Alfred Newman
Dances staged by:	Hermes Pan
Sound:	Alfred Bruzlin, Roger Heman

Story:

In Chicago in the 1920's, Roxie Hart kills her boyfriend and becomes the
center of a sensational trial.

Distribution:

Twentieth Century-Fox

Running Time:

75 minutes

**Moontide   Release date: April 1942

Cast:

Bobo: Jean Gabin, *Anna:* Ida Lupino, *Tiny:* Thomas Mitchell, *Nusty:*
Claude Rains, *Dr. Brothers:* Jerome Cowan, *Woman on Boat:* Helen
Reynolds, *Reverend Price:* Ralph Byrd, *Bartender:* William Halligan,
Takeo: Sen Yung, *Hirota:* Chester Gan, *Mildred:* Robin Raymond, *Pop
Kelly:* Arthur Aylsworth.

Credits:

Screenplay:	John O'Hara
From the novel by:	Willard Robertson
Director:	Archie Mayo
Producer:	Mark Hellinger
Executive Producer:	Darryl F. Zanuck
Cinematography:	Lucien Ballard, Charles G. Clarke
Film Editor:	William Reynolds
Art Direction:	James Basevi, Richard Day
Set Decoration:	Thomas Little

Sound: Eugene Grossman, Roger Heman
Music: Cyril Mockridge, David Buttolph

Story:

A rough seaman falls in love with a woman who has attempted suicide.

Distribution:

Twentieth Century-Fox

Running Time:

94 minutes

Notes:

Johnson did the final draft of the screenplay, but received no screen credit.

**The Pied Piper   Release date: August 1942

Cast:

Howard: Monty Woolley, *Ronnie:* Roddy McDowall, *Nicole:* Ann Baxter, *Major Diessen:* Otto Preminger, *Aristide:* J. Carrol Naish, *Mr. Cavanaugh:* Lester Matthews, *Mrs. Cavanaugh:* Jill Esmond, *Madame:* Ferike Boros, *Sheila:* Peggy Ann Garner, *Willem:* Merrill Rodin, *Pierre:* Maurice Tauzin, *Rose:* Fleurett Zama, *Frenchman:* William Edmunds, *Foquet:* Marcel Dalio, *Mme. Bonne:* Marcelle Corday, *Mme. Rougeron:* Odette Myrtil.

Credits:

Screenplay: Nunnally Johnson
From the novel by: Nevil Shute
Director: Irving Pichel
Producer: Nunnally Johnson
Executive Producer: Darryl F. Zanuck
Cinematography: Edward Cronjager
Film Editor: Allen McNeil
Art Direction: Richard Day, Maurice Ransford
Set Decoration: Thomas Little
Music: Alfred Newman

Story:

Howard, a confirmed bachelor, is asked to escort a group of children out of France at the beginning of World War II. The group gets larger as they get closer to the coast. Howard outwits a Nazi Major to complete the escape.

Distribution:

Twentieth Century-Fox

Running Time:

88 minutes

**Life Begins at Eight-Thirty   Release date: December 1942

Cast:

Madden Thomas: Monty Woolley, *Kathi Thomas:* Ida Lupino, *Robert:*

Cornell Wilde, *Mrs. Lothian:* Sara Allgood, *Barty:* Melville Cooper, *Gordon:* J. Edward Bromberg, *Officer:* William Demarest, *Producer:* Hal K. Dawson, *Sergeant McNamara:* William Halligan, *Announcer:* Milton Parsons, *Mrs. Spano:* Inez Palange, *Mr. Spano:* Charles LaTorre, *Ruthie:* Fay Helm, *Floorwalker:* Wheaton Chambers, *Policeman:* James Flavin, *Cab Driver:* Bud Geary.

Credits:

Screenplay:	Nunnally Johnson
From the play *The Light of Heart* by:	Emlyn Williams
Director:	Irving Pichel
Producer:	Nunnally Johnson
Executive Producer:	William Goetz
Cinematography:	Edward Cronjager
Film Editor:	Fred Allen
Art Direction:	Richard Day, Boris Leven
Set Decoration:	Thomas Little, Al Orenbach
Sound:	George Leverett, Roger Heman

Story:

Madden Thomas, a once-great actor, has become a drunk looked after by his crippled daughter, Kathi. After an unsuccessful comeback attempt, Thomas realizes he is standing in the way of his daughter's happiness, and he tells her to go with the man she loves.

Distribution:

Twentieth Century-Fox

Running Time:

85 minutes

**The Moon Is Down   Release date: May 1943

Cast:

Colonel Lanser: Sir Cedric Hardwicke, *Mayor Orden:* Henry Travers, *Dr. Winter:* Lee J. Cobb, *Molly Morden:* Dorris Bowdon, *Madame Orden:* Margaret Wycherly, *Lieutenant Tender:* Peter Van Eyck, *Alex Morden:* William Post, *Captain Loft:* Henry Rowland, *George Corell:* E. J. Ballantine, *Peder's Wife:* Violette Wilson, *Captain Bentick:* Hans Schumm, *Major Hunter:* Ernest Dorian, *Lieutenant Prackle:* John Banner, *Annie:* Helene Himig, *Joseph:* Ian Wolfe, *Orderly:* Kurt Kreuger, *Albert:* Jeff Corey, *Schumann:* Louis Arco, *Ole:* Charles McGraw, *Foreman:* Trevor Bardette, *Mother:* Dorothy Peterson.

Credits:

Screenplay:	Nunnally Johnson
From the novel by:	John Steinbeck
Director:	Irving Pichel

Producer:	Nunnally Johnson
Executive Producer:	William Goetz
Cinematography:	Arthur Miller
Film Editor:	Louis Loeffler
Art Direction:	James Basevi, Maurice Ransford
Set Decoration:	Thomas Little, Walter M. Scott
Special Photographic Effects:	Fred Sersen
Music:	Alfred Newman
Sound:	Eugene Grossman, Roger Heman

Story:
Colonel Lanser heads the German army occupying a small town in Norway. The town is at first peaceable, but then resistance to the Nazis begins.

Distribution:
Twentieth Century-Fox

Running Time:
90 minutes

**Holy Matrimony   Release date: August 1943

Cast:
Priam Farll: Monty Woolley, *Alice Challice:* Gracie Fields, *Clive Oxford:* Laird Cregar, *Mrs. Leek:* Una O'Connor, *Mr. Pennington:* Alan Mowbray, *Dr. Caswell:* Melville Cooper, *Duncan Farll:* Franklin Pangborn, *Lady Vale:* Ethel Griffies, *Henry Leek:* Eric Blore, *Mr. Crepitude:* George Zucco, *Critics:* Fritz Feld, William Austin, *Judge:* Montagu Love, *John Leek:* Richard Fraser, *Harry Leek:* Whitner Bissell.

Credits:

Screenplay:	Nunnally Johnson
From the novel *Buried Alive* by:	Arnold Bennett
Director:	John Stahl
Producer:	Nunnally Johnson
Executive Producer:	William Goetz
Cinematography:	Lucien Ballard
Film Editor:	James B. Clark
Art Direction:	James Basevi, Russell Spencer
Set Decorations:	Thomas Little, Paul S. Fox
Music:	Cyril J. Mockridge
Sound:	E. Clayton Ward, Roger Heman

Story:
Artist Priam Farll returns to England to be knighted. When his valet dies, Farll takes his identity to avoid publicity. Farll marries Alice and begins a new life, which is disrupted when he begins painting again and is accused of forging Farll's work.

Distribution:
Twentieth Century-Fox

Running Time:
87 minutes

**Casanova Brown   Release date: August 1944

Cast:
Casanova Q. Brown: Gary Cooper, *Isabel Drury:* Theresa Wright, *Mr. Ferris:* Frank Morgan, *Madge Ferris:* Anita Louise, *Mrs. Drury:* Patricia Collinge, *Mr. Drury:* Edmund Breon, *Dr. Zerneke:* Jill Esmond, *Monica:* Mary Treen, *Mrs. Ferris:* Isobel Elsom, *Butler:* Halliwell Hobbes.

Credits:

Screenplay:	Nunnally Johnson
From the play *The Little Accident* by:	Thomas Mitchell and Floyd Dell
Based on the novel *Bachelor Father* by:	Floyd Dell
Director:	Sam Wood
Producer:	Nunnally Johnson
Cinematography:	John Seitz
Film Editor:	Paul Weatherwax
Art Direction:	Perry Ferguson
Set Decoration:	Julia Heron
Music:	Arthur Lange
Sound:	Ben Winkler

Story:
On the eve of his marriage to Madge, Casanova Brown discovers he is about to become the father of a child by Isabel Drury, to whom he was very briefly married the year before. Isabel indicates that she is going to give up the baby for adoption. After the baby is born, Caz kidnaps it and tries to take care of it. He and Isabel decide to remarry.

Distribution:
RKO-Radio

Running Time:
94 minutes

**Woman in the Window   Release date: October 1944

Cast:
Richard Wanley: Edward G. Robinson, *Alice Reed:* Joan Bennett, *Frank Lalor:* Raymond Massey, *Dr. Barkstane:* Edmund Breon, *Heidt:* Dan Duryea, *Inspector Jackson:* Thomas E. Jackson, *Mazard:* Arthur Loft, *Mrs. Wanley:* Dorothy Peterson, *Steward:* Frank Dawson, *Elsie:* Carol Cameron, *Dickie:* Bobby Blake.

Credits:

Screenplay: Nunnally Johnson
From the novel *Once*
   Off Guard by: J. H. Wallis

Director: Fritz Lang
Producer: Nunnally Johnson
Cinematography: Milton Krasner
Film Editors: Gene Fowler, Jr., Marjorie Fowler
Art Director: Duncan Cramer
Set Decoration: Julia Heron

Story:

Richard Wanley has sent his wife and children to the country for the summer. One night, after dinner at his club, he meets a woman whose portrait he has seen in an art gallery window. She invites him to her apartment to show other sketches by the same artist. Shortly after they arrive at the apartment, they are interrupted by her jealous boyfriend, who threatens her. Wanley saves her, but kills the friend in the process. He disposes of the body, but Wanley and the woman are later blackmailed by the man's bodyguard.

Distribution:
RKO-Radio

Running Time:
99 minutes

**The Keys of the Kingdom   Release date: December 1944

Cast:

Father Francis Chisholm: Gregory Peck, *Dr. Willie Tulloch:* Thomas Mitchell, *Rev. Angus Mealy:* Vincent Price, *Mother Maria Veronica:* Rosa Stander, *Francis* (as a child): Roddy McDowall, *Rev. Hamish MacNabb;* Edmund Gwenn, *Monseignor Sleeth:* Sir Cedric Hardwicke, *Nora* (as a child): Peggy Ann Garner, *Nora:* Jane Ball, *Dr. Wilbur Fiske:* James Gleason, *Agnes Fiske:* Anne Revere, *Lisbeth Chisholm:* Ruth Nelson, *Joseph:* Benson Fong, *Mr. Chia:* Leonard Strong, *Mr. Pao:* Philip Ahn, *Father Tarrant:* Arthur Shields, *Aunt Polly:* Edith Barrett, *Sister Martha:* Sara Allgood, *Lieutenant Shon:* Richard Loo, *Sister Clotilde:* Ruth Ford, *Father Craig:* Kevin O'Shea.

Credits:

Screenplay: Joseph L. Mankiewicz, Nunnally Johnson
From the novel by: A. J. Cronin
Director: John M. Stahl
Producer: Joseph L. Mankiewicz
Cinematography: Arthur Miller
Film Editor: James B. Clark

Art Direction:	James Basevi, William Darling
Set Decoration:	Thomas Little, Frank E. Hughes
Special Photographic Effects:	Fred Sersen
Sound:	Eugene Grossman, Roger Heman

Story:

Father Francis Chisholm comes to China as a young missionary and grows to accept not only the Chinese and the Protestant missionaries, but also his own flaws.

Distribution:

Twentieth Century-Fox

Running Time:

137 minutes

Notes:

Johnson completed a first draft screenplay in 1943 before leaving Fox. After he left, the project was taken up and considerably rewritten by Joseph Mankiewicz. Johnson's script treats Father Chisholm's experiences almost as an adventure story, while Mankiewicz's script and film contain more personal drama. There is also in Johnson's script an even greater acceptance of other religions on Chisolm's part than in Mankiewicz's.

**Along Came Jones Release date: June 1945

Cast:

Melody Jones: Gary Cooper, *Cherrie:* Loretta Young, *George Fury:* William Demarest, *Monte Jarrad:* Dan Duryea, *Avery de Longpre:* Frank Sully, *Ira Waggoner:* Walter Sande, *Leo Gledhill:* Don Costello, *Luke Packard:* William Robertson, *Pop de Longpre:* Russell Simpson, *Sheriff:* Arthur Loft, *Boone:* Lane Chandler, *Kriendler:* Ray Teal

Credits:

Screenplay:	Nunnally Johnson
From the story "Useless Cowboy" by:	Alan LeMay
Director:	Stuart Heisler
Producer:	Gary Cooper
Executive Producer:	William Goetz
Cinematography:	Milton Krasner

Story:

Melody Jones is mistaken for a dangerous gunfighter.

Distribution:

RKO-Radio

Running Time:

90 minutes

**The Southerner   Release date: August 1945

Cast:

Sam: Zachary Scott, *Nona:* Betty Field, *Granny:* Beulah Bondi, *Daisy:* Bunny Sunshine, *Joe:* Jay Gilpin, *Harmie:* Percy Kilbride, *Ma:* Blanche Yurka, *Tim:* Charles Kemper, *Revers:* J. Carrol Naish, *Finlay:* Norman Lloyd, *Doctor:* Jack Norworth, *Bartender:* Nestor Paiva, *Lizzie:* Estelle Taylor

Credits:

Screenplay:	Jean Renoir and Hugo Butler
Based on the novel *Hold Autumn in Your Hand* by:	George Perry Sessions
Director:	Jean Renoir
Producer:	David L. Loew, Robert Hakim
Cinematography:	Lucien Andriot
Music:	Werner Jansen
Film Editor:	Gregg Tallas

Story:

Sam and Nona, a poor Texas farm couple, try to overcome problems of poverty, disease, and floods while waiting for a big harvest that never comes.

Distribution:

United Artists

Running Time:

91 minutes

Notes:

Although he did not receive screen credit, Johnson wrote the first draft of the screenplay with Renoir, based on Hugo Butler's adaptation of the novel. William Faulkner subsequently worked on the screenplay, also without credit.

**The Dark Mirror   Release date: October 1946

Cast:

Terry Collins/Ruth Collins: Olivia de Havilland, *Dr. Scott Elliott:* Lew Ayres, *Detective Stevenson:* Thomas Mitchell, *Rusty:* Richard Long, *District Attorney Girard:* Charles Evans, *Franklin:* Gary Owen, *George Benson:* Lester Allen, *Mrs. Didrickson:* Lela Bliss, *Miss Beade:* Martha Mitrovich, *Photo-double:* Amelita Ward.

Credits:

Screenplay:	Nunnally Johnson
Based on a story by:	Vladimir Pozner
Director:	Robert Siodmak

Producer:	Nunnally Johnson
Cinematography:	Milton Krasner
Film Editor:	Ernest Nims
Special Photographic Effects:	J. Devereaux Jennings, Paul Lerpas
Production Design:	Duncan Cramer
Costume Design:	Irene Sharaff
Sound:	Fred Lau, Arthur Johns
Set Decoration:	Hugh Hunt
Dialogue Director:	Phyllis Loughton
Music:	Dimitri Tiomkin

Story:
A doctor is killed, and several witnesses recognize the girl coming out of his apartment. The girl, however, has a twin sister, and the police call in a psychiatrist who is an expert on twins to try to tell them apart.

Distribution:
Universal-International

Running Time:
85 minutes

The Senator Was Indiscreet   Release date: December 1947

Cast:
Senator Melvin G. Ashton: William Powell, *Poppy McNaughton:* Ella Raines, *Lew Gibson:* Peter Lind Hayes, *Valerie Shepherd:* Arleen Whelan, *Houlihan:* Ray Collins, *Farrell:* Allen Jenkins, *Dinty:* Charles D. Brown, *Waiter:* Hans Conried, *Oakes:* Whit Bissell, *Woman at Banquet:* Norma Varden, *"You Know Who":* Milton Parsons, *Frank:* Francis Pierlot, *Helen:* Cynthia Corley, *Indians:* Oliver Blake, Chief Thunder Cloud, Chief Yowlachie, Iron Eyes Cody, *Politicos:* Boyd Davis, Rodney Bell.

Credits:

Screenplay:	Charles MacArthur
From the story by:	Edwin Lanham
Director:	George S. Kaufman
Producer:	Nunnally Johnson
Associate Producer:	Gene Fowler, Jr.
Cinematography:	William Mellor
Film Editor:	Sherman A. Rose
Art Direction:	Bernard Herzbrun, Boris Leven
Set Decoration:	Russell A. Gausman
Sound:	Leslie I. Carey
Music:	Daniele Amfitheatrof

Story:
Senator Ashton decides to run for President since he considers himself

unqualified for anything else. He keeps announcing he is not a candidate, which, of course, makes him one. He convinces the party bosses he should be a candidate by showing them the diary he has kept. The diary is stolen by a woman working for Ashton's opposition. It is recovered by a newspaperwoman who publishes the contents.

Distribution:
Universal-International

Running Time:
81 minutes

**Mr. Peabody and the Mermaid   Release date: August 1948

Cast:
Mr. Peabody: William Powell, *Mermaid:* Ann Blyth, *Mrs. Peabody:* Irene Hervey, *Cathy Livingston:* Andrea King, *Mike Fitzgerald:* Clinton Sundberg, *Dr. Harvey:* Art Smith, *Major Hadley:* Hugh French, *Colonel Mandrake:* Lumsden Hare, *Basil:* Frederick N. Clark, *Lieutenant:* James Logan, *Wee Shop Clerk:* Mary Field, *Mother:* Beatrice Roberts, *Nurse:* Cynthia Corley, *Waiter:* Tom Stevenson, *Lady Trebshaw:* Mary Somerville, *Waiter:* Richard Ryan, *Boy:* Bobby Hyatt, *Sidney:* Ivan H. Browning

Credits

Screenplay:	Nunnally Johnson
From the novel	
Peabody's Mermaid by	Guy and Constance Jones
Director:	Irving Pichel
Producer:	Nunnally Johnson
Associate Producer:	Gene Fowler, Jr.
Cinematography:	Russell Metty
Film Editor:	Marjorie Fowler
Underwater	
Cinematography:	David S. Horlsey
Art Direction:	Bernard Herzbrun, Boris Leven
Set Decoration:	Russell A. Gausman, Rubey R. Levitt
Sound:	Leslie Carey, Corson Jowett
Music:	Robert Emmett Dolan

Story:
Approaching fifty, Mr. Peabody tells his doctor about his discovery of a mermaid while on vacation. The doctor puts it down as a symptom of Peabody's hitting the "air pocket" of fifty.

Distribution:
Universal-International

Running Time:
89 minutes

**Everybody Does It   Release date: October 1949

Cast:

Leonard Borland: Paul Douglas, Cecil Carver: Linda Darnell, Doris Borland: Celeste Holm, Major Blair: Charles Coburn, Mike Craig: Millard Mitchell, Mrs. Blair: Lucille Watson, Wilkins: John Hoyt, Rossi: George Tobias, Hugo: Leon Belasco, Make-up Man: Tito Vuclo, Carol: Geraldine Wall, Mrs. Craig: Ruth Gillette, Chamberlain: Gilbert Russell, Grand Priest: John Ford, Housekeeper: Mae Marsh.

Credits:

Screenplay:	Nunnally Johnson
From the novel *Career*	
In C Major by:	James M. Cain
Director:	Edmund Goulding
Producer:	Nunnally Johnson
Cinematography:	Joseph LaShelle
Film Editor:	Robert Fritch
Art Direction:	Lyle Wheeler, Richard Irvine
Set Decoration:	Thomas Little, Paul S. Fox
Sound:	Eugene Grossman, Roger Heman
Musical Direction:	Alfred Newman
Music and Italian	
Lyrics:	Mario Castelnuovo-Tedesco

Story:

Doris Borland wants to be an opera singer, but her husband, Leonard, is discovered to have the talent. He goes on tour with singer Cecil Carver, but his first appearance in an opera is a disaster.

Distribution:

Twentieth Century-Fox

Running Time:

98 minutes

Notes:

This film was a remake of *Wife, Husband and Friend*.

**Three Came Home   Release date: February 1950

Cast:

Agnes Keith: Claudette Colbert, Harry Keith: Patric Knowles, Betty Sommers: Florence Desmond, Colonel Suga: Sessue Hayakawa, Henrietta: Sylvia Andrew, Sister Rose: Phyllis Morris, George: Mark Keuning, Lt. Nekata: Howard Chuman, Woman Prisoners: Drue Mallory, Carol Savage, Virginia Keiley, Mimi Heyworth, Helen Westcott.

Credits:

Screenplay:	Nunnally Johnson

From the book by:	Agnes Keith
Director:	Jean Negulesco
Producer:	Nunnally Johnson
Executive Producer:	Darryl F. Zanuck
Cinematography:	Milton Krasner
Film Editor:	Dorothy Spencer
Music:	Hugo Friedhofer
Musical Direction:	Lionel Newman
Art Direction:	Lyle Wheeler, Leland Fuller
Set Decoration:	Thomas Little, Fred J. Rode
Sound:	Clayton Ward, Roger Heman

Story:

The true story of Mrs. Agnes Keith's year in a Japanese prisoner-of-war camp in the Philippines.

Distribution:

Twentieth Century-Fox

Running Time:

106 minutes

The Gunfighter   Release date: July 1950

Cast:

Jimmy Ringo: Gregory Peck, *Peggy Walsh:* Helen Westcott, *Sheriff Mark Strett:* Millard Mitchell, *Molly:* Jean Parker, *Mac:* Karl Malden, *Hunt Bromley:* Skip Homeier, *Charlie:* Anthony Ross, *Mrs. Pennyfeather:* Verna Felton, *Mrs. Devlin:* Ellen Corby, *Eddie:* Richard Jaeckel, *First Brother:* Alan Hale, Jr., *Second Brother:* David Clark, *Third Brother:* John Pickard, *Jimmie:* B. G. Norman, *Mac's Wife:* Angela Clarke, *Jerry Marlowe:* Cliff Clark, *Alice Marlowe:* Jean Inness, *Archie:* Eddie Ehrhart, *Pablo:* Albert Morin, *Swede:* Kenneth Tobey, *Johnny:* Michael Branden, *Barber:* Eddie Parkes.

Credits:

Screenplay:	William Bowers, William Sellers
Original screen story:	William Bowers and Andre de Toth
Director:	Henry King
Producer:	Nunnally Johnson
Cinematography:	Arthur Miller
Film Editor:	Barbara McLean
Art Direction:	Lyle Wheeler, Walter M. Scott
Music:	Alfred Newman
Sound:	Alfred Bruzlin, Roger Heman

Story:

Jimmy Ringo, escaping from three brothers who are determined to kill him, stops in a small town to try to convince his wife to come away with him. He is tired of being a gunfighter and wants to "retire," but he is constantly being challenged by young gunfighters who want to make names for themselves.

Distribution:
Twentieth Century-Fox

Running Time:
84 minutes

Notes:
Final rewrite was done by Nunnally Johnson.

**The Mudlark
Release date: December 1950

Cast:
Queen Victoria: Irene Dunne, *Disraeli:* Alec Guinness, *Wheeler:* Andrew Ray, *Lady Emily Prior:* Beatrice Campbell, *John Brown:* Finay Currie, *Lt. Charles McHatten:* Anthony Steele, *Sgt. Footman Naseby:* Raymond Lovell, *Lady Margaret Prior:* Marjorie Fielding, *Kate Noonan:* Constance Smith, *Slattery:* Ronan O'Casey, *The Watchman:* Edward Rigby, *Herbert:* Robin Stevens, *Sparrow:* William Strange, *General Sir Henry Ponsonby:* Kynaston Reeves, *Tucker:* Wilfred Hyde White, *Hammond:* Ernest Clark, *Assistant Lt. of Police:* Eric Messiter, *Princess Christian:* Pamela Arliss.

Credits:

Screenplay:	Nunnally Johnson
From the novel by:	Theodore Bonnet
Director:	Jean Negulesco
Producer:	Nunnally Johnson
Cinematography:	Georges Perinal
Film Editor:	Thelma Myers
Art Direction:	C. P. Norman
Music:	William Alwyn
Special Effects:	W. Percy Day

Story:
A Cockney waif falls in love with a picture of Queen Victoria and sneaks into Windsor·Castle to see her.

Distribution:
Twentieth Century-Fox

Running Time:
99 minutes

**The Long Dark Hall
Release date: May 1951

Cast:
Arthur Groome: Rex Harrison, *Mary Groome:* Lilli Palmer, *Sheila Groome:* Tania Heald, *Rosemary Groome:* Henrietta Barry, *Mary's Mother:* Dora

Sevening, *Mary's Father:* Ronald Simpson, *Chief Inspector Sullivan:* Raymond Huntley, *Sgt. Cochran:* William Squires, *Supt. Maxey:* Ballard Berkeley, *The Man:* Anthony Dawson, *Sir Charles Morton:* Denis O'Dea, *Clive Belford:* Anthony Bushell, *Judge:* Henry Longhurst, *Rose Mallory:* Patricia Wayne, *Mrs. Rogers:* Brenda DeBanzie.

Credits:

Screenplay:	Nunnally Johnson
Additional Scenes and Dialogue:	W. E. C. Fairchild
From the novel *A Case to Answer* by:	Edgar Lustgarden
Directors:	Anthony Bushell, Reginald Beck
Producer:	Peter Cusick
Cinematography:	Wilkie Cooper
Film Editor:	Tom Simpson
Art Direction:	George Patterson
Music:	Benjamin Frankel

Story:

A man is accused of murdering his girl friend. The real murderer tries to turn the man's wife against him during the investigation and trial.

Distribution:

Eagle Lion Classics-United Artists

Running Time:

86 minutes

Notes:

Johnson wrote this script while at Universal, and the script was subsequently sold to Huntington Hartford, who produced the film in England.

**The Desert Fox   Release date: October 1951

Cast:

Erwin Rommel: James Mason, *Dr. Karl Strolin:* Cedric Hardwicke, *Frau Rommel:* Jessica Tandy, *Hitler:* Luther Adler, *General Burgdorf:* Everett Sloane, *Field Marshall Von Rundstadt:* Leo G. Carroll, *General Fritz Bayerlein:* George Macready, *Aldinger:* Richard Boone, *Col. Von Stauffenberg:* Eduard Franz, *Desmond Young:* Himself, *Manfred Rommel:* William Reynolds, *General Schultz:* Charles Evans, *Admiral Ruge:* Walter Kingsford, *Keitel:* John Hoyt, *General Maisel:* Don de Leo.

Credits:

Screenplay:	Nunnally Johnson
From the book by:	Desmond Young
Director:	Henry Hathaway
Producer:	Nunnally Johnson
Cinematography:	Norbert Brodine

Film Editor:	James B. Clark
Art Direction:	Lyele Wheeler, Maurice Ransford
Set Decoration:	Thomas Little, Stuart Reiss
Sound:	Eugene Grossman, Roger Heman
Special Photographic Effects:	Fred Sersen, Ray Kellogg
Music:	Daniele Amfitheatrof

Story:

Field Marshall Erwin Rommel is approached to become part of a plot to assassinate Hitler. Rommel reluctantly agrees, but the plot fails, and Rommel is captured and forced to commit suicide.

Distribution:

Twentieth Century-Fox

Running Time:

88 minutes

Phone Call From a Stranger   Release date: February 1952

Cast:

Binky Gay: Shelley Winters, *David Trask:* Gary Merrill, *Dr. Fortness:* Michael Rennie, *Eddie Hoke:* Keenan Wynn, *Sally Carr:* Evelyn Varden, *Marty Nelson:* Warren Stevens, *Mrs. Fortness:* Beatrice Straight, *Jerry Fortness:* Ted Donaldson, *Mike Carr:* Craig Stevens, *Jane Trask:* Helen Westcott, *Marie Hoke:* Bette Davis, *Stewardess:* Sydney Perkins, *Dr. Brooks:* Hugh Beaumont, *Mr. Sawyer:* Thomas Jackson, *Dr. Fletcher:* Harry Cheshire, *Dr. Fernwood:* Tom Powers, *Thompson:* Freeman Lusk, *Doctor:* George Eldredge, *Headwaiter:* Nestor Paiva, *Mrs. Brooks:* Perdita Chandler.

Credits:

Screenplay:	Nunnally Johnson
From the story by:	I.A.R. Wylie
Director:	Jean Negulesco
Producer:	Nunnally Johnson
Cinematography:	Milton Krasner
Film Editor:	Hugh Fowler
Art Direction:	Lyle Wheeler, J. Russell Spencer
Set Decoration:	Thomas Little, Bruce MacDonald
Music:	Franz Waxman
Sound:	Eugene Grossman, Roger Heman
Special Photographic Effects:	Ray Kellogg

Story:

David Trask, a survivor of a plane crash, contacts the relatives of three passengers he met on the plane.

Distribution:
  Twentieth Century-Fox

Running Time:
  96 minutes

**We're Not Married   Release date: July 1952

Cast:
  Ramona: Ginger Rogers, *Steve Gladwyn:* Fred Allen, *Justice of the Peace:*
  Victor Moore, *Annabel Norris:* Marilyn Monroe, *Jeff Norris:* David Wayne,
  Katie Woodruff: Eve Arden, *Hector Woodruff:* Paul Douglas, *Willie Fisher:*
  Eddie Bracken, *Patsy Fisher:* Mitzi Gaynor, *Frederic Melrose:* Louis
  Calhern, *Eve Melrose:* Zsa Zsa Gabor, *Duffy:* James Gleason, *Attorney
  Stone:* Paul Stewart, *Mrs. Bush:* Jane Darwell, *Detective Magnus:* Alan
  Bridge, *Radio Announcer:* Harry Golder, *Governor Bush:* Victor Suther-
  land, *Attorney General:* Tom Powers.

Credits:

Screenplay:	Nunnally Johnson
From the story "If	
I Could Remarry" by:	Gina Kaus and Jay Dratler
Adaptation by:	Dwight Taylor
Director:	Edmund Goulding
Producer:	Nunnally Johnson
Cinematography:	Leo Tover
Film Editor:	Louis Loeffler
Special Montage by:	William Cameron Menzies
Art Direction:	Lyle Wheeler, Leland Fuller
Set Decorations:	Thomas Little, Claude Carpenter
Music:	Cyril Mockridge
Sound:	W. D. Flick, Roger Heman

Story:
  It is discovered that a country justice of the peace illegally married five
  couples. Notification to the couples that they are not married produces
  different reactions.

Distribution:
  Twentieth Century-Fox

Running Time:
  85 minutes

**O. Henry's Full House   Release date: October 1952
"The Ransom of Red Chief" Episode

Cast:
  Sam: Fred Allen, *Bill:* Oscar Levant, *J.B.:* Lee Aaker, *Mr. Dorset:* Irving
  Bacon, *Mrs. Dorset:* Kathleen Freeman, *Ellie Mae:* Gloria Gordon,

Storekeeper: Alfred Mizer, *Yokels:* Robert Easton, Robert Cherry, Norman Leavitt.

Credits:

Director:	Howard Hawks
Producer:	Andre Hakim
Cinematography:	Milton Krasner

Story:
Two inept kidnappers take a young boy who is such a holy terror that nobody wants to pay the ransom.

Distribution:
Twentieth Century-Fox

Running Time:
"The Ransom of Red Chief" episode: 26 minutes *O. Henry's Full House:* 117 minutes

Notes:
Johnson wrote the screenplay. He was so distressed at the changes made by Hawks in both the dialogue and the overall tone that he requested his name be taken off the credits.

**My Cousin Rachel   Release date: December 1952

Cast:
Rachel: Olivia de Havilland, *Philip Ashley:* Richard Burton, *Louise:* Audrey Dalton, *Nick Kendall:* Ronald Squire, *Rainaldi:* George Dolenz, *Ambrose Ashley:* John Sutton, *Seecombe:* Tudor Owen, *Reverend Pascoe:* J. M. Kerrigan, *Mrs. Pascoe:* Margaret Brewster, *Mary Pascoe:* Alma Lawton, *Pascoe Daughters:* Ola Lorraine, Kathleen Mason, *Signora:* Argentini Brunetti, *Caretaker:* Mario Siletti, *Tamblyn:* Lumsden Hare, *Lewin:* Trevor Ward, *Philip–Age 10:* Nicholas Koster, *Philip–Age 15:* Robin Camp, *Foreman:* Victor Wood.

Credits:

Screenplay:	Nunnally Johnson
From the novel by:	Daphne de Maurier
Director:	Henry Koster
Producer:	Nunnally Johnson
Cinematography:	Joseph LaShelle
Film Editor:	Louis Loeffler
Art Direction:	Lyle Wheeler, John de Cuir
Set Decoration:	Walter M. Scott
Music:	Franz Waxman
Sound:	Alfred Bruzlin, Roger Heman
Special Photographic Effects:	Ray Kellogg

Story:

Philip Ashley falls in love with, Rachel, the widow of his guardian, even though he suspects that she murdered the guardian. Philip marries Rachel, and then he begins to believe she is trying to murder him also.

Distribution:

Twentieth Century-Fox

Running Time:

98 minutes

How To Marry a Millionaire   Release date: November 1953

Cast:

Loco: Betty Grable, *Pola:* Marilyn Monroe, *Schatze Page:* Lauren Bacall, *Freddie Denmark:* David Wayne, *Eben:* Rory Calhoun, *Tom Brookman:* Cameron Mitchell, *J. Stewart Merrill:* Alex D'Arcy, *Waldo Brewster;* Fred Clark, *J. D. Hanley:* William Powell, *Mr. Otis:* Tudor Owen, *Man at Bridge:* Emmett Vogan, *Model:* Charlotte Austin.

Credits:

Screenplay:	Nunnally Johnson
Based on the play	
The Greeks had a	
Word for It by:	Zoe Akins
And the play *Loco* by:	Dale Eunson, Katherine Albert
Director:	Jean Negulesco
Producer:	Nunnally Johnson
Cinematography:	Joe MacDonald
Film Editor:	Louis Loeffler
Art Direction:	Lyle Wheeler, Leland Fuller
Musical Direction:	Alfred Newman
Incidental Music:	Cyril Mockridge
Sound:	Alfred Bruzlin, Roger Heman

Story:

Three models in New York pool their resources to find millionaires to marry, with varying degrees of success.

Distribution:

Twentieth Century Fox

Running Time:

95 minutes

Night People   Release date: March 1954

Cast:

Van Dyke: Gregory Peck, *Leatherby:* Broderick Crawford, *Hoffy:* Anita Bjork, *Miss Cates:* Rita Gam, *Foster:* Walter Abel, *Sgt. McColloch:* Buddy

Ebsen, *Frederick S. Hobart:* Casey Adams, *Frau Schindler:* Jill Esmond, *Petrechine:* Peter Van Eyck, *Kathy:* Marianne Koch, *Johnny:* Ted Avery, *Burns:* Hugh McDermott, *Whitby:* Paul Carpenter, *Stanways:* John Horsley, *Lakeland:* Lionel Murton.

Credits:

Screenplay:	Nunnally Johnson
From a story by:	Jed Harris, Thomas Reed
Director:	Nunnally Johnson
Producer:	Nunnally Johnson
Cinematography:	Charles G. Clarke
Film Editor:	Dorothy Spencer
Art Direction:	Hanns Kuhnert, Theo Zwierski
Music:	Cyril Mockridge
Musical Direction:	Alfred Newman
Sound:	Hans Wunschel, Roger Heman

Story:

The son of an American industrialist is kidnapped by the East Germans in Berlin. An American colonel in the military police negotiates to get him back.

Distribution:

Twentieth Century-Fox

Running Time:

93 minutes

Black Widow   Release date: November 1954

Cast:

Lottie: Ginger Rogers, *Peter:* Van Heflin, *Iris:* Gene Tierney, *Detective Brown:* George Raft, *Nanny Ordway:* Peggy Ann Garner, *Brian:* Reginald Gardiner, *Claire Amberly:* Virginia Leith, *Ling:* Otto Kruger, *Lucia:* Cathleen Nesbitt, *John:* Skip Homeier.

Credits:

Screenplay:	Nunnally Johnson
From a novel by:	Patrick Quentin
Director:	Nunnally Johnson
Producer:	Nunnally Johnson
Cinematography:	Charles G. Clarke
Film Editor:	Dorothy Spencer
Art Direction:	Lyle Wheeler, Maurice Ransford
Music:	Leigh Harline
Sound:	Eugene Grossman, Roger Heman

Story:

Peter Denver is a Broadway producer. While his wife is out of town he lets

Nanny Ordway write in his apartment. When Nanny is killed, Peter is the prime suspect.

Distribution:
Twentieth Century-Fox

Running Time:
95 minutes

**How To Be Very Very Popular   Release date: July 1955

Cast:
Stormy: Betty Grable, *Curly:* Sheree North, *Wedgewood:* Bob Cummings, *Tweed:* Charles Coburn, *Eddie:* Tommy Noonan, *Toby:* Orson Bean, *Mr. Marshall:* Fred Clark, *Midge:* Charlotte Austin, *Miss Syl:* Alice Pearce, *Flagg:* Rhys Williams, *Moon:* Andrew Tombes, *Cherry Blossom Wang:* Noel Toy, *Chief of Police:* Emory Parnell.

Credits:

Screenplay:	Nunnally Johnson
From the novel *She Loves Me Not* by:	Edward Hope
And the play by:	Howard Lindsay
And the play *Sleep It Off* by	Lyford Moore and Harlan Thompson
Director:	Nunnally Johnson
Producer:	Nunnally Johnson
Cinematography:	Milton Krasner
Film Editor:	Louis Loeffler
Art Direction:	Lyle Wheeler, John De Cuir
Set Decoration:	Walter M. Scott, Chester Bayhi
Music:	Cyril J. Mockridge
Sound:	E. Clayton Ward, Harry M. Leonard

Story:
Two strippers are witnesses to the shooting of a third stripper. The two girls hide out in a college fraternity hall.

Distribution:
Twentieth Century-Fox

Running Time:
93 minutes

**The Man in the Gray Flannel Suit   Release date: April 1956

Cast:
Tom Rath: Gregory Peck, *Betsy:* Jennifer Jones, *Hopkins:* Frederic March, *Maria:* Marisa Pavan, *Judge Bernstein:* Lee J. Cobb, *Mrs. Hopkins:* Ann Harding, *Caesar Gardella:* Keenan Wynn, *Hawthorne:* Gene Lockhart,

Susan Hopkins: Gigi Perreau, *Janie:* Portland Mason, *Walker:* Arthur
O'Connell, *Bill Ogden:* Henry Daniell, *Mrs. Manter:* Connie Gilchrist,
Edward Schultz: Joseph Sweeney, *Barbara:* Sandy Discher, *Pete:* Mickey
Maga, *Mahoney:* Kenneth Tobey, *Florence:* Ruth Clifford, *Miriam:* Geral-
dine Wall, *Johnson:* Alex Campbell, *Freddie:* Jerry Hall.

Credits:

Screenplay:	Nunnally Johnson
From the novel by:	Sloan Wilson
Director:	Nunnally Johnson
Producer:	Darryl F. Zanuck
Cinematography:	Charles G. Clarke
Film Editor:	Dorothy Spencer
Art Direction:	Lyle R. Wheeler, Jack Martin Smith
Set Decoration:	Walter M. Scott, Stuart A. Reiss
Music:	Bernard Herrmann
Sound:	Alfred Bruzlin, Harry Leonard

Story:
Tom Rath is a young executive who is offered an important job as assistant
to a company president. He turns it down because of family problems.

Distribution:
Twentieth Century-Fox

Running Time:
153 minutes

**Oh Men! Oh Women!   Release date: February 1957

Cast:
Arthur Turner: Dan Dailey, *Mildred Turner:* Ginger Rogers, *Dr. Alan
Coles:* David Niven, *Myra Hagerman:* Barbara Rush, *Cobbler:* Tony
Randall, *Mrs. Day:* Natalie Schafer, *Miss Tacher:* Rachel Stephens, *Dr.
Krauss:* John Wengraf.

Credits:

Screenplay:	Nunnally Johnson
From the play by:	Edward Chodorov
As produced on the stage by:	Cheryl Crawford
Director:	Nunnally Johnson
Producer:	Nunnally Johnson
Cinematography:	Charles G. Clarke
Film Editor:	Marjorie Fowler
Art Direction:	Lyle Wheeler, Maurice Ransford
Set Decoration:	Walter M. Scott, Stuart A. Reiss
Music:	Cyril Mockridge
Sound:	Alfred Bruzlin, Harold Root

Story:

Dr. Alan Coles is a psychoanalyst who thinks he is above such human emotions as jealousy. He discovers he is not when he learns of his fiancée's previous relationships with two men.

Distribution:

Twentieth Century-Fox

Running Time:

90 minutes

Notes:

Although the writing credits for the film are listed above, in fact they did not appear in the film. Because Chodorov had been blacklisted, his name was now allowed to appear on the screen. Johnson had his own name removed from the writing credits in protest.

**The True Story of Jesse James   Release date: March 1957

Cast:

Jesse James: Robert Wagner, *Frank James:* Jeffrey Hunter, *Zee:* Hope Lange, *Mrs. Samuels:* Agnes Moorehead, *Cole Younger:* Alan Hale, *Remington:* Alan Baxter, *Rev. Jethro Bailey:* John Carradine, *Ann:* Rachel Stephens, *Dr. Samuels:* Barney Phillips, *Jim Younger:* Biff Elliot, *Major Cobb:* Frank Overton, *Attorney Walker:* Barry Atwater, *Rowena Cobb:* Marian Seldes, *Askew:* Chubby Johnson, *Charley,* Frank Gorshin, *Robby:* Carl Thayler, *Hollstron:* John Doucette

Credits:

Screenplay:	Walter Newman
Based on a screenplay by:	Nunnally Johnson
Director:	Nicholas Ray
Producer:	Herbert B. Swope, Jr.
Cinematography:	Joe MacDonald
Film Editor:	Robert Simpson
Art Direction:	Lyle R. Wheeler, Addison Hehr
Set Decoration:	Walter M. Scott, Stuart A. Reiss
Music:	Leigh Harline
Sound:	Eugene Grossman, Harry M. Leonard

Story:

Jesse James is considered an outcast by his neighbors because he fought for the South in the Civil War. He becomes an outlaw as an expression of his resentment.

Distribution:

Twentieth Century-Fox

Running Time:
93 minutes

Notes:
Nominally, this was a remake of Johnson's screenplay for the 1939 film, but in fact it bears no resemblance to it.

**The Three Faces of Eve   Release date: September 1957

Cast:
Eve: Joanne Woodward, *Ralph White:* David Wayne, *Dr. Luther:* Lee J. Cobb, *Dr. Day:* Edwin Jerome, *Secretary:* Alena Murray, *Mrs. Black:* Nancy Kulp, *Mr. Black:* Douglas Spencer, *Bonnie:* Terry Ann Ross, *Earl:* Ken Scott, *Eve–Age 8:* Mimi Gibson.

Credits:

Screenplay:	Nunnally Johnson
From the book by:	Corbett H. Thigpen, M.D., and Hervey M. Cleckley, M.D.
Director:	Nunnally Johnson
Producer:	Nunnally Johnson
Cinematography:	Stanley Cortez
Film Editor:	Marjorie Fowler
Art Direction:	Lyle Wheeler, Herman A. Blumenthal
Set Decoration:	Walter M. Scott, Eli Benneche
Music:	Robert Emmett Dolan
Sound:	W. D. Flick, Frank Moran
Narration:	Alistair Cooke

Story:
The true story of a woman with a split personality who developed yet a third personality.

Distribution:
Twentieth Century-Fox

Running Time:
95 minutes

**The Man Who Understood Women   Release date: December 1959

Cast:
Willie Bauché: Henry Fonda, *Ann Garantier:* Leslie Caron, *Marco Raniere:* Cesare Danova, *Preacher:* Myron McCormick, *LeMarne:* Marcel Dalio, *G.K.:* Conrad Nagel, *Baron:* Edwin Jerome, *Kress:* Harry Ellerbe, *Milstead:* Frank Cady, *Soprano:* Bern Roffman, *French Doctor:* Ben Astar.

Credits:

Screenplay:	Nunnally Johnson

From the novel
The Colors of the Day

by:	Romain Gary
Director:	Nunnally Johnson
Producer:	Nunnally Johnson
Cinematography:	Milton Krasner
Film Editor:	Marjorie Fowler
Art Direction:	Lyle Wheeler, Maurice Ransford
Set Decoration:	Walter M. Scott, Paul S. Fox
Sound:	Charles Peck, Harry M. Leonard
Music:	Robert Emmett Dolan

Story:

Willie Bauché, a genius-type movie director, marries his star, Ann Garantier. She finds him more interested in business than in her, and she has an affair with a French soldier of fortune. In the end, she returns to Willie.

Distribution:
Twentieth Century-Fox

Running Time:
105 minutes

The Angel Wore Red   Release date: September 1960

Cast:

Soledad: Ava Gardner, *Arturo Carrera:* Dirk Bogarde, *Hawthorne:* Joseph Cotten, *General Clave:* Vittorio DeSica, *Cannon Rota:* Aldo Fabrizi, *Insurgent Major:* Arnoldo Foa, *The Bishop:* Finlay Currie, *Mercedes:* Rossana Rory, *Captain Botargas:* Enrico Maria Salerno, *Father Idlefonso:* Robert Bright, *Jose:* Franco Castellani, *Mac:* Bob Cunningham, *Major Garcia:* Gustavo DeNardo, *Captain Trinidad:* Nino Gastelneuvo.

Credits:

Screenplay:	Nunnally Johnson
From the novel *The Fair Bride* by:	Bruce Marshall
Director:	Nunnally Johnson
Producer:	Goffredo Lombardo for Titanus-Spectator Productions
Cinematography:	Guiseppe Rotunno
Film Editor:	Louis Loeffler
Art Direction:	Pier Filippone
Music:	Bronislau Kaper

Story:

Arturo, a priest, leaves the church the day the Spanish Civil War starts. He falls in love with a prostitute. He uses the relic from the local church to save a group of prisoners.

Distribution:
Metro-Goldwyn-Mayer

Running Time:
99 minutes

**Flaming Star Release date: December 1960

Cast:
Pacer: Elvis Presley, *Clint:* Steve Forrest, *Roslyn Pierce:* Barbara Eden, *Neddy Burton:* Delores DelRio, *Pa Burton:* John McIntire, *Buffalo Horn:* Rudolph Acosta, *Dred Pierce:* Karl Swenson, *Doc Phillips:* Ford Rainey, *Angus Pierce:* Richard Jaeckel, *Dorothy Howard:* Ann Benton, *Tom Howard:* L. Q. Jones, *Will Howard:* Douglas Dick, *Jute:* Tom Reese, *Ph'sha Knay:* Marian Goldina, *Ben Ford:* Monte Burkhart, *Hornsby:* Ted Jacques, *Indian Brave:* Rodd Redwing, *Two Moons;* Perry Lopez.

Credits:
Screenplay:	Clair Huffaker, Nunnally Johnson
From the novel by:	Clair Huffaker
Director:	Don Siegel
Producer:	David Weisbart
Cinematography:	Charles G. Clarke
Film Editor:	Hugh S. Fowler
Art Direction:	Duncan Cramer, Walter M. Simonds
Set Decoration:	Walter M. Scott, Gustav Bernsten
Music:	Cyril Mockridge
Sound:	E. Clayton Ward, Warren B. Delaplain
Technical Advisor:	Colonel Tom Parker

Story:
Pacer, a half-breed, finds his loyalties divided when the Indians go on the warpath against the white settlers.

Distribution:
Twentieth Century-Fox

Running Time:
92 minutes

Notes:
Johnson completed his draft of the script in 1958; it remained unproduced for two years.

**Mr. Hobbs Takes a Vacation Release date: July 1962

Cast:
Mr. Hobbs: James Stewart, *Peggy:* Maureen O'Hara, *Joe:* Fabian, *Byron:* John Saxon, *Mrs. Turner:* Marie Wilson, *Reggie McHugh:* Reginald Gardiner, *Katey:* Lauri Peters, *Marika:* Valerie Varda, *Janie:* Lili Gentle,

Mr. Turner: John McGiver, *Susan:* Natalie Trundy, *Stan:* Josh Peine, *Brenda:* Minerva Urecal, *Danny Hobbs:* Michael Burns, *Plumber:* Richard Collier.

Credits:

Screenplay:	Nunnally Johnson
From the novel *Mr. Hobbs' Vacation* by:	Edward Streeter
Director:	Henry Koster
Producer:	Jerry Wald
Associate Producer:	Marvin Gluck
Cinematography:	William C. Mellor
Film Editor:	Marjorie Fowler
Art Direction:	Jack Martin Smith, Malcolm Brown
Set Decoration:	Walter M. Scott, Stuart A. Reiss
Music:	Henry Mancini
Sound:	Alfred Bruzlin, Warren Delaplain

Story:

Mrs. Hobbs convinces Mr. Hobbs that the whole family, married children and all, should vacation together. They move into an old house near the beach and discover the problems of too much togetherness.

Distribution:
Twentieth Century-Fox

Running Time:
116 minutes

**Take Her, She's Mine   Release date: November 1963

Cast:

Frank Michaelson: James Stewart, *Mollie:* Sandra Dee, *Anne:* Audrey Meadows, *Pope-Jones:* Robert Morley, *Henri:* Philippe Forquet, *Mr. Ivor:* John McGiver, *Alex:* Robert Denver, *Linda:* Monica Moran, *Adele:* Cynthia Pepper, *Sarah:* Jenny Maxwell, *M. Bonnet:* Maurice Marsac, *Miss Wu:* Irene Tsu, *Liz:* Charla Doherty, *Policeman:* Marcel Hillaire, *Stanley Bowdry:* Charles Robinson.

Credits:

Screenplay:	Nunnally Johnson
From the play by:	Phoebe and Henry Ephron
Director:	Henry Koster
Producer:	Henry Koster
Cinematography:	Lucien Ballard
Film Editor:	Marjorie Fowler
Art Direction:	Jack Martin Smith, Malcolm Brown
Set Decoration:	Walter M. Scott, Stuart Reiss

| Sound: | W. D. Flick, Elmer R. Raguse |
| Music: | Jerry Goldsmith |

Story:
Frank Michaelson has difficulty adjusting when his daughter goes away to college.

Distribution:
Twentieth Century-Fox

Running Time:
98 minutes

**The World of Henry Orient   Release date: May 1964

Cast:
Henry Orient: Peter Sellers, *Stella:* Paula Prentiss, *Isabel Boyd:* Angela Lansbury, *Frank Boyd:* Tom Bosley, *Mrs. Gilbert:* Phyllis Thaxter, *Valerie Boyd:* Tippy Walker, *Marian "Gil" Gilbert:* Merrie Spaeth, *Boothy:* Bibi Osterwald, *Joe Byrd:* Peter Duchin, *Sidney:* John Fiedler, *Store Owner:* Al Lewis, *Doctor:* Fred Lewis, *Emma:* Philippa Bevans, *Kafritz:* Jane Buchanan.

Credits:

Screenplay:	Nora Johnson, Nunnally Johnson
From the novel by:	Nora Johnson
Director:	George Roy Hill
Producer:	Jerome Hellman
Cinematography:	Boris Kaufman, Arthur J. Ornitz
Film Editor:	Stuart Gilmore
Music:	Elmer Bernstein

Story:
Two teenage girls develop a crush on concert pianist Henry Orient. They follow him around, interrupting his liaisons with married women.

Distribution:
United Artists

Running Time:
106 minutes

**Dear Brigitte   Release date: February 1965

Cast:
Professor Leaf: James Stewart, *Kenneth:* Fabian, *Vina:* Glynis Johns, *Pandora:* Cindy Carol, *Erasmus:* Billy Mumy, *Upjohn:* John Williams, *Dr. Voker:* Jack Kruschen, *The Captain:* Ed Wynn, *George:* Charles Robinson, *Dean Sawyer:* Howard Frieman, *Terry:* Jane Wald, *Brigitte Bardot:* Herself.

Credits:

Screenplay:	Hal Kanter
From the novel	
Erasmus with Freckles	
by:	John Haase
Director:	Henry Koster
Producer:	Henry Koster
Cinematography:	Lucien Ballard
Film Editor:	Marjorie Fowler
Art Direction:	Jack Martin Smith, Malcolm Brown
Set Decoration:	Walter M. Scott, Steve Potter
Music:	George Dunning
Sound:	Alfred Bruzlin, Elmer Raguse

Story:

An eight-year-old mathematical genius has a crush on Brigitte Bardot.

Distribution:

Twentieth Century-Fox

Running Time:

100 minutes

Notes:

Johnson wrote the screenplay for the film, and Hal Kanter was brought on the project to write the final sequences and some revisions. Johnson asked to have his name taken off the credits.

**The Dirty Dozen   Release date: June 1967

Cast:

Major Reisman: Lee Marvin, *General Worden:* Ernest Borgnine, *Joseph Wladislaw:* Charles Bronson, *Robert Jefferson:* Jim Brown, *Victor Franko:* John Cassavetes, *Sgt. Bowren:* Richard Jaeckel, *Major Armbruster:* George Kennedy, *Pedro Jiminez:* Trini Lopez, *Capt. Stuart Kinder:* Ralph Meeker, *Col. Dasher-Breed:* Robert Ryan, *Archer Maggott:* Telly Savalas, *Vernon Pinkley:* Donald Sutherland, *Samson Posey:* Clint Walker, *General Denton:* Robert Webber, *Milo Vladek:* Tom Busby, *Glenn Gilpin:* Ben Carruthers, *Roscoe Lever:* Stuart Cooper, *Corp. Morgan:* Robert Phillips, *Seth Sawyer:* Colin Maitland, *Tassos Bravos:* Al Mancini, *Pvt. Gardner:* George Ronbrick.

Credits:

Screenplay:	Nunnally Johnson, Lukas Heller
From the novel by:	E. M. Nathanson
Director:	Robert Aldrich
Producer:	Kenneth Hyman
Cinematography:	Edward Scaife
Film Editor:	Michael Luciano

Art Direction:	W. E. Hutchinson
Special Effects:	Cliff Richardson
Music:	Frank de Vol

Story:

Major Reisman is given the job of training a group of convicted criminals into a special attack organization. He succeeds, and the group attacks a German officers' headquarters.

Distribution:

Metro-Goldwyn-Mayer

Running Time:

150 minutes

Produced Stage Plays of Nunnally Johnson

**Shoot The Works

Produced at the George M. Cohan Theatre, New York City, 21 July 1931. 87 performances.

A Review assembled by Heywood Broun and Milton Raison.

Contributors:

Heywood Boun	A. Robinson
H. I. Phillips	Dorothy Parker
Peter Arno	Nunnally Johnson
Sig Herzig	E. B. White
Edward J. McNamara	Jack Hazzard
Michael H. Cleary	Irving Berlin
Philip Chagrig	Max Lieb
Jay Gorney	Nathaniel Lieb
Dorothy Fields	E. Y. Harburg
Ira Gershwin	Jimmie MacHugh
Alexander Williams	Vernon Duke
Robert Stolz	Herbert Goode
	Walter Reisch

Principal Performers:

Heywood Broun	Julie Johnson
William O'Neal	Imogene Coca
Johnny Boyle	Frances Dewey
George Murphy	Margot Riley
Jack Hazzard	Francis Nevins
Edward J. McNamara	Virginia Smith
Al Gold	Lee Brody
Percy Helton	Lela Manor
Edgar Nilson	Lila Manor

Notes:

Shoot the Works was conceived by Heywood Broun as a way to give hundreds of out-of-work actors jobs. Johnson wrote some of the between-scenes dialogue.

250

**Dark Eyes

Produced at the Belasco Theatre, New York City, 14 January 1943. 174 performances.

Credits:

A play by:	Elena Miramova and Eugenie Leontovich
Produced by:	Jed Harris

Cast:

Larry Field: Carl Gose, *Willoughby:* Oscar Polk, *Grandmother Field:* Minnie Dupree, *Pearl:* Maude Russell, *Helen Field:* Anne Burr, *Prince Nicolai Toradje:* Geza Korvin, *Natasha Rapakovitch:* Eugenie Leontovich, *Tonia Karpova:* Elena Miramova, *Olga Shmilevskaya:* Ludmilla Toretzka, *John Field:* Jay Fassett

Notes:

Johnson's friend, producer Jed Harris, asked Johnson to put this play, which had been written by its two stars, "into English." He received no writing credit on it.

**The World's Full of Girls

Produced at the Royal Theatre, New York City, 6 December 1943. 9 performances.

Credits:

A comedy in three acts by:	Nunnally Johnson
Based on the novel *Till I Come Back to You* by:	Thomas Bell
Produced and staged by:	Jed Harris
Settings:	Stewart Chaney

Cast:

Mr. Bridges: Thomas W. Ross, *Mrs. Bridges:* Eva Condon, *Dave:* Thomas Hume, *Hannah:* Julie Stevens, *Florrie:* Gloria Hallward, *Adele:* Francis Heflin, *Nick:* Walter Burke, *Edward:* Charles Lang, *Miley:* Berry Kroeger, *Sally:* Virginia Gilmore, *Sergeant Synder:* Harry Bellaver, *Mel Fletcher:* John Conway, *Mrs. Fletcher:* Cora Smith.

Notes:

The text of this play was published in the February 1944 issue of *Theatre Arts* magazine.

**Park Avenue

Produced at the Shubert Theatre, New York City, 4 November 1946. 72 performances.

Credits:

A musical comedy
  in two acts by: Nunnally Johnson, George S. Kaufman
Produced by: Max Gordon
Music: Arthur Schwartz
Lyrics: Ira Gershwin
Orchestration: Don Walker

Cast:

Carlton: Byron Russell, *Ned Scott:* Ray McDonald, *Madge Bennett:* Martha Stewart, *Ogden Bennett:* Arthur Margetson, *Mrs. Sybil Bennett:* Leonora Corbett, *Charles Crowell:* Robert Chisholm, *Mrs. Elsa Crowell:* Mata Errolle, *Reggie Fox:* Charles Purcell, *Mrs. Myra Fox:* Ruth Matteson, *Richard Nelson:* Raymond Walburn, *Mrs. Betty Nelson:* Mary Wickes, *Ted Woods:* Harold Mattox, *Mrs. Laura Woods:* Dorothy Bird, *James Meredith:* William Skipper, *Mrs. Beverly Meredith:* Joan Mann, *Mr. Meacham:* David Wayne, *Freddie Coleman:* Wilson Smith, *Carole Benswanger:* Virginia Gordon.

**Henry Sweet Henry

Produced at the Palace Theatre, New York City, 23 October, 1967. 80 performances.

Credits:

A musical based on the
  novel *The World of*
  Henry Orient by: Nora Johnson
Book by: Nunnally Johnson
Music and Lyrics: Bob Merrill
Produced by: Edward Specter Productions and Norman
                             Twain
Director: George Roy Hill
Choreography: Michael Bennett
Musical Direction and
  Vocal Arrangements: Shepard Coleman
Scenery and Lighting: Robert Randolph
Costumes: Alvin Colt
Orchestration: Eddie Sauter
Dance Music: William Goldenberg, Marvin Hamlisch
Production Stage
  Manager: William Dodds
Stage Manager: Henry Clark

Cast:

Kafritz: Alice Playten, *Valerie Boyd:* Robin Wilson, *Miss Cooney:* Barbara Beck, *Marian Gilbert:* Neva Small, *Henry Orient:* Don Ameche, *Stella:* Louise Lasser, *Mrs. Gilbert:* Trudy Wallace, *Usherette:* Julie Sargant, *Mrs.*

Boyd: Carol Bruce, *Russ:* John Mineo, *Captain Kenneth:* George McJames, *Hal:* Robert Iscove, *Policeman:* Gerard Brentte, *Mr. Boyd:* Milo Boulton, *Policeman:* Charles Rule, *Big Val:* K. C. Townsend.

Notes:
This was a musical adaptation of the same novel Johnson had adapted into a film three years before.

**Darling of the Day

Produced at the George Abbott Theatre, New York City, 27 January, 1968. 31 performances.

Credits:

A musical based on the novel *Buried Alive* by:	Arnold Bennett
Music:	Jule Styne
Lyrics:	E. Y. Harburg
Produced by:	The Theatre Guild and Joel Schenker
Director:	Noel Willman
Choreography:	Lee Theodore
Musical Director and Vocal Arrangements:	Buster Davis
Scenery:	Oliver Smith
Costumes:	Paoul Pene du Bois
Lighting:	Peggy Clark
Dance Music:	Trude Rittman
Orchestration:	Ralph Burns
Production Manager:	Phil Friedman
Stage Managers:	Michael Sinclair, Phil King

Cast:
Oxford: Peter Woodthorpe, *Priam Farll:* Vincent Price, *Henry Leek:* Charles Welch, *Old Gentleman:* Carl Nicholas, *Lady Vale:* Brenda Forbes, *Cabby:* Ross Miles, *Doctor, Judge:* Leo Lyden, *Alice Challice:* Patricia Routledge, *Daphne:* Joy Nichols, *Alf:* Teddy Green, *Bert:* Marc Jordan, *Rosalind:* Beth Howland, *Sidney:* Reid Klein, *Attendant:* Larry Brucker, *Frame Maker:* Paul Eichel, *Duncan:* Mitchell Jason, *Equerry, Constable:* John Aman, *The King:* Charles Gerald, *Mrs. Leek:* Camila Ashland, *Curates:* Herb Wilson, Fred Siretta, *Pennington:* Michael Lewis

Notes:
This was a musical adaptation of the same novel Johnson had adapted into the film *Holy Matrimony.* Johnson requested his name be taken off the credits.

Published Short Stories of Nunnally Johnson

The Smart Set

Ashes to Ashes	May 1923
Scarehead	May 1923
I Owe It All to My Wife	July 1923
Doing Right by Nell	November 1923
Futility	November 1923
The Ad Section	January 1924
The Happy Ending	March 1924
Where Is Thy Sting?	March 1924
Twins	June 1924

Saturday Evening Post

Rollicking God	11 October 1924
Hero	14 March 1925
Lovelorn	28 March 1925
Hearse Horse	11 April 1925
Laughing Death	25 April 1925
Death of an Infinitive Splitter	5 September 1925
Love of a Moron	27 February 1926
His Name in the Papers	13 March 1926
Fame Is a Bubble	3 April 1926
Rough House Rosie	12 June 1926
It Probably Never Happened	10 July 1926
Portrait of the Writer	16 October 1926
Straight from New York	30 October 1926
Lady of Broadway	9 July 1927
Good Little Man	8 October 1927
An Artist Has His Pride	3 December 1927
Belting Bookworm	7 January 1928
Anti-New York	11 February 1928
Comedy	17 March 1928
Young Poison	7 April 1928

Divine Afflatus	28 April 1928
The Actor	26 May 1928
Private Life of the Dixie Flash	2 June 1928
New York—My Mammy	8 September 1928
Who's Who, and Why	29 September 1928
World's Shortest Love Affair	27 October 1928
Simple Honors	22 December 1928
Pain in the Neck	20 April 1929
Not if You Gave It to Me	11 May 1929
Pagliacci Blues	22 June 1929
Mlle. Irene the Great	5 October 1929
One Meets Such Interesting People	30 November 1929
Victim of the War	27 December 1929
Faunthorpe's Folly	8 February 1930
Away from It All	15 February 1930
Sugar in Corn Bread!	1 March 1930
Burgler's Bride	12 April 1930
France on Two Words	26 April 1930
Those Old Pals of Hers	3 May 1930
Twenty Horses	17 May 1930
There Ought to Be a Law	26 July 1930
Artist Relaxed	19 July 1930
How to Treat Reporters	2 August 1930
It's in the Blood	30 August 1930
Women Have No Sense of Humor	13 September 1930
Here We Go A-Nutting	27 September 1930
Perfect Crime Case	11 October 1930
Back to Barrie	15 November 1930
Woman at the Wheel	27 December 1930
Lowest Form of Humor	January 1931
Dixie Bell	28 February 1931
Woman's Touch	21 March 1931
Nightmare	4 April 1931
Angler's Prayer	25 April 1931
Lion of the Bronx	6 June 1931
Author! Author!	4 July 1931
Man on Horseback	11 July 1931
Submachine-Gun School of Literature	3 October 1931
Pillar of Strength	17 October 1931
Josie	24 October 1931
Stage-Struck	14 November 1931
No Hits, No Runs, One Error	19 December 1931
Will You Please Stop That?	9 April 1932
Man Who Made a Speech	9 July 1932
Krazy	30 July 1932
Blood from the Moon	12 November 1932

They Laughed!   December 1932
Once a Sucker   14 January 1933
Wizard   3 June 1933
Twelfth Baronet   26 August 1933
Clothes Make the Man   21 October 1939

American Mercury

Nathalia from Brooklyn   September 1926
Shocking Care of Gregory Ellwood   April 1930
Lulabel the Lulu   September 1933

Colliers

Noise Off-Stage   3 October 1925

Bibliography

Agee, James. *Agee on Film*. Boston: Beacon Press, 1964.

Allvine, Glendon. *The Greatest Fox of Them All*. New York: Lyle Stuart, 1969.

Balio, Tino. *United Artists: The Company Built by the Stars*. Madison: The University of Wisconsin Press, 1976.

Blesh, Rudi. *Keaton*. New York: The Macmillan Co., 1966.

Blotner, Joseph. *Faulkner, A Biography*. New York: Random House, 1974.

Bluem, A. William, and Squire, Jason E., eds. *The Movie Business: American Film Industry Practice*. New York: Hastings House, 1972.

Bluestone, George. *Novels into Film: The Metamorphosis of Fiction into Cinema*. Berkeley: The University of California Press, 1957.

Bogdanovich, Peter. *John Ford*. Berkeley: The University of California Press, 1968.

Brown, Karl. *Adventures with D. W. Griffith*. New York: Farrar, Straus & Giroux, 1973.

Brownlow, Kevin. *The Parade's Gone By*. New York: Alfred A. Knopf, 1968.

Capra, Frank. *The Name Above the Title*. New York: The Macmillan Co., 1971.

Corliss, Richard. *Talking Pictures: Screenwriters in the American Cinema*. Woodstock, New York: The Overlook Press, 1974.

Curti, Carlo. *Skouras*. Los Angeles: Holloway House, 1967.

Dardis, Tom. *Some Time in the Sun*. New York: Charles Scribner's Sons, 1976.

Eells, George. *Hedda and Louella*. New York: G.P. Putnam's Sons, 1972.

French, Philip. *The Movie Moguls: An Informal History of the Hollywood Tycoons*. London: Weidenfeld and Nicolson, 1969.

French, Warren. *Filmguide to The Grapes of Wrath*. Bloomington: Indiana University Press, 1973.

Froug, William. *The Screenwriter Looks at the Screenwriter*. New York: The Macmillan Company, 1972.

Gish, Lillian, with Ann Pinchot. *The Movies, Mr. Griffith and Me*. New York: Prentice-Hall, 1969.

Goldman, William. *The Season: A Candid Look at Broadway*. New York: Harcourt, Brace & World, 1969.

Guild, Leo. *Zanuck: Hollywood's Last Tycoon*. Los Angeles: Holloway House, 1970.

Gussow, Mel. *Don't Say Yes Until I Finish Talking: A Biography of Darryl F. Zanuck*. Garden City, New York: Doubleday & Co., 1971.

Hampton, Benjamin. *History of the American Film Industry: From its Beginnings to 1931*. (*A History of the Movies*. New York: Covici, Friede, 1931.) Reprint, New York: Dover Publications, 1970.

Haskell, Molly. *From Reverence to Rape: The Treatment of Women in The Movies*. New York: Holt, Rinehart and Winston, 1974.

Hecht, Ben. *A Child of the Century*. New York: Simon & Schuster, 1954.

Higham, Charles. *Hollywood at Sunset*. New York: Saturday Review Press, 1972.

Higham, Charles, and Greenberg, Joel. *The Celluloid Muse: Hollywood Directors Speak*. London: Angus & Robertston, 1969.

Huettig, Mae D. *Economic Control of the Motion Picture Industry*. Philadelphia: The University of Pennsylvania Press, 1944.

Jacobs, Lewis. *The Rise of the American Film: A Critical History*. New York: Harcourt, Brace and Co., 1939. Reprint. New York: Teachers College Press, 1967.

Kael, Pauline. *I Lost It at the Movies*. Boston: Little, Brown and Co., 1965.

Kael, Pauline. *Kiss Kiss Bang Bang*. Boston: Atlantic-Little, Brown, 1968.

Kawin, Bruce. *Faulkner on Film*. New York: Ungar, 1977.

Knight, Arthur. *The Liveliest Art: A Panoramic History of the Movies*. New York: The Macmillan Co., 1957.

Latham, Aaron. *Crazy Sundays: F. Scott Fitzgerald in Hollywood*. New York: The Viking Press, 1971.

Leuchtenberg, William. *The Perils of Prosperity 1914-1932*. Chicago: The University of Chicago Press, 1958.

Macgowan, Kenneth. *Behind the Screen: The History and Techniques of the Motion Picture*. New York: Delacorte Press, 1965.

May, Henry F. *The End of American Innocence (1912-1917)*. New York: Alfred A. Knopf, 1959.

Parish, James Robert. *The Fox Girls*. New Rochelle, New York: Arlington House, 1971.

Powdermaker, Hortense. *Hollywood: The Dream Factory*. Boston: Little, Brown and Co., 1950.

Rosten, Leo C. *Hollywood: The Movie Colony: The Movie Makers*. New York: Harcourt, Brace and Co., 1941.

Sinclair, Utpon. *Upton Sinclair Presents William Fox*. Los Angeles: Sinclair, 1933.

Taylor, Deems; Peterson, Marcelene; and Hale, Bryant. *A Pictorial History of the Movies*. New York: Simon and Schuster, 1950.

Teichmann, Howard. *George S. Kaufman: An Intimate Portrait*. New York: Atheneum, 1972.

Warshow, Robert. *The Immediate Experience: Movies, Comics, Theatre, and Other Aspects of Popular Culture*. Garden City, New York: Doubleday & Co., 1962.

Wilk, Max. *The Wit and Wisdom of Hollywood*. New York: Atheneum, 1971.

Index

Page numbers in italics refer to pages on which cast and credits for plays and films may be found.